JOURNEY
TO THE
CENTERS OF
THE MIND

JOURNEY TO THE CENTERS OF THE MIND

Toward a Science of Consciousness

Susan A. Greenfield

W. H. Freeman and Company
New York

Library of Congress Cataloging-in-Publication Data

Greenfield, Susan.
  Journey to the centers of the mind : toward a science of
consciousness / Susan A. Greenfield.
      p.   cm.
  Includes bibliographical references (p.   ) and index.
  ISBN 0-7167-2723-4 (hbk.)
  1. Consciousness—Physiological aspects. 2. Cognitive
neuroscience. I. Title.
QP411.G69 1995
153—dc20   94-45848
                                                                CIP

Printed in the United States of America

1 2 3 4 5 6 7 8 9 0 VB 9 9 8 7 6 5

CONTENTS

PREFACE

I first performed a dissection on the human brain more than twenty years ago. At the time I was tantalized by the thought that a scrap of brain tissue might readily disintegrate from the apparently solid mass and, were it not for protective gloves, lodge beneath my fingernails. It is perhaps macabre, but nonetheless intriguing, to wonder what that particular scrap of brain was actually for: Did it generate a love of Beethoven? Was it a memory of a particular summer day? Would it have caused the person to fidget while speaking? In short, how do our very personalities and mental processes, our "states of consciousness," derive from a slurry of tissue with the consistency of a soft-boiled egg? The brain is a tangible physical organ constituted from molecules; but that collection of molecules seems mockingly remote from the insubstantial, complex, transient thoughts that combine to endow us with conscious awareness. Even then, while floundering in the tangle of Latin names labeling every nook and cranny of tissue, the stark truth was that I held in one hand the pickled essence of what had once been someone's individuality.

Since that time I have been plagued by our apparent inability to formulate even the dimmest vision of the physical basis of our "state of mind." Perhaps my awe and frustration would have remained unfocused and undeveloped had it not been for a chance turn in conversation one night over dinner in a Chinese restaurant with the philosopher Susan Hurley. We started discussing the physical basis of consciousness from our respective and widely different standpoints. Rapidly it became clear that a debate between philosophers and neuroscientists would be enormously revealing and valuable, not only in clarifying areas of formerly esoteric mystery but also perhaps in enabling us to make more progress together than we could ever achieve in isolation. I approached Colin Blakemore, then the head of my department (the Laboratory of Physiology), and together we organized a series of debates, each between a philosopher and a neuroscientist on a particular theme. These sessions took place on cold and dark autumn and winter evenings in Oxford, with minimal publicity, and even that confined to the university. Nonetheless more than a hundred people consistently turned out each time, and frequently stayed in heated discussion until after midnight. Such was our success, and the demand for an increased understanding of the mind-brain, that we were persuaded to take a step we had never originally envisaged and publish the presentations.

Listening to the debates, and subsequently editing (with Colin Blakemore) *Mindwaves,* sharpened my interest further in the type of contribution that neuroscience could make to the question. The more I heard, read, and thought about it, the more it seemed incredible that mere molecules could in some way constitute an inner vision, idea, or emotion, or—even more astounding—that they could generate the subjectivity of an emotion. Yet how else could we explain why, in cases of brain death where there is no brain activity, there is never any consciousness? Consciousness is continuous with the brain's activity and must emerge from it.

Despite the seemingly obvious truth that the brain generates consciousness, there are those who think that it is premature to use the rigors of science to explore a topic that cannot be defined satisfactorily. The psychologist Stuart Sutherland is widely quoted as claiming, "Consciousness is a fascinating phenomenon; it is impossible to specify what it is, what it does or why it evolved. Nothing worth reading has been written on it." Perhaps it is the utter subjectivity of the concept that makes it so alarming and unpalatable. After all, the clarion call of all scientists is "objectivity." Even the accepted writing style in research papers is to abjure any use of "I" or "we" in favor of insipid and often clumsy phrases such as "a stock solution was made up." If neutrality is the key to good science and if good science is indeed founded on the making of objective measurements, then how are scientists to tackle something that is above all so subjective, so confined to the individual?

To date there have been various ways of coping with this dilemma. Some scientists opt out altogether, waiting for someone else to convert consciousness obligingly and miraculously into a nonsubjective phenomenon. Once this transformation has taken place, objective measurements can be made, with an operational definition of consciousness akin to declaring that we know when a solution is hot because we can measure the rising temperature. Others have already capitulated and claim that there is, after all, no subjectivity, no self in consciousness, and that consciousness can be studied as a series of sequential snapshots of ongoing brain states, and hence even modeled on a computer. Still another group, the physicalists, believe that although consciousness is generated by the brain, it is such a special property that it currently defies scientific understanding.

Those going along with these sorts of premises may well find themselves intellectually becalmed. There appears to be no obvious strategy for exploring the physical basis of consciousness while at the same time preserving its quintessential subjective phenomenology. What I have tried to do in this book, however, is to present a possible way forward. The most sensible and obvious place to start seemed to be with a survey of what has been said already. The relevant disciplines are now so widely disparate that it is easy for scientists and philosophers to polarize, and for scientists themselves to get blinkered by one particular approach or technique. It was for me a valuable and urgently needed exercise to compare ideas gleaned from philosophy, cognitive psychology, basic neuroscience, computation, brain damage studies, animal behavior, and developmental psychology before introducing any pet theories of consciousness of my own. It was also important to strip away any subject-related jargon and see if there were any common themes that could act as clues for how to proceed. Hence the first five chapters are, I hope, no mere rehashing; rather, they play an integral part in the development of the theory presented in the later chapters.

Even though I am a neuroscientist, writing unequivocally from a neuroscientist's perspective, the theory itself is not inspired by a purely scientific contemplation of the brain. Many scientists, from both physical and biological backgrounds, have tackled the question of consciousness by starting with the properties of the physical brain, and then trying to see how consciousness might be tacked on post hoc as an all-or-none entity. Here I present a reverse strategy. The theory starts as just that, a theory, prompted by examining consciousness itself. From there we are then able to see how any or all of the possible features of consciousness can be accommodated in the brain.

One of the most basic features of consciousness emphasized here is that consciousness grows as the brain does. Consciousness is not all-or-none but increases and deepens as the brain becomes more sophisticated and as one progresses from fetus to neonate to child. In addition, it is possible to imagine that even as adults our consciousness will also be variable in depth, momentarily shrinking and expanding in accordance with our interaction with the outside world as we live out our lives. Charged with these ideas, the advantage of then turning to neuroscience is that it offers us an opportunity to see how such shifting degrees of consciousness might really match up with shifting, ever changing combinations of neurons.

In this spirit, the aim of writing this book was to harness what we know about brain chemistry and brain electricity to help see how we might, one day, formulate the physical basis of the phenomenological sensation of consciousness. At this particular moment, however, there are no instant answers, no magic bullets, and no trendy catchphrases that sum it all up. Surely we need first to be able to correlate purported mental events with actual events in the brain that are free of metaphor and grounded firmly in current scientific knowledge. As this correlation becomes tighter and more detailed, the nearer we will come to an understanding of how consciousness can be generated by populations of neurons. I have tried to focus on this issue: how to come to terms with the generation of consciousness by the brain. This book offers a tentative step forward to strengthening the connection between the phenomenology and the physiology of consciousness, of offering a framework for explaining one in terms of the other. As such, I hope the book will contribute as one of the voices for neuroscience in the current, ever burgeoning debate. Above all, I hope that it will be easily understandable to the non-neuroscientist. I have made it one of my highest priorities to explain any facts, phenomena, or concepts in terms readily accessible to the general reader.

Many people have knowingly and unknowingly helped me write this book. Among those who never realized they were making any contribution are the medical students at Lincoln College, who, over the last decade, have put me through my paces and have helped me work out ideas on brain function during tutorials on neuroscience. In this regard I would also like to thank my friend and colleague John Stein, who has time and again acted as a wily and uncompromising critic during wide-ranging discussions. In addition I am grateful to my research group for their continued support while this project was under way, and most of all to my parents for a lifetime of encouragement. Of those who have had a more immediate role, I am indebted to Elizabeth Clark not only for her excellent secretarial services but also for her unflagging cheerfulness and interest. Several distinguished authorities have also provided invaluable contributions by reading the manuscript and making extremely helpful comments; accordingly, I am indebted to Gary Aston-Jones, Patricia Churchland, Gordon Claridge, Marianne Fillenz, George Graham, Jeffrey A. Gray, Richard L. Gregory, J. Allan Hobson, Ron Hoy, Bryan Kolb, Steven Rose, and Christine A. Skarda. Finally, there are two people without whom this book would truly not have been possible and to whom any expressions of thanks would always be insufficient: one is my husband, Peter, and the other my editor, Jonathan Cobb.

Susan A. Greenfield
Oxford, England
March 1995

chapter one

THE
PROBLEMS OF
CONSCIOUSNESS

Locked away in our brains is an absolute and inviolate individuality, a personal inner privacy of cascades of thoughts and feelings to which no one else has automatic access. As long as you can avoid any severe cranial trauma or anesthetist's ministrations, and as long as you can evade sleep, you can peer from this inner world, perhaps reacting to and interacting with the outside world of objective time and space, but all the time remaining distinct from it. This inner world of your particular consciousness arises from a kaleidoscope of memories, prejudices, hopes, habits, and emotions which are constantly expanding and enriching your life as you develop. It is a world that respects neither conventional space nor time: It is composed of incessantly shifting scenes, some hazy and some almost real, some rooted in history, fear, or fantasy, and others a seemingly faithful reproduction of the immediate outside. Inside our heads is a world contemptuous of clocks where we live out the slow-motion scene of an accident or, immersed in a thriller, remain unaware that a whole morning has flown. For most of us, consciousness is at the root of the purpose of modern life: After all, we spend most of our existence striving to heighten, broaden, divert, or simply indulge it.

But how is the trick of deincarnation achieved? What special property is actually built into the brain to generate this inner world of consciousness? There is no little creature in the deepest recesses between your ears to appreciate all that is going on: There is no brain within the brain. There is a morass of a hundred billion brain cells that generate electricity and release minute quantities of chemicals. Nothing is translated back again from nervous impulses, decoded into colors, shapes, or smells. Brain electricity and brain chemistry are ultimately all there is to your mind.

Our secret inner world, our consciousness, is the ultimate enigma of the brain and the most baffling problem that that same brain will ever ask itself about itself. We are about to embark on a journey, a journey into neuroscience, to try to resolve this enigma. As you stare at this page, what might be going on at this very moment in the tangible mass of tissue behind your eyes to create a private, subjective experience? Immediately, of course, we run into problems.

The Problem of Definition

"Experience is never limited, and it is never complete; it is an immense sensibility, a kind of huge spiderweb of the finest silken threads suspended in the chamber of consciousness, and catching every airborne particle in its tissue." So Henry James (1888) captured the essence of states of awareness without any attempt at a definition. Few would deny that we experience consciousness most of the time we are not asleep; yet it is like clutching at air when it comes to explaining what we actually mean by the concept. So what is the problem?

We can practice first with some straightforward definitions and see how we normally go about things. A mouse is a small rodent; a table is a piece of furniture; love is an emotion; the retina is a sense organ. It is easy to see from these examples that when we make a stab at defining something, we usually start by referring to a larger group or set, such as rodents, furniture, emotions, or organs. We could even categorize tricky entities such as unicorns and Santa Claus by referring to the set of mythical concepts.

But what about an entity that is so all-embracing that it cannot fit into any category, however large? The largest and most embracing entity would seem to be the universe. Of course we could always seize on the very uniqueness and all-inclusive nature of the universe to define it as "all there is." But then someone could argue back that unicorns and Santa Claus do not exist in actuality, although they are both far from being mere nonsense words. Hence in a sense these mythical entities *exist*. Our mental world, our consciousness, stretches beyond the physical world and everything observable that it contains to embrace imaginary concepts and events such as a green sky, humanoid Martians, time travel, and so on. Moreover, the individual inner state of consciousness really is a consistent, complete, and autonomous world. Toward the end of Shakespeare's *Richard II*, the king, alone in a dungeon in Pomfret Castle with presumably little to stimulate his senses, muses:

> *My brain I'll prove the female to my soul,*
> *My soul the father; and these two beget*
> *A generation of still-breeding thoughts,*
> *And these same thoughts people this little world*
> *In humours like the people of this world.*
>
> Act v, Scene v

Our imagination seems boundless: Consciousness is more encompassing than the universe. It is the ultimate superset; no wonder it is hard to define. On the other hand, some might argue that we could relegate consciousness to a lesser status, make it merely part of a larger set by dismissing it simply as "a property of the brain," on a level with many other humdrum features such as the peculiar grayish color or soft-boiled egg consistency. Although this might serve as a definition of sorts, it is not adequate: Consciousness is far from humdrum. Such a definition would have ignored the quintessential subjectivity of consciousness that prevents it from being lined up with other properties of the brain. *There are simply no terms of reference, no framework for capturing an objective description of the subjective.*

An alternative approach for coming to grips with the problem of definition is to resort to a grapeshot approach and attempt to convey a sense of the concept through a range of particular and personalized examples. "Bliss was it that dawn to be alive, / But to be young was very heaven"; "As soon as she saw him she felt traces of the old flame creep beneath her limbs"; "Do I dare / Disturb the universe?" From these diverse examples, we could compile a list of some of the facets or effects of consciousness. Such a list might read something like this: a feeling of being special, perhaps the most important person alive; a cohesiveness of values and attitudes over time, amounting to a unified concept of self; a blurring of past, present, and future so that any ongoing experience is colored by what we hope, fear, and remember; a sense of spontaneity and proactivity that elevates us above mere machines responding robotically to instructions from outside forces.

We all "know" what consciousness is, but find it impossible to articulate using an objective frame of reference. Hence the fascination and frustration of the subject. Whichever way we might characterize it phenomenologically, consciousness is ultimately the very essence of ourselves. But there are those who might argue that soul and mind also capture our individuality. So how might consciousness be distinguished from these two terms?

Soul, Mind, and Consciousness

For some, such as Plato (c. 428–c. 348 B.C.) and René Descartes (1596–1650), the term soul had clear theological associations that rendered it immune from study. At the end of the eighteenth century, the same wariness was apparent, for different reasons, in the attitudes of Immanuel Kant (1724–1804) and Charles Bonnet (1720–1793), who both shrank from ever being able to attempt to explain "the great phenomenon of the union between body and soul." Soul was simply not physical in the sense that the brain was. Others, such as Thomas Willis (1621–1675) and Robert Whytt (1714–1766), argued that the soul was virtually indistinguishable from mind, effectively a mortal entity that was an integral part of the brain, toward the front end and "equipped with dioptric mirrors" (see Mazzolini 1991).

The crucial difference as to whether or not soul and mind are interchangeable hinges on whether or not we are speaking of immortality. For those who believe in the existence of a soul that has the chief characteristic of being immortal, such an entity would be, by definition, independent of the physical and mortal basis of mind. But it is this physical basis of mind, not the immortal qualities of soul, that is my only concern in this book. However, in cases where soul is used as a term for the mental properties of the brain, we shall consider it interchangeable with mind, in that use of one or the other simply reflects the preoccupations and tastes of a particular era.

What about distinguishing consciousness from mind? When we fall asleep, we would probably admit to a loss of consciousness, but we would probably not regard ourselves as having relinquished our minds. Mind, then, has a more inclusive, permanent, and enduring connotation that survives the fleeting moment and is somehow tied up with our integral and continuing personalities. Consciousness, on the other hand, is suggestive of more transient states in the here and now.

Moments of Consciousness and Arousal

If consciousness is only some fleeting state of our highly individual minds, perhaps there is not so looming a problem after all. Let's consider another transient state, arousal. In everyday language we think of it as underscoring extreme emotions such as anger or love. Indeed, in evolutionary terms an aroused state serves to prepare us for action of some kind, whether it is to save, propagate, or maintain life. The changes that occur when the body is highly aroused are often dubbed the "fight or flight" response. They consist of sweating, an increase in heart rate and blood pressure, a cessation of digestion of food, and removal of blood from the skin in order to divert it to meet the more urgent demands of the vital organs for oxygen. This response is frequently elicited in situations where life is not literally threatened but is interpreted as such, as in a heated argument. Could this background tone to our experiences be the same as consciousness?

Fighting and fleeing are extreme examples of arousal. It is less obvious perhaps that arousal, in physiological terms, is not just the fight or flight response. In a less obtrusive fashion it is constantly with us: We can think of it for the moment as an energizing power permeating the brain as well as the body. Arousal is best thought of, physiologically, as some type of generalized activation of brain cells caused by certain chemicals pulsing through the brain (Steriade and Buzsaki 1990). Another way of looking at it is as the most basic behavior we have. It is not an independent, optional course of action but to greater or lesser extents pervades all we do. In extreme examples, arousal can be conspicuous by its low levels (sedation) as well as by its high levels (hyperactivity and distraction).

But now it seems that the features of arousal, as described here, are starting to have an uncanny resemblance to some of the features of consciousness. Both are always with us while we are awake and both are dramatically reduced when we are asleep. How, then, might arousal differ, if at all, from consciousness? In terms of the brain, a state of high arousal is registered as intense activity of brain cells recorded from electrodes on the scalp. When arousal is measured, it is not an all-or-none phenomenon but, rather, is graded, a sort of continuum. At one end of the continuum of arousal, we are in nondreaming stages of sleep, we are unconscious. Interestingly enough, it is when we are unconscious in this way that it is *easier* to be awakened than when we are dreaming (Rechtshaffen et al. 1966). It is when we are dreaming, however, and we are in rapid eye movement (REM) sleep that, according to recordings from electrodes placed on the scalp, the brain is relatively more aroused than in dreamless stages of non-REM sleep.

If arousal were the single factor responsible for consciousness, indeed, if it were synonymous with consciousness, then it would be hard to explain why the high arousal accompanying conscious dreams is transformed *less* readily into wakening consciousness than the total lack of consciousness of deep sleep, where arousal is lower. If consciousness were simply arousal, then we would expect that the more aroused we were, the easier it would be to be affected by the ring of an alarm clock or the shaking of a shoulder. There must, therefore, be an additional factor relevant to dreams, and thus consciousness, that is not directly related to arousal. We shall attempt to discover what this additional factor might be later in the book. For the time being, the important point to establish is that arousal and consciousness are *not* synonymous; rather, arousal is most likely to be a contributing factor.

Given that they can be distinguished from each other, how do mind and arousal relate to consciousness? Mind, in our everyday understanding, is long lasting in that it endures as long as the

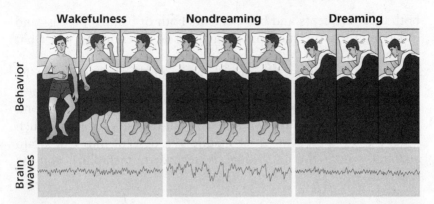

The three major stages involved in sleep, as shown by changes in body movement and brain waves. In the first stage, wakefulness, there is continuous voluntary movement, and low-amplitude, high-frequency brain waves can be recorded on the electroencephalogram. However, once a person is asleep, brain waves become slower and develop a characteristic large amplitude. Body movement, tossing and turning, still occurs occasionally. When dreaming, however, there is far less movement than in nondreaming sleep—almost as if the sleeper were paralyzed. Brain waves, though, once again resemble those of the awake state. (After J. Carey, ed., *Brain Concepts: Sleep and Dreaming* [Washington, D.C.: Society for Neuroscience, 1991].)

brain does. Consciousness, however, is relinquished every night. In a folklore psychology use of the term, it is a phenomenon with some continuity throughout each day that transcends our moment-to-moment existence in an unbroken stream. Almost seventy years ago the pioneering neurologist Henry Head described the seamless continuity of consciousness as "a march of events with a definite temporal relation; the response obtained from any one point, at a particular moment, depends on what has happened before" (1926). After all, few would confess to a series of ruptures in consciousness during a day at the office, as though our brains were governed by a system operating like traffic lights, where we were forever in a stop-go situation.

By contrast, arousal is far more fickle. It can fluctuate appreciably over shorter time periods and *contribute* to our experiences of awareness throughout the day without being the pivot of consciousness. Arousal is clearly a process, whereas mind is generally regarded as an entity. Consciousness spans the bridge between both these concepts and has elements both of being a process and of having the more substantive qualities of an entity. So just what are these qualities?

Perhaps the most obvious property of mind that cannot be attributed to arousal is a continuity of individuality. As the anesthetist looms over you on the threshold of the operating room, you would not claim that you were about to lose your mind. Such a phrase is reserved for utter madness, a descent into true brain anarchy where the individual is regarded, metaphorically, as falling apart.

The Problem of Self

Although it might seem like quibbling to stress the difference in permanence between mind and consciousness, such a distinction proves critical when it comes to deciding if we have any enduring individuality. In considering consciousness, philosophers such as Derek Parfit and Daniel Dennett concentrate on whatever mental state prevails and disregard any enduring self that might be independent of that current conscious experience. To explain the subjective feel of consciousness, Parfit (1989) proposes the Buddhist bundle theory, which suggests that different streams of potential consciousness exist. Whichever one dominates at any one time gives you a sense not only of a certain conscious view of the world but also a sense of identity. In a similar vein, Dennett (1991) envisages the brain processing incoming information in a continuing sequence that can be sampled at different stages, so that there are multiple drafts of any one event; whichever draft is dominating amounts to your current consciousness.

It is easy to see that these scenarios, where the fleeting moment dictates your mental state, are better described as a *process* consciousness at work rather than reflecting the static presence of an *entity*, the mind. But the philosopher Thomas Nagel suggests that this is not enough; a fleeting snapshot type of consciousness does not encapsulate the idea of a highly subjective, personalized view of the world. Nagel (1986) argues that individual beliefs, desires, traits, and so forth that make up a person *should* survive the radical break in consciousness that occurs in the total oblivion of sleep or anesthesia, that there is something more to being a person than a snatched moment of consciousness.

This idea seems plausible as long as we accept that the mind and brain are two faces of the same coin, that the mental life of any one individual (one's mind) is not transferable to any other brain. Most of us like to think that even when our brain sleeps there will be a consistency in our consciousness when we wake up again.

The reason Dennett rejects the idea of an enduring mind or self is because it seems to conjure up a lasting and fixed property in the brain, a region of unchanging, inflexible mechanism committed specifically to the generation of consciousness. Instead, Dennett suggests, our mental states are a kind of ecosphere of ideas, tunes, and catchphrases (dubbed by the biologist Richard Dawkins as "memes") that harmoniously blend. In this way, the mind is constituted of elements presumably more flexible and labile than those that make up the original idea of a rigid and constant self. These memes organize themselves, according to Dennett, as an ever adapting ecosystem where all participants altruistically aid and abet the well-being of the whole. There is no need to invoke a boss to organize this inner world any more than a super-ant is needed to organize an anthill.

This concept of a kind of brain ecosphere is not actually inconsistent with Nagel's idea of a long-lasting individuality. One can very easily imagine that individual brains, or rather their intrinsic neuronal connections, are gradually shaped by experience, and that in turn these modifications to the brain are constantly modifying the mind and hence the consciousness of an individual throughout life. Far from disproving the concept of a self with a continuity of mind, the notion of a neuronal ecosphere offers a very plausible basis for it. The fact that the self can evolve does not invalidate its existence.

Can we sniff out this self in any way at all? The only outward signs we have of what is going on inside someone else's brain are the movements that person makes. Such movements, of course, cannot capture the subjective feelings or private reflections that constitute a consistent self, but they can in particular cases indicate a highly individual consistency in the way the brain is working. A good reason for not dismissing the idea of an evolving yet consistent self comes from a consideration of a commonplace yet remarkable phenomenon—handwriting.

Handwriting, especially a signature, is the only universally accepted outward sign of an individual. Moreover, it is a sign that is accepted as consistent. Handwriting is not merely a product of a group of individual muscles in the arm and shoulder happening on their own to produce a particular pattern on a page. If an individual loses the use of his hands, his signature written with the mouth or feet is still recognizable as written by the same person (Cohen and Wander 1993). Similarly, in Parkinson's disease, where one aspect of the poverty of movement is tiny writing (micrographia), the individuality of the signature remains. True, our handwriting becomes modified as we grow up, but that reflects an evolving individual, not a transient one. In regression analysis, when patients are hypnotized back to stages in their childhood, their handwriting also regresses. The individual is still lurking.

The significance of different types of handwriting in revealing quirks of our personality is still controversial. Nevertheless, the mere fact that we produce, day after day, a consistent signature that is not merely a trick of our arm muscles suggests a distant and pale echo of a singular and cohesive union of brain states that could be regarded as a self. We are, however, far too early in our journey to speculate as to how these physical brain states might work to give a consistency of consciousness. But the scenario of building a conscious self can be appreciated phenomenologically.

Everything we see, hear, taste, touch, and smell is laced with associations from previous experiences. At the very least these associations are able to give significance to the world around us, unlike the world of a newborn infant, a world of meaningless abstract forms and sounds. Much more than helping us simply to recognize tables and chairs, as we journey through life, experience piles on particular associations as a tourist gathers souvenirs. But these associations cannot *in themselves* account for consciousness. Such associations can reasonably be assumed to contribute to a consistent profile of individuality and to survive nighttime breaks in consciousness. Hence these experience-related associations are not synonymous with consciousness. Rather, the neuro-ecosphere, built up slowly by a lifetime's conglomeration of associations, determines the *quality* of our conscious experience, however it has come about. Whether we view a dog with fear or happiness, a sunset with nostalgia or cynicism, depends upon what has happened to us in the past. As we get older, the associations are richer, while some objects might trigger more associations than others. In this way consciousness may become deeper than at other times. Our consciousness is not all-or-none but a variable phenomenon that grows as we do. Even in adult life it might shrink or expand according to where we are and what we happen to be doing and, most importantly, what the focus of our consciousness is.

But how is a focus of consciousness determined? This question poses a critical problem which theories of bundles or multiple drafts evade. It is not clear as to *who* or *what* decides what multiple draft or what stream in a bundle should dominate consciousness at any one time. We are left to suppose there is some sort of randomized surfacing of brain states into consciousness, like the chance selection of numbered Ping-Pong balls bouncing haphazardly on puffs of air in a lottery machine. Such a neuro-lottery would be a very unlikely and unhelpful way of determining the salient consciousness as we go through life.

Dennett answers the question of "Who's in charge?" by replying "First one coalition and then another, shifting in ways that are not chaotic, thanks to good meta-habits that tend to entrain coherent, purposeful sequences rather than an interminable helter-skelter power grab." It would certainly be a very bizarre situation indeed if the mind were freewheeling by producing randomized and distinct types of consciousness that had nothing at all to do with where we were or what we were doing. But it is not good enough to say simply that there must be some sort of organization, albeit unspecified and indescribable, for interfacing our consciousness with the world around us. Just what sort of scheme must it be? The problem is that it is not at all clear how multiple consciousness might be integrated into a smooth working system without an executive command for ordering the sequential probing. Who would call the shots? Surely there must be an alternative to the unrealistic scenario of the neuro-lottery, an alternative where the predominating conscious state is somehow linked to the environment and the needs of the individual.

The Problem of Brain Events

The next and most critical point is that we still have no idea how such evolving states in the brain are actually translated into a moment of consciousness. Nagel proposes that certain special brain events have in some way a final property of consciousness that is particular for any individual brain. So far, however, no one has come up with any idea as to what these brain events might be that, *unlike other brain events,* can conspire to generate consciousness. What makes them so special? These events would have to be more than the associative links among brain cells, forged gradually by experience. After all, you are not conscious all the time of everything that you remember. Some temporary, additional occurrences would have to take place for consciousness of a particular moment or object to happen. It is this permissive feature of the brain, the final feature or process, that is not just a necessary but also a sufficient condition for consciousness, that is the ultimate mystery. We need to know what other brain events occur in addition to associative pairings. Most accounts of consciousness stay at the level of metaphors, such as multiple drafts (Dennett 1991), bundles (Parfit 1989), and internal logician (Harth 1993). Such terms do not help identify any immediately obvious and real neurophysiological counterparts. The problem has gone unsolved as to what real events in the brain are the truly relevant brain events.

Finding an Answerable Question

The ultimate question is: How exactly does nervous tissue cause consciousness? No one has the faintest idea how even to approach this question; nor can anyone conceptualize the types of answers that would be satisfactory, let alone the types of experiments that might demonstrate such causality. Up against such a soaring cliff face, it is easy to sympathize with the shrugs of indifference of many scientists. Of course, we could modify our aims. It would be a great advance at least to identify what happens in the brain that is not just necessary but is *sufficient* for consciousness. It might then be possible to describe how such events are reflected in behavior, even if we cannot as yet explain how it is all done, how an effective deincarnation takes place. This is the particular quest for understanding consciousness in this book.

Like others before me, I shall be probing around in the physical brain, trying to find unusual or interesting features and events that might or might not match consciousness. Other scientific forays have remained firmly rooted inside the physical brain and have treated the phenomenon of consciousness as an ethereal black box, a mysterious entity that is squeezed into neuronal circuitry, almost as an afterthought, at the end of an extensive excursion into neuroscience. Although we shall be making many forays into the brain, we shall also be standing back repeatedly in an attempt to relate brain events to subjective phenomena. Instead of being placed to the side as an impregnable mystery, consciousness itself must first be characterized, defined in some way, if it is ever to be accommodated in the brain. The big difference, then, in this particular scientific approach is that I shall attempt a working definition of consciousness before actually tackling the enigma of its physical basis.

First we shall see what clues might be learned from surveying normal brain events, computers, brain damage, and animals. Then we shall see if we can analyze the phenomenon of consciousness, describe it in terms of certain properties. Armed with these properties, it will only then be possible to attempt a working definition and from this definition to construct a "theory" of consciousness. This theory will make use of the clues gleaned earlier and, ultimately, will be testable at both levels, those of physiology and of phenomenology.

chapter two

MOLECULES, CELLS, AND MINI-BRAINS

As I walk to my room in Lincoln College from the laboratory at the end of a day, I'm sifting, churning, rejoicing in, and regretting an avalanche of conversations, incidents, phone calls, and ideas. The familiar streets of Oxford, laden with medieval architectural wonders, pass me by as, oblivious, I plod along my programmed ten-year-old route, completely tuned to a special inner world. What is happening in my brain at this point? Brain molecules, brain cells, or something else has to be the critical factor. What *type* of events in the brain can we eventually hope to match up to mental ones such as these? In this chapter we shall take a cursory look at the options that are open to us.

A Substance for Consciousness?

The most basic level possible is the molecular. Is there some special consciousness substance in the brain? This idea is one of the oldest. The ancient Greeks thought that a consciousness substance (thymos) existed in the seat of the mind, which they had originally identified as the lungs. Even when views changed at the end of the sixth century B.C. in favor of the brain as the location of mental activity, the idea of some special consciousness substance persisted.

15

But whereas the air in the lungs was the obvious ethereal substance of thought, the Greeks realized that there was no tidal traffic of air in the brain. The best candidate for a substance of mind in the brain was cerebrospinal fluid, the colorless liquid that flows within the interconnecting cavities (ventricles) lying deep in the brain and bathing the external surface of the brain and spinal cord. Today this fluid is routinely collected in lumbar punctures for diagnosing a host of disturbances in the brain. In the second century A.D., Galen (129–199) proposed that our mental faculties, the psychic pneuma, resided in this fluid, now sometimes referred to rather disparagingly as the "urine of the brain." Cerebrospinal fluid contains salts and sugars as well as diverse substances released from the brain; it contains nothing so special that it could be described as "psychic."

Long after the Greek concept of thymos and Galen's suggestion of the ventricular psychic pneuma, it was still an attractive idea that the soul (this time in the sense of a mortal mind) was amorphous and ubiquitous, distributed throughout the brain as a kind of neuronal marinade. Robert Whytt was an early modern proponent of this idea. He suggested that the "sentient principle" was even present in the spinal cord, since reflexes could still be generated in decapitated frogs. Views of this type, of a special nerve substance, were perpetuated by a movement in Germany, *Naturphilosophie,* at the end of the eighteenth century. The core idea of this romantic movement—led by Goethe, among others—was that brain tissue was driven by an active life force, *natura naturans,* and thus operated in a dynamic, organic, and essentially nonmechanistic fashion. A similar idea had been propounded earlier by Thomas Willis and another pioneer brain researcher, Antoni van Leeuwenhoek (1632–1723), who was the first to study nerve cells using a microscope. They concluded that brain cells contained a special animal spirit or nerve fluid.

While the vitalist terminology expressing the concept of *Naturphilosophie* is now outdated, its central idea should not be dismissed out of hand, even in the computer age. The basic concept is that there is a dynamic and irreducible organic force in all living things. Essentially the mind should be viewed as a special and spontaneously proactive system as opposed to a passive product of physicochemical forces. However, no one has discovered any chemical unique to the brain; but the next level up from molecules, that of brain cells, might hold more promise. What the romantics of *Naturphilosophie* did not know was that the nature of individual cells in the brain does indeed enable them to function simultaneously as independent units and as parts of a complex whole.

Cells of Consciousness

The idea of brain cells also dates from the ancient Greeks. Democritus (c. 460–c. 370 B.C.) argued that there had to be a physical basis for the mind because everything in the universe was composed of small invisible particles; he envisaged the mind as made up of particularly special atoms. It seems remarkable that in a world without microscopes, where there was no evidence of smallness beyond what could actually be seen, it would have been possible to imagine the mind, wherever it was lodged, as being composed of tiny particles. Nevertheless, Democritus was correct in principle. If the brain were pried apart to reveal its smallest working component, you would end up with cells, tiny factories of life about forty thousandths of a millimeter in diameter. The most significant of these cells are, for our present discussion, neurons, the gray cells of everyday expressions (Dowling 1992). Neurons are the principal constituents of the mysterious brain tissue that puzzled our ancestors. It is these brain cells, invisible to the naked eye but actually much larger than atoms, that are the building blocks of all we can ever profess to be.

Neurons can be seen under a microscope, stained into visibility as dark blobs with thin branches emanating from them. But the shape of neurons gave few clues to early scientists as to how they might function. There was a further problem: The very process of marking the cells with a dye killed them. Thus brain cells could only be studied in the same way as pressed flowers, pinned butterflies, or fossils. They had to be kept alive to be appreciated fully. Luigi Galvani (1737–1798) originally suggested that living nerve cells were conductors of electricity. The electric fluid inside the nerves, he thought, emanated from activity in the brain. For almost two hundred years this finding, which could have quite easily supported the idea of a special psychic fluid, remained undeveloped. Then, in the 1950s, a brilliant

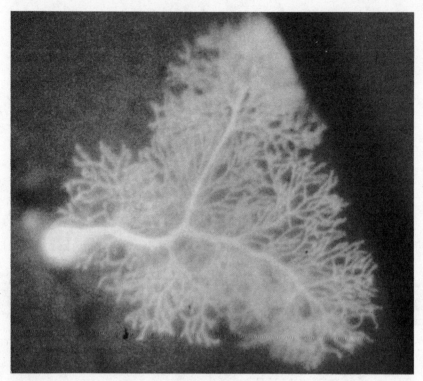

A neuron stained with a fluorescent dye so that the cell body and dendrites can be seen. The dendrites, named from the Greek for "tree," resemble branches emanating out into progressively thinner processes. These dendrites are the main receiving area for inputs from other neurons. The axon, which conducts signals from the cell body to make contact with the dendrites of the next cell, is too thin to be seen. Although almost all neurons have dendrites, a cell body, and an axon, their overall shapes vary enormously, particularly as to the number and size of dendrites. This particular neuron is a typical Purkinje cell, which relays signals from the outer layer of one particular brain region, the cerebellum, to its deep interior. (From R. R. Llinás, ed., *The Biology of the Brain: From Neurons to Networks* [New York: W. H. Freeman and Co., 1988]. Reprinted with permission.)

breakthrough occurred: The physiologists Alan Hodgkin and Andrew Huxley developed a model for describing how living nerve cells could generate electrical signals.

We now know that this electrical activity can be transiently and dramatically changed when a chemical, released by a neighboring brain cell, latches onto the outside of a neuron. This transient change in electrical activity (an action potential) causes the release of a chemical from the second nerve cell, which, in turn, acts on a third, and so on. This repeating chain of electrical and chemical events forms the basis for communication among brain cells. Thanks to an armory of modern techniques by which these physical changes (the change in electrical activity or the release of a particular chemical) can be monitored, we have at last windows on the living brain cell at work as it communicates with its neighbors.

Much is now known about the diversity, elegance, and precision of how brain cells interact. But for the purposes of our present discussion, there are only two very basic facts to grasp. First, brain cells contain no magic property that might be a candidate for consciousness. Neurons differ from other cells in the body only in that they can generate electrical signals. These electrical signals are simply the result of an imbalance of just four types of ions (charged atoms of chloride, calcium, sodium, and potassium), amounting to a net imbalance of charge across the outer wall of the cell, the neuronal membrane. This imbalance of charge generates a potential difference, a voltage. Temporary changes in the state of the membrane cause temporary changes in voltage, as ions flow to and fro. Hence it is possible to create electrical signals, which are the building blocks of brain activity, without any special or magical substance.

The second basic fact about neurons that is relevant here is that the transient changes in the activity of brain cells (the action potentials), which are a measure of their communication with one another, always persist to a certain degree in all living brains, even those in sleeping or anesthetized animals. Conversely, consciousness is often retained in a seemingly viable way in patients who have large populations of neurons destroyed, as happens in a stroke or following accidents. Brain injury may frequently modify consciousness, but it does not necessarily diminish it. Taken together, these facts suggest that consciousness is not a piecemeal commodity parceled out equally as a generic property of all neurons.

If consciousness is a property of the brain but is attributable neither to a special molecule nor to the inherent generic nature of individual brain cells, then the problem of seeing how brain events become mental ones is not readily solved in any obvious

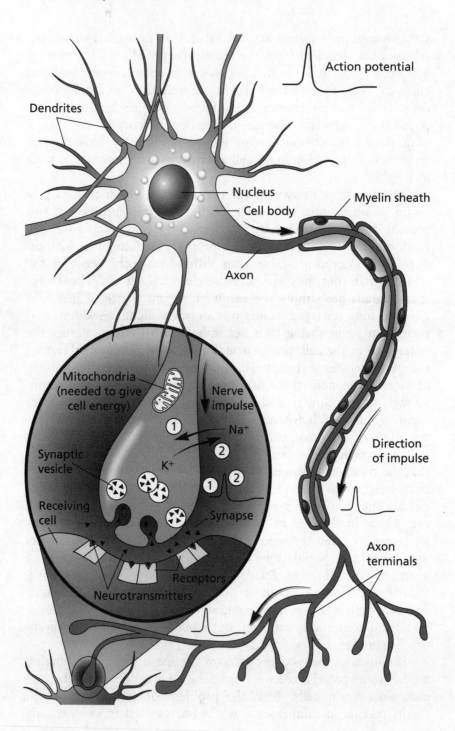

Action potential

Dendrites

Nucleus

Cell body

Myelin sheath

Axon

Mitochondria
(needed to give
cell energy)

Nerve
impulse

Na+

K+

Direction
of impulse

Synaptic
vesicle

Receiving
cell

Synapse

Axon
terminals

Neurotransmitters

Receptors

(Left) Scheme of neuronal communication. An electrical signal is generated in a neuron when sodium and potassium ions become redistributed across the membrane wall, evoking an action potential, a change in electrical activity. Aided by booster stations in the gaps in the insulating myelin sheath, the action potential (also called "impulse") is conducted down the axon to the extremities of the neuron, the axon terminals. The change of voltage in the axon terminals creates the conditions for small packets (vesicles) containing the chemical transmitter to empty out into the gap (synapse) between the first cell and the next. Once it has diffused across the synapse, the transmitter binds to a specific target molecule (receptor), which then causes a change in the potential difference of the next cell. Hence neurons communicate by an electrical signal being encoded into a chemical one, which is then decoded back into an electrical signal in the receiving neuron. (Modified from J. Carey, ed., *Brain Concepts: Sleep and Dreaming* [Washington, D.C.: Society for Neuroscience, 1991].)

way, or indeed by basic common sense. Without some resolution of this problem, we cannot advance much in understanding a host of brain disorders. Parkinson's disease, for instance, is a widespread and severe disorder of movement where the central problem (apart from muscle rigidity and tremor) is that the patient *wants* to move but cannot (Przuntek and Riederer 1989). The mental wish cannot be translated into a physical consequence. Although the patient's muscles can contract appropriately, the ability to energize those muscles is tragically impaired. The physical cause of this phenomenological difficulty is known: It is the loss of a particular chemical (dopamine) in a particular group of cells (nigro-striatal neurons) located deep in the center of the brain. But even with this precise and detailed knowledge, we still have no idea whatsoever why, in that particular part of the brain, dopamine is necessary for the translation of thought into deed.

Another example, given by the philosopher George Graham (1993), is of the phenomenological experience of depression. Although a neuroscientist may state that depression is correlated with a decrease in the levels of a certain class of brain chemicals (amines) (Leonard 1992), that chemical change in itself does not tell us all we may want to know about the state of depression. A full understanding of depression would draw not just on the immediate physical facts but on other, phenomenological factors, such as a divorce or the loss of a job. We cannot simply extrapolate from a physical situation concerning the net status of brain chemicals to a phenomenological one.

There are varying feelings of optimism and pessimism about whether or not we shall ever catch a fair wind in this current stagnant position. Not all philosophers agree that efforts underway to match the physical and the phenomenological will be successful. John Searle (1992) asserts, for example, that the mind obviously arises out of the brain. But he claims that such a dichotomy is misleading and that the two terms can refer to one and the same entity. Yet, at present, there is no available description as to how it happens, any more than it is possible to describe how the sensation of solidity can be reduced to the behavior of molecules. On the other hand, Daniel Dennett (1991) uses an almost identical image to claim the opposite. The properties of gold and silver, such as their glittering, eye-catching appearance, can, he maintains, be explained at the molecular level. Any emergent property should be explicable in terms of the elements from which it arises and which themselves do not possess that property. Hence conscious events should ultimately be explainable in terms of unconscious events.

A serious worry here, as often happens with analogies, is just how appropriate they are. How similar is consciousness to solidity or glitteriness? Of course all three (consciousness, solidity, and glitteriness) are emergent properties—that is, properties literally emerging from a group of components that are themselves lacking that very property. But there is a discrepancy in the actual emphasis placed on the subjectivity of the glitteriness or solidity. The *sensation* of feeling solidity or seeing glitteriness is not intrinsic to an object any more than is the experiencing of beauty, and in this sense Searle's argument seems reasonable—that subjective consciousness is not reducible to the objective elements that cause it. But if we disregard the subjective element of glitteriness and solidity, if we concentrate on why a solid, gold object (even one locked away in a safe) is as it is, then of course we (or at least a chemist) could describe the nonsolid, nonglittery molecular infrastructure that endows the specific object with these properties. But the real question is how far we should disregard the subjective in our consideration of consciousness. Subjectivity is, arguably, the most fundamental property of consciousness, much more so than the mere *feel* of solidity is the defining and pivotal feature of a solid object. The solid object would, arguably, still exist without anyone feeling it, whereas consciousness *cannot* exist if there is no one to experience it.

Consciousness arises from the brain, and the basic components of the brain are neurons. Indeed, it is not in contention that consciousness is an emergent property of neurons but, rather, whether or not we are able to identify the all-important, conceptually unfathomable connection. Tracing the connection between a nugget of gold and solidity or glitteriness is *not* possible if we are after the subjective sensations they produce, but it *is* possible if we concentrate on solidity and glitteriness as nonsubjective phenomena. Similarly, *it is of critical importance to distinguish between identifying what particular elements or events in the brain make up the mind and the subsequent question of how the mind actually emerges from them.* In this book we shall see that the former may be within our grasp, while the latter remains a quest for the future.

The first goal, then, is to identify a class of special brain events that might correlate or match with conscious experiences. For the moment, a fundamental factor that keeps answers to even this first issue so far beyond our grasp is a need to know more about how the brain is organized. True, the brain is composed of chemicals, which are in turn contained in and released by neurons, but as we shall see later on, the real power of the brain resides in the way large aggregates of neurons are organized to yield awesome emergent properties that could never be contemplated by anyone studying a single brain cell. We cannot just switch from a desire to move or from an emotion such as depression to a lone chemical or a solitary brain cell any more than we can explain fully how a car works by simply saying that the amount of fuel is a factor or that the engine needs to be turned on.

A further problem is that an ignorance of what is actually happening in the brain lures us into the use of metaphor. This is all very well as long as we do not start to think we know more about the brain than we actually do. Dennett refers to metaphors as the "tools of thought," but they can actually seduce us into believing that we do literally have drafts, codes, and programs in our brains. If we are to understand the relationship between the physical and the phenomenological, then surely we must understand the physical in its actual, unvarnished, and nonmetaphorical form: a living, breathing assemblage of neurons.

A knife in the back of a corpse tells a detective far from all he wishes to know about that death. In order to explain satisfactorily a knife in the back of a corpse, one needs to know who placed it there and why. Similarly, a plausible physical explanation of the depression of an individual would include not just the level of a chemical but also the connections of different brain cells in diverse brain regions, which would in turn have been caused by myriad external and internal phenomenological factors, including, say, divorce or job loss. So perhaps consciousness is best matched with brain events at the level of particular brain regions.

A Center of Consciousness

If consciousness really is generated by the brain, it must happen somewhere in ordinary physical space. But where? We have just seen that there is neither a special chemical nor, at a level more complex, a general property of individual neurons that is responsible for consciousness. Clearly, then, consciousness does not seep throughout all brain tissue as a wine marinade through a leg of lamb. We need to turn to the next step up in brain organization, that of recognizable and distinct brain regions. Is there a consciousness center, a dedicated region or process of the brain where it all comes together?

Descartes identified the pineal gland, a small region deep in the center of the brain, as the seat of the soul. This was no wild guess, but had a understandable rationale: The brain is symmetrical in that matching distinct regions can be discerned on each side of the brain. There are a few exceptions, of which the solitary pineal gland, in the very center of the brain, may well have been, to Descartes, the most conspicuous. If the soul is indeed in the head, then the pineal gland would seem to be its logical location. For Descartes as well as for Plato, the soul was not the same as mind or consciousness but was a distinct and separate immortal phenomenon. Nonetheless, finding a location for a mortal soul, as for consciousness, has proved equally difficult and indeed has come to be identified with the ideas posed by Descartes.

The elusive location of a consciousness center has been used by Derek Parfit to reject the concept of a lifelong mind and, hence, a self. Since split-brain patients, who have the connections between the two halves of their brain severed, still regard themselves as only one person, Parfit argues there cannot be a single center of consciousness in the normal brain. The concept of an executive region where all inputs into the brain finally cause consciousness has been referred to by Dennett as the Cartesian theater. This theater is a hypothetical command station that effectively enables an enduring and consistent mental state to survive the momentary ebb and flow of consciousness. The Cartesian theater would be no less than the permanent home of the mind, the consciousness center. In a very literal way it would not be a problem for neuroscientists to demonstrate that Dennett was right. Contrary to Descartes' proposition, we can now be certain that no single special area demarcated in the physical brain has the crucial quality of autonomously and uniquely generating consciousness.

But could centers of consciousness exist in some other way? Let us look at the problem from a neuroscientific standpoint. After all, the brain is processing incoming information in *some* way, and we have to find out what that way is. We need to know first not just how neurons work in general but what they actually do in particular. If consciousness is not an inherent and generic property of this smallest component of the brain, a feasible alternative might be that it is localized in some committed region of a nonhomogeneous brain. What happens, then, if we look beyond the generic, disembodied single neuron, if we stand back slightly and survey the brain with a wider and weaker lens?

The brain can readily be divided into conspicuous anatomical regions, many of which can be easily discerned with the naked eye. These regions are often set apart, one from the other, by clear physical boundaries, just as countries frequently are. In the brain the natural boundaries occur where there are obvious differences in simple physical appearance: A brain region may be delineated by a fluid-filled cavity (ventricle) or by a bundle of stringy white tissue (fiber track.) It may contain many densely packed brain cells, thus appearing a different color from adjacent regions, or it may be actually pigmented (see England and Wakely 1991). A legitimate question to ask would be whether or not consciousness

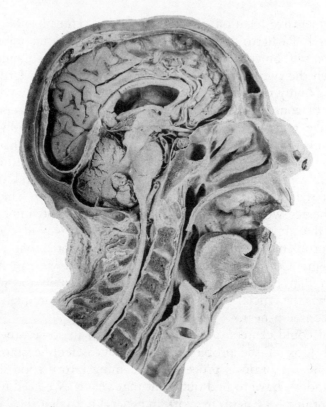

Brain regions, shown in situ. Even with the naked eye, it is possible to distinguish one major brain region from another. (From M. A. England and J. Wakely, *A Colour Atlas of the Brain and Spinal Cord* [London: Wolfe, 1991]. Reprinted with permission.)

might be localized in one of these specific regions. A corollary question, and one that is easier to tackle experimentally, would be: What are the functions of each of these brain regions?

This issue has been pursued ever since scientists were aware of the existence of different brain regions. In the seventeenth century Thomas Willis proposed that there could be seats of memory. A little later this type of localization of function was challenged by experiments on living animals. Luigi Rolando (1773–1831) endeavored to make the "mute pulp" of the brain speak by cutting out or stimulating different areas and observing the effect of these procedures on the behavior of animals. He concluded that different brain regions had different functions. By contrast, Marie-Jean-Pierre Flourens (1794–1867) proposed that all parts of the brain participated in all functions, for all functions appeared to grow weaker as he rather ghoulishly removed progressively more of the brain.

As soon as different brain regions were identified and classified by anatomists, a very basic and persistent debate was kindled: Does each region have a separate function, or does the brain work as a flexible whole, wherein the regions might be interchangeable? In favor of the localization of function is the undeniable fact that damage to specific brain regions leads to specific deficits—for example, the Parkinsonian inability to move. On the other hand, we know that after a stroke the ensuing paralysis can sometimes be compensated for by other groups of neurons gradually taking over the job of the damaged tissue. Similarly, certain brain regions are closely associated with the function of vision; but there are as many as thirty such areas located throughout the brain.

Neither of the two extreme standpoints in the controversy is really accurate. There are no rigid separate functions for each particular brain region, but at the same time the brain does not function as a homogeneous mass. Rather, different brain regions have different and flexible roles in a coordinated, integrated brain. In this spirit, an ingenious compromise between these two positions was proposed as far back as the nineteenth century by the English neurologist John Hughlings Jackson (1835–1911). Jackson suggested that brain regions had different functions, but they were organized in a hierarchical fashion, such that the *relations* among regions were critical in determining a final global output from the brain (Kennard and Swash 1989). As a vindication of his theory, he pointed to certain brain disorders where specific regions are destroyed and which are characterized by an unleashing of symptoms normally kept in check. These include tremor and the wild involuntary movements of Huntington's chorea. Jackson's theory was to have a great impact on Sigmund Freud (1856–1939), who used the idea of repression of lower functions to explain the control exerted by the rational consciousness—the "ego" over the instinctive and passionate "id." The beauty of Jackson's concept is that it reconciled the ideas of separate brain functions with that of a unified brain. But there are problems with a hierarchical organization of the type Jackson proposed: What function within what structure should be placed at the top, and where does consciousness fit in?

In building up an integrated view of the brain from its gross, recognizable parts, it would be straightforward if we could adopt an intuitively comfortable approach and say that each region has a certain function, such as pleasure, conscience, motor control, and so on. But such easy compartmentalization does not exist. For a neuroscientist, therefore, it is easy to sympathize with Dennett and Parfit as they reject the concept of self on the grounds of there being no plausible center for consciousness. The essential difficulty is how we match the phenomenology, the net outward behavior or sensation, with the internal workings of neurons in a given region.

Localization of Functions

Attempts to match mind and brain, phenomenological and physical, have relied on three basic strategies of brain investigation: stimulation, destruction, and recording. By stimulating brain regions electrically, it was hoped to see some relationship between the region so modified and any change in thought or behavior. This procedure would enable us to identify the function of any brain area. Stimulation of gross regions is used very little nowadays, as there may well be no change in outward behavior at all. If a particular region is stimulated, then there is either too much electric current spread to be comparable with the impulses normally at work in the brain or not enough to recruit the relevant neurons.

When it comes to the rationale of selective destruction by experiments or disease, it is questionable if such scenarios help us understand the actual physical neuronal infrastructure leading to changes in mood or actions. An old argument used to illustrate this type of shortcoming is that if a tube were removed from a radio, which then started to howl, you would not say that the function of the tube was to inhibit howling. The data from clinical observations of brain damage therefore have to be interpreted with caution.

A third strategy, which is today by far the most popular, is to record the activity of individual brain cells, usually in nonhumans. In these types of experiments an electrode is placed just outside a neuron so that it is sensitive to changes in the traffic of ions into and out of the cell when an action potential is generated. The greater the frequency of action potentials, the more "active" the cell is deemed. The idea, then, is to relate the activity of the neuron being recorded to whatever function might be occurring at the time. Many scientists argue that this is the best way of coming to terms with the problem of extrapolating to mind from brain. After all, we are letting the brain work without excessive or unnatural stimulation or destruction. We are letting the relationship between physical and phenomenological unfold spontaneously before our eyes. But this very advantage imposes yet another logical constraint, albeit of a different type.

In experiments recording electrical activity, there is no clear causal relation between the discharge of the neuron in question and the concomitant behavior. How would we know if one were a direct consequence of the other? If a red monitor light comes on when I switch on an iron, can I assume that that red light causes the iron to become hot? This is a particularly important point because one of the more ubiquitous features of the nervous system is that neurons are often activated in just such a way (known as corollary discharge) that they might *register* events and send appropriate signals to other parts of the brain but do not necessarily *mediate* those events (Humphrey and Freud 1991). If the red light were broken, the iron would work just the same. The red light is only indicating an event; it is not causing anything to happen. It could thus be the case that if we show that a brain cell is more active during a certain behavior, this increased activity may not have been necessary at all for the actual execution of that original behavior. The function of that cell, much less the general area in which it is located, could not then be claimed with any validity to be the function mediating that particular behavior.

This issue brings us to another problem associated with inferences made from recording neuronal activity. We cannot assume that all neurons within a delineated brain area behave uniformly, any more than we can imagine that all members of a football team play the same position. In addition, a brain area is composed of more complex subpopulations of cells, so that they resemble countless football games occurring simultaneously—but at the same time imagine such games relating to each other as in a tournament. How erroneous it would be to bypass these neuronal subpopulations in the hope that a single cell (an isolated player) would reflect anything truly meaningful or informative regarding the output of a whole region of the brain (the final result of the tournament). An analogy that perhaps might be more apt, since it involves vastly larger numbers, is a presidential election. Would the behavior of just one voter be a faithful barometer of the final voice of the nation, or of the state, or even of the city?

Although monitoring simultaneous behavior and cell activity might give us some clues about the type of function with which the respective brain area might be associated, more questions are generated than answered concerning the importance of that single cell. Is there one complex context, such as walking-in-the-country-on-a-summer-morning-eating-an-apple-and-listening-to-a-robin, for which the cell might be active *and no other*? What about if one were eating a pear, or listening to a warbler, or wearing heavy boots rather than sandals? We could go on *ad absurdum* giving ever more specialized contexts for our single cell. The problem would come, of course, if that cell happened to die (as tens of thousands are claimed to do each day), or if the number of contexts which we encountered as we grew up exceeded the number of available neurons. It is unlikely that individual neurons themselves are the critical entity, nor is their spontaneous activity likely to be the only brain event that we need to know about. Hence recording single cells will only give us a limited amount of information.

We must be careful about what we can expect of single cells and even of a single brain region, even though it is composed of millions of cells. The integration of perceptual awareness with appropriate behavioral responses hinges on the integrity of the brain as a whole, not of putative constituent mini-brains, whether they are single cells or even single brain regions. By compartmentalizing the brain, we concentrate on the trees at the expense of the forest; by focusing on how brain regions are different in what they do, we ignore the question of how they work together.

If we were analyzing why a particular football team was successful, we would not be concerned so much with the respective merits of the individual players but with how they interacted to produce the net behavior. We might indeed study an individual player's sleep patterns, or discover what he had for breakfast, or trace his daily routine, or go so far as to measure his reaction time. All of these factors might contribute to the individual's performance and hence to the ultimate outcome of a game. On the other hand, while exploring the lifestyle of this single player it would be all too easy to forget that he was part of a football team at all. Such is the problem with the study of a *single* cell and in turn a *single* brain region: We might conveniently forget about any global function of the brain, such as consciousness.

If consciousness therefore is not generated exclusively in any one area, we need to think along more dynamic lines. It is not so important how the brain is statically constituted into recognizable, anatomical regions. Rather, the crucial question is what it is happening anywhere and everywhere when it is active, performing one of its functions. Instead of starting with a brain area and trying to find it a function, we can *start* with a function and see how it is generated when several brain regions work in parallel.

Delocalization of Functions

Over thirty years ago two neurophysiologists, David Hubel and Torsten Wiesel (1962), made a discovery that was to win them the Nobel Prize. They showed that neurons in a particular brain region do not all behave in the same way. Instead, groups of neurons became active under very specific and diverse conditions. Hubel and Wiesel were working on the visual system, and they were able to show that different neurons in the outer and evolutionarily newest part of the brain, the cortex, became active if different patterns of light were presented before the eyes. The patterns could come from either a spot of light or a bar that was stationary or moving in a particular direction. For example, for a particular neuron to become excited, the bar might have to be in a very specific orientation, perhaps moving in a certain direction. Some cells turned out to be fussier than others in the conditions required to activate them. These findings soon prompted speculation as to how the brain, in particular the visual system, might work.

Clearly, there could be a hierarchical system of visual processing, with the least fussy cells at the bottom forming inputs to progressively more selective neurons until at the very top there would be only one or two cells responding to a highly particular sight, perhaps even one as specific as your grandmother or a yellow Volkswagen. Although it is well established now that the visual system works in relay stations from the retina through the brain into the cortex, no one now really believes in the idea of a "grandmother cell." An immediate problem is the simple numerical one of not having enough neurons to account for all the sights we might see in our lifetime. An alternative view, suggested by more recent experiments, is that the brain does not work by the convergence required of a hierarchy as much as it does by divergence or parallel processing. In this scheme different systems of the brain would not feed into each other like railway tracks at Grand Central Station but, rather, work independently and simultaneously in parallel.

In the late 1980s several neuroscientists demonstrated that the brain uses at least two distinct paths of neuronal relays for processing different aspects of the same visual object—its form, color, and movement (Livingstone and Hubel 1988; Van Essen et al. 1992). Even at the first stage of visual processing in the retina, two different types of cells are sensitive to different aspects of an object and again at the second stage of processing in the brain. At the third processing point these separate aspects of visual processing are still segregated and indeed do not come together but diverge further to different parts of the brain at the final stage. If we were to localize the function of seeing, it is clear that we would have to implicate diverse brain regions at each relay to accommodate the fact that an apparently unitary process, seeing an object, is actually constructed by the brain from multiple parallel procedures or streams.

A basic concern here is that there is still a poor match between the schemes of philosophers and those of neuroscientists. What the neuroscientists have come up with so far as "streams" is not to be confused with the "drafts" of Dennett or the "bundles" of Parfit. A real-life, neuroscientific parallel draft or stream still leaves us with the problem of where, even just for that particular moment, it all comes together as a glorious symphony of consciousness. Such individual, real-life, complementary drafts on their own would be of little help, since they would be like motion without form or like the grin on the cat in *Alice in Wonderland*. By contrast, the philosophers' hypothetical draft or bundle is in itself a complete and multifaceted whole, however fleeting. The draft used by Dennett in his multiple drafts model of consciousness is no less than the whole, miraculous experience of consciousness in a blink of time, a complete and consistent scene, *not* a disembodied physical feature within one's sensory modality.

There is also another, more immediate, consideration. If this type of parallel processing does occur, then inevitably we will always be looking at more than one brain region to locate a single function. What we perceive as a smooth and single function is splintered into countless scattered shards by the distributed nature of brain organization. Sooner or later, however, we *do* perceive the world around us as single united entities combining form and motion. So if parallel processing occurs, how does it finally all come together? Not only is the pure parallel processing scheme conceptually hard to accept, but there is also empirical evidence that the segregated pathways are not as separate as initially imagined. Rather, they overlap in their functioning. For example, neurons sensitive to color are also activated by inputs from the stream primarily associated with detection of motion (Martin 1992). The distinct functions attributed to separate neuronal pathways turn out to be in some cases rather blurred because one system can, after all, do part of the job of another.

So, then, what is the alternative? If brain processes are organized along neither strictly parallel nor strictly hierarchical schemes, how will we ever be able to tackle the issue of the center of consciousness? In a sense the solution lies in the problem. With respect to localizing function, the problem with both the parallel processing schemes as well as the original scenario of Hubel and Wiesel was that all the experimental rationale was founded on the strategy we looked at a little earlier: correlating an event in the outside world with the activities of single autonomous neurons. Let us return to our analogy of the football player and think instead of neurons functioning in teams. Clearly, the activity of a single cell will not be very informative, but if we start to record from groups of interrelated neurons, more meaningful events might emerge. This rationale is precisely the one currently being adopted with burgeoning enthusiasm in neuroscience.

Neurons can team up and function in networks that can span anatomical divisions of gross brain regions, and these networks can be organized partly in a hierarchical and partly in a parallel fashion. This scheme reconciles at least some of the purely neuroscience problems, such as how to explain the anatomical observations concerning parallel neuronal pathways that are nonetheless cross-linked. Another happy aspect is that such a scheme would ensure that a neuron was not just lying around idle on the off chance that you might, for a second time in your life, walk in the woods while eating an apple at precisely the same moment that a robin was singing, and so on. If a neuron can participate in different groups, then there is much more of a chance that it might be used over and over again in different ways. Such economy of brain cells is much more what we could realistically expect of the brain, given the myriad processes of which it is capable. The concept of neuronal networks, however, still leaves open, for the time being, the mystery as to how a network might become, if only transiently, transformed into the physical basis of a moment of consciousness.

So what have we learned so far? Any explanation of consciousness will need to be able to localize the phenomenon in the brain in a way that neither invokes a specialized and committed center nor leaves neurons with some generic special property. The only alternative is that groups of neurons work together and that some groups of neurons become, in some way, *temporarily* special for a period of time. We will have to incorporate into any neurobiological theory of consciousness a physical basis of shifting populations of neuronal networks with no direct or fixed correspondence to anatomically recognized divisions of the brain. But it could be argued that if the workings of large groups of neurons, albeit in some as yet unspecified way, is all there is to consciousness, and if these neurons are obeying certain known principles, then surely there is no insurmountable mystery. On the face of it, it would seem perhaps a straightforward matter to generate consciousness, perhaps even in nonbiological but comparable systems. We turn, then, to consider the plausibility of a mechanical account of consciousness.

chapter three

MECHANICAL MINDS

"Thought is a priority of matter." It is for this type of claim, made over two hundred and fifty years ago, that Julien Offroy de La Mettrie (1709–1751) has gained a place in history (Hollander 1920). Given the religious climate of his times, it is not surprising that La Mettrie eventually fled his native France for Holland on account of his uncompromising view that the human brain was distinguishable only quantitatively, not qualitatively, from other kinds of machines. Persecuted subsequently by the Dutch, La Mettrie eventually found refuge in Berlin, where he died at the age of forty-two. However, his mechanistic view of the brain and indeed the mind, encapsulated in the title of his book, *L'Homme-machine,* has endured. In addition to religious opposition, there were critics who thought La Mettrie wrong for equally powerful but more secular reasons.

These vociferous "romantic" opponents to the concept of a mechanical brain were those in the *Naturphilosophie* movement, whom we met in Chapter 2. Two basic philosophies were in direct opposition: In one view the brain was the passive vehicle of physicochemical forces that, once identified, would turn out to be essentially banal; in the other view brain tissue was proactive, organic, and, above all, special in some way. In this chapter we shall explore some of the nuts and bolts of the physical brain as a possible key to understanding how consciousness is actually realized or incarnated. If we wished to study the principles of flight, we would not restrict ourselves to studying birds; we might gain great insights by examining different flying machines, such as hot-air balloons, helicopters, jets, and so forth. In this spirit, let us consider computers. Might a computer, one day, have consciousness?

Conscious Computers

Ever since the computer HAL "died" in the film *2001*, the concept of a mechanistic mind has generated an ambivalent fascination. It is both exciting and terrifying that an entity so palpably different from us, not made of flesh and blood, could be nonetheless so similar, seemingly alive, and, above all, conscious. Of course we can dream of very clever machines that are humanlike, such as HAL, or that are more broadly just magical devices enabling time travel, as in *Back to the Future*, or teletransportation, as in *Star Trek*. But we might just as easily dream of truly enchanted entities such as the fairies Oberon and Titania in *A Midsummer Night's Dream*, since we cannot actually prove that any of these imaginings is not possible. In general, nonevents cannot be falsified. How would you prove, for example, that fairies do not exist?

We will only be able to say whether a computer is conscious once we have first resolved what we mean by consciousness. As yet we have no test whereby we can say, "Consciousness occurs when X happens." We have no operational definition with which to tackle the issue of conscious computers to any advantage. Furthermore, responses of just any kind are not signs of awareness: A pocket calculator or our own knee jerk does not necessarily entail consciousness. By the same token, consciousness does not necessarily elicit a response. The listless sea of faces that can stare back blankly during a lecture are those of presumably conscious individuals, even though not a muscle seems to twitch and there is no outward sign of a working mind. Objective, measurable responses have no obvious or immediate link with understanding consciousness. Thus, for our purposes and for the moment, the issue of conscious computers is a dead end. We might gain more insight by pursuing the separate issue of whether or not the brain works like a computer. If so, we will be able to apply computational principles to constructing a theory of consciousness.

Computational Processing

There are some obvious similarities between the brain and a computer. The computer is the first device in human history not geared to perform just one job, like a washing machine, or a range of particular jobs, like a hammer, but is built as a noncommitted system that can perform a vast range of diverse functions, just like the brain. Both computers and brains are highly complicated and superficially mysterious entities with obvious inputs and outputs. Moreover, the outputs or responses can be learned or modified by both the brain and a computer. Since there can be an infinite variety in exactly what is learned, both systems can be endowed with a certain semblance of individuality. Indeed, we even speak of personalizing our relatively small-capacity home computers. The learning potential of both the brain and a modern computer is enormous, and in many respects the computer *seems* superior in its accuracy of recall, its speed of operation, and its reliability of performance.

There is an even more seductive potential similarity between the brain and a computer. If we look inside the "black box" of a computer, we can readily distinguish the hardware, the actual physical construction of the machine, from the software, the less tangible programs. How tempting it would be to ascribe a similar terminology to the brain as hardware, with the substanceless mind as software. At the same time, we could turn to the latest sophisticated computers and focus on features such as parallel processing in the hope that analogous features in the brain then could be better appreciated in terms of the overall working of the system. Proponents of mechanical minds like to use the power of computers, which arises from their ever growing complexity, to refute objections from those who think that brain tissue is in some way different. This is why Dennett (1991) claims it is unfair to argue that the brain is nonmechanical simply because it is not like a pocket calculator. Instead, we need to appreciate the similarities between the brain and modern parallel processing devices.

This line of reasoning is one of the central tenets of computational neuroscience.

Computational neuroscience seems intuitively wrong as the key to consciousness, for two unjustified reasons—banality and incredulity. It feels almost humiliating to accept that all we may be ultimately is a mechanistic, plodding series of operations that can be simulated on a computer. On the other hand, such a dreary series of events is also literally incredible. It is impossible to imagine how the ceaseless traffic of ions across the wall of a brain cell can be converted into the essence of our subjectivity and personality. These reservations, however, really do not stand up for very long. Some computers are far from banal; furthermore, incredulity was fortunately not perceived as a serious consideration by Nicolaus Copernicus (1473–1543) when he proposed that the earth revolved round the sun, or by Orville and Wilbur Wright when they persisted with a flying machine.

In order to assess the validity of the computational approach for eventually understanding consciousness, we need to compare briefly the nuts and bolts of brains and computers. The computer in common use is serial and digital. This means that it processes one job at a time in a yes-no, on-off fashion. Well over thirty years ago, much was made of the fact that neurons also seemed to have two unambiguous states, excited and inhibited. Excitation and inhibition occurred when the sharp, transient change in voltage across the membrane (the action potential) did or did not occur. We saw in Chapter 2 that the generation of an action potential in a brain cell leads to the release of a chemical transmitter which latches onto a neighboring cell, so that this second cell in turn is either inhibited or excited. The presence of an action potential shows that a brain cell is at work and communicating with other neurons. It was thus natural to view the occurrence of these action potentials as similar to the binary modes of a digital computer.

Soon, however, it became apparent that neurons were far from digital in their operation. The events *leading up* to the generation of an action potential are actually graded (analog). But that is not all. We now know that there are many types of ion traffic across the membrane that can occur in the absence of action potentials. These other ionic conductances confer on each type of neuron the propensity for particular patterns of response. Sometimes there is even an oscillating bi-stability, as the neuron rhythmically changes from more to less excitable entirely on its own in a continuous cycle. These responses, which do not necessarily lead to the generation of action potentials, will nevertheless *bias* the neuron to be more or less active. In this way the fluxes of ions that predispose a neuron to respond in a variety of ways confer on the brain an enormous flexibility and versatility. Such modulatory ionic events in the brain are not digital, but analog. In this respect they differ from most conventional computers.

Another critical feature of neurons that makes them hard to compare with computer nodes is that their very *shape* dictates how they communicate with one another. On the face of it, this could seem bizarre in that it is not immediately obvious how a brain cell might vary in shape or how the basic principle of communication, which we met in Chapter 2, might itself vary. There are at least fifty basic neuronal shapes in the brain which can affect the efficiency of signaling. For example, neurons with very long dendrites, extensions that are similar to long limbs, could receive incoming signals mainly at the extremities of these extensions, the neuronal equivalent of fingertips. Because the electrical signal has a relatively long way to travel from the extremity to the main body of the cell, and because the "limb" along which it is conducted is not like copper wire but a highly imperfect conductor of electricity, the signal may degrade considerably before it reaches its destination. Thus only signals that are initially relatively powerful will get through. Another important feature is the actual size of neurons. Small cells are excited more easily than larger ones (because the smaller cells have a higher resistance, and so any current produced as an incoming signal is transformed into a larger voltage).

Size, then, and the number and length of processes that extend from a cell are critical factors in its behavior. Therefore the seemingly easy metaphor of hardware and software does not really work as an analogy for the brain. The actual shape of the nodes of a computer gives no clue regarding the type of responses it might make. The hardware gives little information about the software, which is programmed well after the computer is built. By contrast, the physical shape of neurons in the brain goes a long way in determining neuronal response; the "hardware" and the "software" are effectively one and the same.

Even so, computational neuroscience in recent years has managed to circumvent these problems by looking beyond individual neurons toward the overall functioning of the brain. We have already seen in Chapter 2 that the interactions between neurons and neuronal aggregations are most accurately described as networks (a combination of hierarchies and parallel processors). If a neuron is part of a net, many potential difficulties in understanding how the real brain works can be accommodated (Churchland and Sejnowski 1992). First, instead of having just one function, a neuron can participate in different networks serving several functions, just as a single person can be part of a football team, a family, a rock-and-roll dance duo, a church choir, and myriad other groupings. The combinations that can be made from a group of components vastly exceed the number of the components themselves. Thus it is easy to see how the idea that neuronal networks are the functional building blocks of the brain immediately circumvents the problem of not having enough neurons to perform all the tasks we would expect.

In addition, the incorporation of neurons into a network makes possible a certain amount of redundancy, if we assume several neurons can do the same job. Such redundancy acts as insurance against the death of an otherwise unique single cell. Most important of all, once neurons are incorporated into a network, they can be changed in some way through inputs from other neurons. We have seen that it would be impossible to explain how a single cell might know in advance that it should respond when, say, grandmother comes into view. However, once a neuron is part of a network, the potential for *communication* among cells can be exploited, and learning can take place.

Learning is the key property of neurons in groups that cannot be accomplished by a neuron in isolation. It is the phenomenon of learning, or, less anthropomorphically, adaptation, that is the central event studied by computationalists in their attempts to reconstruct what they regard as a critical, perhaps *the* critical, feature of the brain. By studying the shifting relations among neurons in a network, computational scientists try to model aspects of the brain. Does this modeling of neuronal networks throw light on brain function, most specifically on consciousness? Or was Tomaso Poggio right when he cynically remarked in 1988 that "the only thing neural networks have in common with the human brain is the word neural."

The Model Brain

A computational model is based on the idea that neuronal networks receive distinct inputs which are subsequently transformed within the net by a set of mathematically expressible rules, or algorithms, to give a final output. An algorithm is a well-defined and completely inflexible operation that can be applied automatically in a procedure regardless of any other factors. The simplest and least flexible arrangement would be a network organized so that the relations among neurons remain fixed. In such a setup the group of cells would function as a straightforward input-output device, scarcely more sophisticated than a slide rule or an elementary dictionary. However, the input-output relations do not have to be predetermined; the algorithms need not be defined in advance but can emerge from the network as it operates.

The particular advantage of a *group* of model neurons is that we can make the hypothetical cells respond differentially to the same input; we can bias the sensitivity of a cell to a subsequent input, just as different individuals might respond with different sensitivities to someone shouting. Some people might ignore the shouting until it has gone on for several minutes, and even then some might remain impervious, while others might react as soon as a voice is raised. This idea of weighting the responses of neurons in a group means that we have a wider range of outputs for a specified input. But the most valuable aspect of all in computational neuroscience is that, just as a soldier might learn to respond quickly to the commands of a drill sergeant, the weighting for each individual neuron can be changed through experience.

The power and potential of an adjustable bias in neuronal responses was first explored nearly fifty years ago by the visionary psychologist Donald Hebb, who suggested that the more two neurons communicate with each other, the easier communication becomes (1949). In his view, weighting the extent of communication among various neurons is not random but actually the result of experience or learning. In this way the very nature and quantity of messages coming into a network of neurons might modify how those messages are subsequently processed. The more that certain contacts among neurons are used, the more efficient those particular contacts become. We would thus have a dynamic model that is at least theoretically able to account for the adaptation that we know has to be constantly occurring in the brain, especially if we are to understand how we can adapt through experience. Once the feature of weighting is incorporated into a computer model, the next step for computationalists is to build feedback processes into the model. The output then also becomes a kind of input and influences subsequent events in the network. But is this really how the brain works, and, most important, is it all we need to know in order to explain consciousness?

A Computational Mind

The first issue concerns what is actually fed into any model brain: How accurately do the particular features of whatever input is introduced correspond to the real world? After all, we do not know a priori what features of the outside world the brain normally seizes on as important. This question is also of concern to computationalists. Two leading advocates of the computational approach, Terrence Sejnowski and Patricia Churchland, have confessed that "simulating the world is as hard as simulating the brain" (1992).

Another implicit difficulty in studying consciousness is related to what goes in and what comes out of a computational model. Computationalists frequently refer to the "encoding of vectors," implying that at some stage a signal, a message, or information is about to be decoded. Nothing could be further from the truth. There is no little person inside the brain translating nerve impulses back into light flashes, tones, and tastes. Perhaps the nearest the brain gets to decoding is the ultimate translation of brain activity into some kind of responsive behavior. The only time an input gives rise to a clear, invariant output is in the case of reflexes, such as the knee jerk in response to a tap on the knee. And that behavior does not involve the brain at all! Usually when the brain is involved, movements or behaviors do not bear an invariant and direct relation to any inputs. What you see, smell, hear, taste, and feel is not encoded to give a subsequently decoded, stereotyped *unconscious* response. Rather, all incoming information is stored like credit in a bank, to be used to advantage at a later, unspecified date as part of your idiosyncratic repertoire.

A further problem in modeling the brain as a forerunner to modeling the mind is the need for such a model to encompass several levels. Levels, in this case, refer to the different degrees of detail with which the brain can be described. There is the chemical level of molecules which gives rise to the level of brain cells which eventually leads to the level of net response, the final output of behavior. Perhaps the most successful model constructed to date is the one (mentioned in Chapter 2) by Alan Hodgkin and Andrew Huxley in their theoretical reconstruction of the action potential (1952). More recently other ionic events have been faithfully modeled, including the autorhythmicity of cells, in which the excitability of the neuron oscillates on its own like a one-person band without any external help (Llinás 1988a). This highly reductionist level of modeling has the advantage of possibly giving rise to previously unenvisioned events *within the context studied,* rather like new chess strategies might emerge from a committed chess-playing computer. But a chess-playing computer will never be expected to compose a symphony; thus these reductionist models are similarly constrained. We would not expect a model of, say, the influx of sodium ions through a particular ion channel ever to generate spontaneously and independently a model for learning and still less one for consciousness.

The problem of levels is not that one level is a more accurate barometer of neuronal events than another but, rather, of translating one level in terms of another. This difficulty is best illustrated by one of the most intensively investigated phenomena in the brain, long-term potentiation, which some neuroscientists believe lies at the very core of our ability to learn and to remember.

The Mechanism of Learning

Over twenty years ago two electrophysiologists, Tim Bliss and Terje Lomo (1973), made a surprising discovery in the course of their experiments. They observed that, when stimulated intensively, neurons become more sensitive to subsequent stimulation for several hours later. Bliss and Lomo named their discovery long-term potentiation (LTP). LTP is most readily demonstrated like this: A cell in a slice of tissue taken from any one of several particular brain areas is kept alive in a dish in vitro and is electrically stimulated so that it excites a neighboring cell. This stimulation is then repeated over and over again at a high frequency. Now comes the interesting part. If a solitary weak stimulus is subsequently applied some time later (long term), the degree of excitation (potentiation) is massively enhanced.

The discovery of this phenomenon was hailed with great excitement because it seemed to provide the physical evidence for Hebb's ideas of strengthening the communication among neurons, the very essence of weighting. Furthermore, the actual events underscoring LTP can be fairly well traced to the level of the participating chemicals. The cornerstone for the entire event is a special type of docking zone (receptor) for the chemical on the external surface of the target neuron. Receptors usually act as intermediaries between the released chemical and the target neuron. When a particular chemical fits into a receptor, it acts as a trigger to open or close channels in the cell membrane for the subsequent passage of a particular ion in or out of the cell. Because the voltage is thus changed, the excitability of the neuron is altered. However, the receptor that is pivotal to our story is special in that when a transmitter binds to it, there is usually no change in its excitability (Watkins 1989).

The obstinacy of this receptor means that even though the chemical is released from a neighboring cell, it will initially have no effect; it attaches to a target that does nothing with it, as though receiving a present but not unwrapping it. But the same chemical can also attach to more willing, less fussy types of receptors which respond readily and let positively charged sodium ions flood into the neuron. The neuron thus becomes more excited, regardless of the lack of participation of the special, fussy receptor. If the stimulation is continued, a large amount of transmitter will be released continuously onto the unfussy target, and the cell will be excited for a sustained period.

But the trick really lies in the special property of the uncooperative, dormant target receptor. What is special is that if the cell is excited for a sustained period of time, the consequent, prolonged change in potential difference across the cell membrane causes the target area suddenly to come to life. It is as though shouting and shouting at someone finally makes that person open the present. What actually happens when the target comes to life is that the sustained excitement, the new voltage caused by activating the unfussy target, removes a plug of magnesium from the channel. Once the plug is no longer obstructing the channel, activation of the special target begins and lets not just sodium but also calcium ions into the neuron. Calcium is a far more versatile and powerful ion inside a neuron than is sodium. Once in the interior of the cell, these calcium ions can promote many changes, such as the activation of genes. And once certain genes are activated, the neuron may change the amounts and types of particular chemicals it contains and even undergo a modification in its overall appearance. Thus it will have adapted over a period of time to the sustained increase in input; its response will have become weighted to respond in different ways to future signals.

Since LTP is thoroughly documented from the bottom up, from its chemical nuts and bolts, it is hardly surprising that it is one of the richest areas for the computational modeler to go prospecting. Indeed, some of the most powerful models are currently being constructed around the algorithm of LTP. If anything is a barometer of the success of the computational approach, it is LTP. So how does it fare?

Our first stumbling block is that so far LTP has only been truly demonstrated in artificial laboratory experiments. Sustained stimulation can show electrophysiological potentiation and parallel behavioral evidence of memory, both of which are abolished by a drug that blocks the fussy all-important receptor. But no one has proved conclusively that LTP occurs in the normal animal while it is learning or memorizing some task within its normal repertoire of behavior. Nonetheless, it seems that the intense stimulation of the contrived laboratory protocol, which is needed to induce the potentiated response but which has proved elusive in the normal brain, might still have a real-life counterpart. If incoming messages that converge on a particular neuron are all active simultaneously, then this concerted effort would be sufficient for priming the potentiation, just as several people talking together might be the equivalent of one person shouting (Zalutsky and Nicoll 1990).

A further finding is that when an animal is quiet after a period of exploration, many cells in the critical brain region become active altogether in a synchronized way (Buzsaki 1989). This concerted surge of activity may act like the repeated stimulation in an artificial laboratory situation and produce potentiation after that exploration period. This scenario suggests that you gain

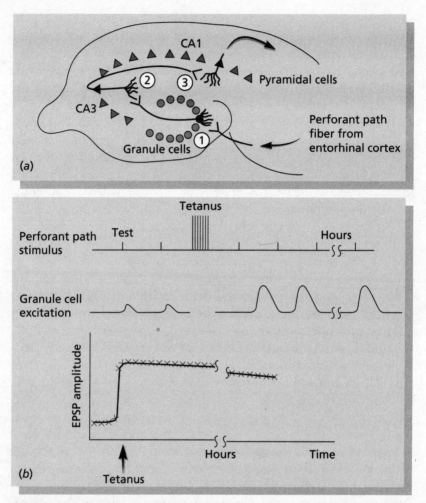

Scheme of long-term potentiation (LTP). (*a*) A schematic drawing of a slice of hippocampus. The regions CA1 and CA3 are called cornu ammonis (Latin for "Ammon's horn"), another name for the hippocampus. Nerve fibers from another brain region, the entorhinal cortex, enter the hippocampus and make contact with cells in the first region, the dentate gyrus (1). In turn, cells in the dentate gyrus make contact with cells in CA3 (2), which make a third relay with output cells in CA1 (3). (*b*) The first trace shows the different electrical stimuli applied to the input fibers. Note that the test stimulus is more modest and briefer than the stronger, repeated tetanus stimulus. The middle trace shows the degree of excitation in the target cells (granule cells) in the dentate gyrus. After the tetanus, the original test stimulus evokes a much larger response. The bottom trace shows the duration and slow decay of this potentiated response over hours. (Modified from Irwin B. Levitan and Leonard K. Kaczmarek, *The Neuron: Cell and Molecular Biology* [Oxford: Oxford University Press, 1991].)

experience for a while and then, during a period of rest, your brain sets in motion LTP, which is responsible for your adapting to or learning from the experience you have just had. This idea is difficult to accept intuitively, since it is hard to know what really constitutes activity.

In the case of sophisticated human animals, we do not have to be on the move in order to gain experience. Would intense thought or stimulating conversation or attendance at a lecture generate activity? It would certainly constitute experience. In the average college day, for example, little provision is made for regular periods of rest after each and every class. If this model were to apply to humans, we would therefore have to imagine that the periods of rest and experience were much longer than in rats; there would have to be periods cycling over day-and-night periods, with LTP occurring only after dark. This scenario leads to the even more farfetched view that learning or memory would be least effective in the morning, at the time most remote from the moment in the following evening when we have a chance to rest and let LTP go to work to consolidate our memories.

A further serious consideration is that over time LTP decays, whereas many of our memories, we hope, are relatively permanent. So it seems that the phenomenon of potentiation at the cellular level does not equate precisely with the learning process. We do not have an exact match between a neurochemical event and a behavioral one. Instead, the former influences the latter in, at most, a necessary but not a sufficient manner. Indeed, it seems the exclusive one-to-one matching between the physical and the phenomenological is even more tenuous than that, since LTP can occur rather promiscuously in a variety of totally different situations. For example, LTP can take place *before* a learning task, thereby facilitating it, rather than being the learning event itself (Alonso et al. 1990). In this case, LTP might only be the first stage in an adaptation process, as its lack of permanency suggests. Alternatively, it might act as some kind of initiating executive switch that somehow sets in motion the learning process rather than actually causing it.

The physiologist Rodolfo Llinás has further demonstrated that the physical events of LTP do not match up exactly with the phenomenological process of memory, since they can be generated under conditions totally different from those associated with memory. Llinás has shown that if inputs to a cell cause an on-off excitement in rapid oscillation (Blake et al. 1988), then a potentiation can also occur *without* the purportedly requisite priming from an initial intense stimulation. This type of LTP, Llinás maintains, is not mediating memory at all, but may represent a requisite condition related to it, such as attention (Alonso et al. 1990).

The loose relationship between the physical mechanism of LTP and the phenomenological process of memory suggests that there are still many difficulties in relating what is going on in the brain leading to the final result, global behavior. The dedicated computationalist might retort that only certain types of behaviors can, after all, be modeled. Let's consider what these behaviors might be. In effect we are about to reverse a previous strategy. Instead of trying to find a behavior to match a neuronal mechanism, as with LTP, we are starting with a behavior and analyzing it in terms of neuronal mechanisms. The important question then focuses on how that behavior is related to consciousness.

Mechanical Behaviors

Perhaps it is not surprising that the behaviors so far successfully modeled computationally have been relatively uncomplicated; they are the sort of movements made by insects or, in the mammalian brain, behaviors that are in a sense insectlike. These simple behaviors do not require many intervening processes between the input and the output. Let's look at a simple movement that rabbits make (Yeo et al. 1983). This movement (the output of a computational system) involves sliding a special, thin nictitating membrane over the eye in response to some kind of mildly aversive trigger, an input, such as a puff of air. If the puff of air is then presented at the same time as a particular noise, say, a loud click, after a while a change occurs. The loud click presented *alone* is enough to act as a trigger for the membrane to slide over the eye, the so-called nictitating membrane response. How might such a clear input-output behavior involving a type of learning be matched with events in the brain itself? And how successfully can it be reproduced or modeled in computational terms?

During the learning process in which the previously neutral click acquires a significance, cells in an area of the brain associated with memory (the hippocampus) become more active. The

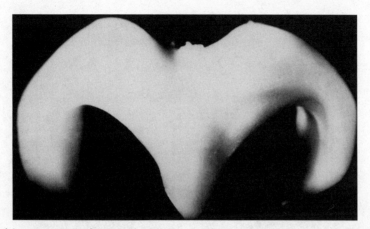

The hippocampus of a rat. This distinctive brain structure, named after the Greek for "sea horse," actually resembles rams' horns in the way it curls around the inner part of the brain. The hippocampus has changed in size, but not markedly in shape, in humans. (Photo courtesy of Dr. J. N. P. Rawlins, Department of Experimental Psychology, Oxford University.)

hippocampus is a large and conspicuous brain region curling from the front of the brain, around the sides, and then forward again, a little like truncated rams' horns. In fact, the structure takes its name from the Greek for "sea horse." It has long been associated with memory, since damage there results in profound amnesia for subsequent events. Indeed, it was in the hippocampus that LTP was first discovered. But it would be a mistake to jump to the conclusion that the hippocampus is necessarily the area where learning always and exclusively takes place. The hippocampal cells may simply be registering that learning is occurring elsewhere—just as we saw in Chapter 2 that a red monitor light on an iron is useful but not necessary for the functioning of the appliance. It turns out that if portions of the hippocampus of a rabbit are selectively destroyed, the animal can still learn to use the sound of the click as a cue to slide the membrane over its eyes.

Instead, it is a brain region known as the cerebellum, the "little brain" that looks like a cauliflower attached rather precariously at the back of the head, that is most crucial. If the cerebellum itself is damaged, then movements become very clumsy

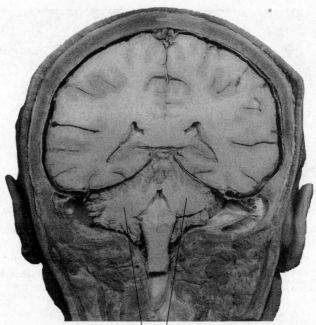

Cerebellum

The cerebellum (in situ), where learning takes place. This brain structure straddles the midline of the back of the brain and is made up of repeating folds, or folia. Apart from size and the percentage of brain it represents, the cerebellum has changed little during animal evolution. (From M. A. England and J. Wakely, *A Colour Atlas of the Brain and Spinal Cord* [London: Wolfe, 1991]. Reprinted with permission.)

(ataxia); there is a loss of sensorimotor coordination, which is effectively an inability to match sensory input with motor output. It is this very type of movement, such as driving a car, playing the piano, or skiing, which we regard as skilled and which is locked into a sequential series of inputs and outputs.

The earliest example of a computational model of such behavior was developed for the cerebellum a few decades ago by the scientist David Marr (1969), who used Hebb's idea of weighting, where communication among brain cells became easier the more it occurred. The essence of Marr's model was to show that if two input messages converged on a cerebellar neuron simultaneously, their joint activity might have the effect of enhancing the sensitivity of the receiving neuron to subsequent inputs. The result of this change in sensitivity might be that if one of these inputs, such as the sound of a click, had been previously ineffective, it would now elicit a response on its own.

In more recent research, the precise neurochemical mechanism underlying this type of adaptation has been suggested to be a variation on long-term potentiation called long-term depression (LTD) (Ito 1987), although this hypothesis remains controversial. Were this type of mechanism operational in the cerebellum, LTP or indeed LTD might well be the answer to a computationalist's dream. The result would be a clear behavior with an anatomical and physiological infrastructure that could be analyzed by computational methods. Computational methods work very well for matching an output to an input and showing how this can be modified over time. But when we ski, drive, or play the piano, we perform these skills automatically. Although we are conscious, we are not consciously planning each movement by which we execute the skill. So, although a simple behavior may be modeled computationally, it is not at all obvious that consciousness is a part of that behavior. On the contrary, when we make a conscious effort to analyze and be aware of our movements as we perform such a skill, we are usually far less adept.

Perhaps it is not surprising that, compared to these mechanical behaviors, we fare less well with modeling more cognitive processes entailing consciousness. A central problem is the nature of the output. In a neuronal net, the processing is distributed: Different aspects of the job are parceled out among individual components but come together again as an output, such as the sliding of a membrane over the eye. It is always a *single* behavior (referred to in computational terms as vector averaging), simply because there can only be any one output or any one movement at any one time. After all, a joint cannot move in two directions or at two different velocities at the same time. However, it is difficult to determine in advance what would be the output of the brain at both the cellular and the behavioral levels once we start dealing with events beyond fixed behaviors—effective reflexes where neuronal mechanism and behavior have a clear one-to-one correspondence. At the cellular level the problem is the one we noted in Chapter 2. Although there is enormous scope in the brain for the distribution of processing, the means for bringing it all together (resynthesis) is far from apparent. Likewise, at the phe-nomenological level, it is worth noting that a nightmare, an inspired insight, or a headache need not give rise to any objective responses in a person. How, then, could we even begin to simulate them computationally?

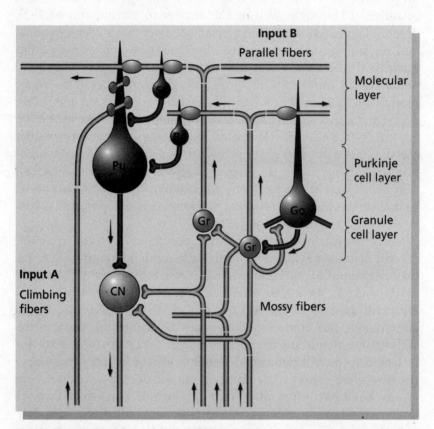

Cerebellar "modular" circuitry: a scheme of the connections between neu-rons in the outer layer (cortex) of the cerebellum. The neurons are orga-nized into repeating modules, one of which is shown here. The Purkinje cell (Pu), shown filled with dye in the illustration on p. 18, is the major cell of this region. It receives two types of inputs directly (climbing fibers, A, and parallel fibers, B), as well as a third, indirect input (mossy fibers). In turn, the Purkinje cell sends the final net signal to neurons deep within the cerebellum, the cerebellar nuclei (CN).

The Robotic Lifestyle: Computers versus Minds

If computers are appropriate models for stimulus-response behavior, the big question is then: To what extent is this type of processing typical of the brain? In the computational model the individual neuron operates on a strict input-output algorithm. Although some of the time our brains might indeed use this type of processing, with groups of brain cells functioning on a simple input-output basis, it seems that any behavioral responses in themselves are not faithful barometers of brain processes. We rarely respond in exactly the same way a second time to a given situation. As yet, neuroscientists are only beginning to appreciate some of the factors involved in learning processes. It is clear, however, that learning, such as discovering the location of food in a maze, involves something between the sensory input and the behavioral output; it requires thought and as such is referred to as a cognitive process. Let us look beyond net outward behavior to see if computation, *irrespective of behavior,* can throw light on the central issue of the processes of the mind itself.

An immediate hurdle in relating consciousness to computational processing concerns the very characteristics of that processing. Two basic physicochemical properties of the brain do not lend themselves readily to invariant algorithmic processing. Most fundamental of all is the problem of numbers. Despite the formidable number of neurons and connections in our brains, we still have only a limited storage capacity for all of the algorithms required for all our mental processes. Another aspect is that there is always some uncertainty in describing neuronal events; neurophysiologists, for example, tend to speak of the *probability,* rather than of the certainty, of particular neurons generating action potentials. If you are recording from a brain cell of an unanesthetized animal, you can never be precisely sure what that neuron will do next in terms of its excitability.

Certain aspects of brain processing are also incompatible with algorithms. As Roger Penrose (1989) has pointed out, it is hard to form fixed and rigid rules for intuition and common sense. Furthermore, our reasoning is not so much a slavish progression from one step to the next but, rather, a confluence of prejudices and insights as well as logic. We can often devise shortcuts for solving a problem, or are sometimes lucky enough to see the answer in a flash. At the very least, it would be rash to assume that *all* of the brain uses algorithmic processing *all of the time*. Probably the most inspired and original thoughts do not depend totally on algorithms. The physicist Niels Bohr is said to have once admonished a student, "You are not thinking, you are just being logical."

It is particularly hard to see how computational processing might, even hypothetically, deal with certain particular features of consciousness. First, our memories are labile and highly subject to revision. How easy it is to tell yourself that someone was not really as angry as you originally thought when you turned up late, or that the red wine you spilled on the white rug was, on reflection, the fault of the cat startling you. How often we rewrite past events, suppressing certain scenes and distorting others, to make ourselves seem braver, cleverer, wittier, or more justified in acting in a certain way. This capricious and inconstant type of memory, which we all display to different extents at different times, is not at all comparable to the rigidly definable and locatable memory of computers. Second, we all have a concept of self. Third, spontaneous mental states such as a nostalgic daydream or a fantasy—which entail neither sensory inputs nor movement outputs but nonetheless need consciousness—are not readily reducible to computation. Fourth, we are able to form abstract concepts such as love, truth, and beauty from the bits and pieces of information flooding into us. Fifth, we are spontaneously active, and our actions are frequently generated from internal thoughts, not external triggers. We cash in the deposits paid to our brains at a much earlier time in a seemingly spontaneous and unpredictable manner.

Although no one really treats the brain anymore as a mere input-output device, all computational models are input driven by some clear trigger. In itself this constraint need not negate a particular model of the brain. After all, our minds are frequently driven by some external sensory inputs. Rather, it is the *shift of emphasis* implied by computation, away from the natural spontaneity of the brain and hence from consciousness, that is so critical. Once an input is specified and the algorithms laid down, we are effectively robots. So why bother with consciousness? Whereas this standpoint might work occasionally—the knee jerk, for example, or running out of the way of a car, or even driving a car much of the time—it certainly does not hold in very many cases. Frequently we are proactive, carrying out various acts that are seemingly spontaneous but far from random, and are thus engaged in voluntary movement. It is possible, therefore, that it is the behavior *not* requiring consciousness (such as stereotyped automatic motor skills) that is best modeled by computation. Just as LTP is not the essence of memory but a possible requirement for it, so computational processing at best may only be a necessary but not a sufficient requirement for processes in the brain leading to consciousness.

One of the most vigorous opponents of the view that an algorithmic, computational basis of consciousness can ever be found is Roger Penrose. He cites a theorem (Nagel and Newman 1959) proposed by the mathematician Kurt Gödel to justify a nonalgorithmic element for consciousness. Gödel's theorem states that the validity of an argument in logic is dependent on premises that are additional to that argument. In mathematics, true propositions are obtained from procedures that are *not* algorithmic, not predetermined by a set of rules. In the same fashion, Penrose observes, our consciousness is governed by something more than a fixed set of rules, more than a series of algorithms. It is only by having some unidentified ability, some sort of insight beyond fixed rules, that we can, for example, discern truth from falsity. Consciousness would be nothing without intuition, common sense, and insight. None of these qualities, as we have just seen, is readily tractable to algorithmic processing. Indeed, if the mind functioned algorithmically, then we would never play a piece of music or go for a walk just because we "felt like it." Every action would have a specified goal and would be done for specified reasons, and with no shortcuts. Such a scenario would cripple the pace of our daily life and turn it irrevocably into a dull routine, all the time!

Another problem with having a purely computational mind concerns the localization of function in the brain. After all, algorithms are nothing in themselves; they have to be interpreted for a particular meaning, for each context. Where and how would this interpretation take place? Where and how would it be laid down, so that whenever someone gives you something you must say thank you? If receiving an object was a frequently repeated part of your job on an assembly line, or if the object in question was a baton in a relay race, or a hand grenade with the pin pulled out, this behavior of saying thank you would be inappropriate. Certainly, there is no obvious site in the brain, nor anything there to decipher the signals, to tell you automatically to say thank you or not. In this vein, even advocates of a mechanical mind, such as Churchland and Sejnowski, claim that "motives, moods, and appetites may be part and parcel of information processing to a degree hitherto unsuspected" (1992).

It appears, then, that consciousness is not reducible to computation and that computation can occur without consciousness. Irrespective of whether or not some of the brain works some of the time like a computer, we need more for an explanation of the physical basis of consciousness. When we disparagingly refer to someone as a robot, it is exactly the apparent lack of emotion, indeed, of consciousness, to which we are referring. Hence, in a search for the physical basis of consciousness, we need to continue to seek special features of the real brain.

chapter four

DISRUPTED
MINDS

Everyone has some idea of the devastating consequences of stroke, head wounds, or neurosurgery, where patients speak and/or act in a conspicuously abnormal way. Has the actual consciousness of these people been altered? We might expect to learn a great deal by seeing how apparent states of consciousness change when brains have been damaged in different ways. This rationale is a little like observing a person not just as he or she normally is, but thirsty in a desert or nervous before an interview. In such a wide range of extreme situations, we would be able to infer much more about the basic nature of that individual. In the scenarios we are about to look at, the exacting situations of brain damage might indeed help us understand more about consciousness.

In the cases of brain damage that we shall be examining, the patients are not unconscious but apparently very much aware of the world around them. Consciousness has been not abolished, but modified. What is changed in each case is a particular aspect of consciousness. If we close our eyes, our visual awareness of an object vanishes, but not consciousness in general. The important issue to bear in mind here is that consciousness is multimodal; it is not normally parceled out according to our senses. When our inner memories dominate, for example, in a daydream, who is to say if any aspects of our sensory systems are at work. Normal global consciousness is a symphony of senses and memories, and as such is extremely difficult to disentangle if we are looking for its physical origin. A good starting point might be to take examples where only one sense is affected and then see what deductions can be made about changes in ensuing consciousness.

Blindsight

In 1917 the British neurologist George Riddoch was working as a captain in the Royal Army Medical Corps. While treating soldiers with head wounds incurred in the trenches during World War I, he noticed a strange phenomenon. Blinded patients could apparently grasp an object in motion and indicate the direction of motion, yet they denied being able to see the object. Because this finding seemed so illogical and bizarre, it was conveniently ignored in subsequent exploration of the visual system for over half a century.

In the early 1970s, however, the psychologist Larry Weiskrantz (1980) was working with people who had suffered limited damage to the brain. There was restrictive damage to certain brain regions because the local blood supply had been cut off due to a blocked blood vessel, leaving a group of cells deprived of oxygen, a stroke. Weiskrantz found that some patients, for whom the stroke occurred in an area toward the back of the brain, could not consciously see an object in front of them in certain places within their field of vision. Yet, in a very revealing experiment, he asked these patients to guess if a light had flashed in their region of blindness, even though it was accepted that they could not consciously "see" the flash. Incredibly, some patients performed this task considerably above the chance probability that would be the case if they were truly guessing, and almost as well as if they could see.

Were these people conscious of the object, after all? A typical case was patient DB, who was completely blind in his left visual field after undergoing brain surgery yet who subsequently performed well in reaching for objects. Weiskrantz and his colleagues reported: "Needless to say, [DB] was questioned repeatedly about his vision in his left half-field, and his most common response was that he saw nothing at all. . . . When he was shown his results, he expressed surprise and insisted several times that he thought he was just 'guessing.' When he was shown a video film of his reaching and judging orientation of lines, he was openly astonished" (1974). Weiskrantz aptly dubbed this paradoxical phenomenon blindsight. Blindsight patients must possess some kind of visual ability, but this ability has become totally dissociated from conscious awareness of events in certain parts of the visual field. So where and when does consciousness of these events normally fit in?

An obvious place to start is to identify the brain region that is damaged in blindsight patients. Since the time of Riddoch, it has been clear that the problem has nothing to do with the retina or the deeper subcortical parts of the brain, but rather with the outer layer, the cortex itself. We saw in Chapter 2 that visual processing can occur in parallel, where motion and form are each analyzed separately. Even within the brain area concerned with motion, however, there is no single executive area responsible. The physiologist Semir Zeki (1993) has highlighted at least two critical parts of the cortex, regions V1 and V5. If V5 is damaged, then so is perception of motion. If V1 is damaged but V5 remains intact, then signals can be recorded from neurons in V5 that correlate with the presentation of a moving object. However, the patient may deny being aware of anything at all, hence blindsight.

The critical factor for conscious vision, Zeki proposes, is that these two particular parts of the cortex (V1 and V5) should be able to interact. Not only must V1 be able to send signals to V5, but there must be a reciprocal arrangement whereby region V1 is, in return, kept informed of what is happening in region V5. The two regions must be able to sustain a dialogue. If left to their own devices, the neurons in V1 will not register, for example, the global direction of movement. On the other hand, we have seen that it is not enough if the neurons in V5 work away by themselves, sensitively monitoring motion of an object. What is needed for the normal *awareness* of motion, it would seem, is that certain neurons in V1 and V5 be active simultaneously in a cooperative fashion. The neurons in each of these two regions not only discharge in response to the motion of an object as it happens but actually emit signals in synchrony, oscillating at the same frequency. It is this oscillation, this neuronal cooperativity, that Zeki maintains is crucial for the conscious perception of movement.

The idea of consciousness arising from brain regions that, by working together, achieve more than their mere sum, is not new. In a loose way we saw in Chapter 1 that neuronal populations must have some sort of emergent property in order for us to explain consciousness. It could be that the only physical solution to the conundrum of the Cartesian theater, the delocalization of consciousness, is to imagine that the special factor additional to normal, ongoing brain events is that several brain regions must work transiently together. By their reverberating interaction, their temporary and transient dialogue, somehow consciousness is generated.

Certain physical connections among brain regions may well need to be intact, and a dynamic, resonating dialogue among parts of the cortex may well be necessary in order to explain the paradox of blindsight. But if we do not look beyond these anatomical and physiological explanations of events within the brain itself, we may miss some critical clues to understanding consciousness. A vital phenomenological feature of blindsight is that it can, in some cases and under certain conditions, be reversed.

A clue to understanding the problem of blindsight is to examine more closely the incoming signals, the very stimuli about which the subject is making guesses. It is possible that in blindsight these signals are simply too weak, that they are not big enough or are not moving fast enough. As far as reception and processing of these signals in the brain is concerned, the problem is not one of needing more neuronal connections; the neurons of our visual system are very sensitive to stimulation and there are an adequate number of neurons surviving in appropriate areas in blindsight patients. Instead, the problem may be one of overcoming an increased degree of resistance (inhibition) in the processing of visual signals. When an area of the cortex damaged in blindsight is similarly damaged in animals under experimental conditions, anatomists observe an increase in an inhibitory chemical messenger along the early stages of the visual pathway (Cowey and Stoerig 1992). We might theorize that if a visual signal is made more intense in terms of its particular features, the problem of blindsight may be overcome. There is some evidence that this idea is plausible.

For example, if an object moves at a greater velocity than before, patients frequently become conscious of the object

(Weiskrantz 1989), even without being invited to guess, and without any evident surprise. But we can go further and envisage that stimuli can be made stronger, not just in terms of their physical properties but also in their psychological strength and their relevance to the individual. Dennett gives a good example of this type of psychological strength by describing how hard it was as a child to find a thimble in the game of hunt the thimble, even though the thimble may have been right in front of his nose. We are all familiar with looking for something we cannot consciously "see," something that is in plain view and that our visual system is presumably processing. Once the thimble was found, its significance was strengthened so that thereafter it would not be camouflaged among the everyday bric-a-brac of the average living room. Using this line of reasoning, Dennett (1991) suggests that the all-important aspect of blindsight guessing is the guessing itself; by inviting a patient to guess, the situation is made just that much more special or stronger. A sensory signal impinging on the brain could be strong in either a literal sense (brighter/bigger/noisier) or in a less obvious psychological or cognitive sense. Examples of the latter might include associations of reward or punishment, or having been singled out as the object of a search or an experiment. Presumably, at the levels of neurons themselves, these stronger stimuli can overcome possible higher degrees of resistance typically present in the brains of blindsight patients.

Studies of blindsight can provide a signpost in our journey toward discovering the physical basis of consciousness. We are either conscious or unconscious of things according to their importance, strength, or intensity. In turn, this strength of objects of our consciousness might determine the extent of the dialogue among participating brain regions. In cases where only part of a neuronal population is destroyed, increasing the strength of the stimulus might recruit more neurons and thus increase the probability of a dialogue being reestablished and actual consciousness of an object being restored.

A variation of this idea was proposed by Flohr (1991), who suggested that consciousness depended not so much on the *extent* of neurons recruited but, rather, on the *rate* at which the recruitment happened. If the time taken for assemblies of neurons to form fell below a critical level, then consciousness did not occur. Hence, in blindsight, there may be some form of enhanced inhibitory process or chemical that slows down the rate by which neurons signal one another to form a working group. Both Flohr's scheme and the one I propose are similar. Flohr emphasizes the temporal dimension, namely, the rate of neuronal recruitment, whereas the alternative idea here stresses the numbers and thus the spatial extent of a temporary neuronal group. According to these schemes, it might be possible to explain how blindsight could be overcome in some cases. A stronger signal in either physical or psychological terms might be able to offset or compensate for an enfeebled recruitment process of groups of neurons.

So far we have two clues about the phenomenology of consciousness: first, that it depends on a focus that is literally or psychologically strong, and second, that it might depend spatially and/or temporally on the extensive, rapid recruitment of a population of brain cells. These brain cells would span different brain regions or different parts of the cortex to constitute a temporary working assembly where all member neurons resonated or discharged in the same way. The more powerful the recruiting signal, the greater the likelihood that such assemblies would be established and consciousness ensue.

The idea that consciousness might arise from a transiently formed neuronal assembly can also be inferred from research outside of the visual system. The physiologist Benjamin Libet (Libet et al. 1979) stimulated part of the cortex that is linked to the sensation of touch (the somatosensory cortex). It is possible to do this in unanesthetized patients undergoing neurosurgery because there are no receptors for pain in the brain. When Libet stimulated this part of the cortex, he asked the subject to report feeling a tingle, similar to a weak electrical stimulation on the skin. Usually the patients reported being conscious of such a sensation, but always a good half a second after the stimulation was delivered. One interpretation of this finding is that a sufficiently extensive population of neurons has to be recruited for consciousness to occur, but that such recruitment can take at least half a second.

In a later series of experiments (Libet et al. 1991), Libet demonstrated the equivalent of blindsight in the somatosensory system. Following direct stimulation of part of the thalamus, patients sometimes felt a tingle, sometimes not. In any event, Libet asked them to respond if they were aware of the stimulation. When a patient claimed, even in the case of a very brief stimulation, that he had just guessed, his performance was well above random. So again we can see that intensity of stimulus might recruit a corresponding assembly of neurons and that both factors, *strong stimulus* and *assembly of neurons,* are necessary for consciousness. These ideas are supported by the characteristics of a completely different type of brain damage, prosopagnosia.

Prosopagnosia

Prosapognosia can be regarded as the opposite of blindsight. In blindsight there is recognition without awareness, whereas in prosopagnosia there is awareness without recognition. Imagine a situation where someone could not recognize by sight an individual whom they had known for years. Prosopagnosia, from the Greek, literally means a failure to recognize faces. Prosopagnosic patients are neither blind nor intellectually impaired; they can interpret facial expressions and they can recognize their friends and relations by name or voice. But they do not recognize faces as such, not even their own in a mirror.

In one critical aspect, however, prosopagnosia may be similar to blindsight. Recordings in electrodermal skin conductance, which measures the sweatiness of the palms and, thus, arousal, show that although patients claim no recognition, there is an increase in arousal when familiar faces are presented. It would seem that these patients are *subconsciously* registering the significance of certain faces but are simply unaware that they are doing so. Just as blindsight can be suppressed under some conditions, so can prosopagnosia. The special conditions are those of associative priming, where all the faces share a well-known common factor (Young and De Haan 1992). For example, a patient unable to recognize the face of Princess Diana might be able to do so if she had first seen a picture of Diana's estranged husband, Prince Charles, but not if the priming face was of a celebrity unconnected with the Princess of Wales, such as the late John Lennon. Similarly, if faces are shown of people from the same professional category or the same television soap opera, then the patient is more readily able to recognize individual faces.

One explanation of this effect is that certain cases of prosopagnosia are due to the fact that the stimulus of the face itself is too weak to induce recognition. If we can talk about recognition in this way, as though the object to be recognized needed to be made in some way stronger, then we can see that the prosopagnosia might sometimes disappear. The critical factor is that the object has to be made, by covert association, sufficiently strong. Perhaps we can regard associative priming, which makes recognition easier for some prosopanosics, as a type of psychological strengthening of the stimulus. This contrived strengthening of the stimulus would thus be a determining factor in linking physical features with any significance. As with blindsight, it is possible that a strong stimulus with many associations might somehow recruit a significant number of neurons for a particular impairment in consciousness to be overcome.

An interesting feature of prosopagnosia is that it is not necessarily restricted to human faces. In two notable examples, a dog expert has shown deficits in recognizing the faces of particular dogs and a farmer in recognizing particular cows. The critical issue is not one of failing to recognize a category of objects—patients can recognize a face as a face as easily as they can recognize a door as a door. Rather, the impairment is in recognizing a particular face, or a particular cow, or a particular dog. Hence, in these examples of not recognizing nonhuman faces, the patients had to be experts in dogs and cows, respectively. Most of us would probably not have been able to differentiate cow faces in the first place! Here, then, is an impairment of consciousness, linked not to just one modality (vision) but to a particular *aspect* of vision—consciousness of the full significance of a particular object. Again, we are dealing with a rather artificial situation, one small flaw in the tapestry of our global consciousness. Moreover, it is a flaw that can be adequately offset as soon as we bring in other sensory modalities. When a prosopagnosic patient hears the voice of a person he or she has been unable to recognize visually, the problem of recognition disappears.

So how much do these sensory-specific disorders actually help us understand consciousness in general? After all, we saw at the beginning of this chapter that usually our impression of the external world is of an integrated multimodal whole, whereas our inner cognitive world of hope and fantasy is rarely purely visual, auditory, or tactile. For our normal, global consciousness there must be a means of transcending individual sensory modalities. We saw in

Chapter 2 that there is no apparent Cartesian theater where it all comes together. How might recruitment of neuronal assemblies actually generate the tiny bit of consciousness previously absent?

Although we cannot tackle these issues immediately, it seems plausible that strength of stimulus and recruitment of dynamic neuronal assemblies are in some way relevant. In fact, the idea of neuronal assemblies works well with the proposals made in Chapter 1, where it was suggested that consciousness is variable and could thus grow with the brain. A variable consciousness would fit in readily with varying sizes of neuronal populations, which might in turn depend on the strength of the stimulus, the focus of consciousness *at any one time*. For our normal, global consciousness, the neuronal assembly would not be restricted to modality-specific parts of the cortex, but would range freely across large banks of neurons throughout the brain. But suppose this unfettered recruitment of cells was stymied because the brain was functionally split in two. What would happen then?

The Split Brain

Not only is the brain normally divided into regions which are symmetrical about the middle, but the outer parts of the brain form two distinct, divided hemispheres. In a normal situation, these two hemispheres are linked by bundles of fibers crossing between them. There are times, however, when it is beneficial to cut these connections. For example, in cases of severe epilepsy, surgical intervention prevents the spread of the seizure from one part of the brain to the other. The patient is thus left with a split brain (Gazzaniga et al. 1962). One might imagine that such patients then have *two* consciousnesses, especially since the two hemispheres constitute the most sophisticated parts of the brain believed to be involved in intellectual activities, the cortex.

The classic experiment showing that the two halves of the brain can work independently of each other was performed by Ronald Myers and Roger Sperry in 1953. Cats were divided into three groups. In the control group were animals on whom no surgery had been performed. In the second group, the cats' brains were only partially split; one of two fiber tracks (optic chiasma or corpus callosum) had been severed, thus preventing the transfer of

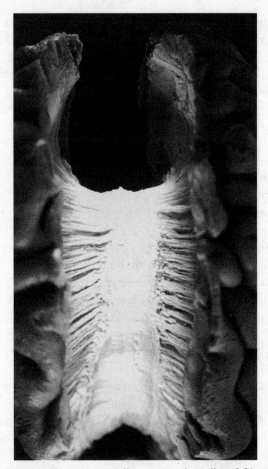

The corpus callosum. The corpus callosum is a bundle of fibers that effect the transfer of information and learning between the two cerebral hemispheres. It is this massive connection that is severed in split-brain cases. (From M. A. England and J. Wakely, *A Colour Atlas of the Brain and Spinal Cord* [London: Wolfe, 1991]. Reprinted with permission.)

visual information between the two hemispheres. In the third group both tracks were cut, effectively isolating one side of the visual cortex from the other; these animals were truly comparable, in terms of the visual system, to split-brain patients.

All three groups of cats were then trained to discriminate between a circle and a square in order to obtain a food reward, while wearing a patch on one eye. All groups performed equally well, showing that one half of the brain could work as effectively on its own as when the two halves were in communication. However, when the patch was then transferred to the other eye, a telling difference among the groups became apparent. The cats with the split brain performed as though they had never learned the task at all. Compared to the other two groups, where what had been learned on one side of the brain was transferred to the other, the split-brain cases behaved very differently. On being presented with a stimulus, the side that had previously been deprived of visual information by the patch now responded in a new way; it had not received any of the vital information from the other side.

Experiments with human split-brain patients confirm that the two halves can work independently of each other. This observation was also first made by Sperry, and it continues to be the basis of debate on what we can infer about consciousness. For example, a patient is asked to retrieve an object, the name of which is flashed briefly on a card: KEY is flashed to the left eye and RING to the right. The patient then retrieves a key with his left hand and a ring with his right, but denies he has seen KEY. Results of this type led Sperry to conclude that there are "two free wills in one cranial vault." So is it possible to have two sets of consciousness?

The psychologist Donald Mackay found no evidence that this should be so. Indeed, one of his patients asked, "Are you guys trying to make two people out of me?" (1989). Mackay concluded that consciousness arises as a result of traffic to and from many brain regions, some of them within the central part of the brain, well below the cortex and far below the area that is cut apart in split-brain patients. The problem with the split-brain cases does not seem to be one of consciousness but, rather, of the extent of the sensory input reaching either hemisphere. If the two hemispheres are isolated, then the amount of sensory input reaching each one is halved. However, just because less visual information is coming in does not mean that split-brain patients are only half conscious. Consciousness may be variable, but it does not depend on the degree of incoming information from any one sensory modality. If one is in a quiet, dark room, one would certainly not claim that consciousness was automatically diminished, although it would obviously be different. Split-brain cases, then, can be used to show that the halves of the brain process incoming information separately, but one is not able to infer anything meaningful about consciousness. In the examples discussed so far, we have tried to fit consciousness in at the end, taking first the clinical paradigm and then asking if and at what stage we could tack on awareness. A fresh angle on the phenomenology of brain damage as a clue to understanding consciousness has recently been suggested by the neurologist Israel Rosenfield (1992).

Loss of Memory

Rosenfield's approach is different in that it takes consciousness as a starting point and interprets all pathologies as disruptions in this central and common state. He argues that modifications to consciousness are best illustrated with cases of memory impairment.

Memory appears to be inextricably linked to consciousness. After all, if you are not conscious you can remember nothing, and if you are conscious your interpretation of the world around you is dependent on what has happened to you previously. Hence any traumatic change in memory, such as a memory loss, would in effect be a change in consciousness. In such cases the problem is not that the individual has forgotten something which he knows he should remember; rather, he acts as though he never knew it in the first place. This kind of memory deficit is quite different from the type of memory problems that are exhibited by a computer. With the machine, memory is stored in designated areas, within circuits that are readily localizable, and that can be called into play or left unused until the appropriate time. But there is no evidence of specific memory traces stored in the human brain in a comparable manner.

Memory, like vision, is distributed as a function in the brain. Damage to different parts of the brain may result in problems with different aspects of memory, but there is no single memory center containing neuronal groups that generate a fenced and inviolate memory of a particular moment or even of a particular object. Not only do different brain regions play a part in memory, but the actual neuronal mechanisms of memory can also vary (Desimone 1992). The versatility and widespread distribution of memory mechanisms might account for the difficulty, as we saw in Chapter 3, in showing that a mechanism such as LTP is operational in normal learning and memory. Further, this delocalization also illustrates why memory is so hard to pin down in physical terms through experimentation. Steven Rose (1992) investigated the natural behavior pattern of chicks to peck at small objects in their field of vision. He demonstrated that chicks learn to avoid pecking at a chrome bead dipped in a bitter-tasting liquid, not because they remember the bead as such but because different parts of the chick brain process separately the shape, size, and color of an object associated with something unpleasant that should be avoided. In multiple brain regions, each different physical aspect of the bead is simultaneously associated with the subjective sensation of unpleasantness. There is no one single place where that association is made.

When people lose their memory, it is not a matter of simply deleting a particular memory trace. Rather, there is a colossal change in global consciousness, and this transformation is explainable, according to Rosenfield (1992), as a basic problem concerning awareness of time. In cases of amnesia a distinction is commonly made between long-term memory and short-term memory. This comparison seems quite logical, since some patients retain memories of events remote in time but remember nothing of recent events—hence, short-term memory deficit. Other patients remember nothing of the past, but recall immediate events quite well—an obvious problem with long-term memory.

Rosenfield reinterprets these conditions in terms of an upheaval in consciousness. The problem is not, he maintains, one where some memories are stored differently from others and there is difficulty in retrieving one sort or the other. Instead, Rosenfield views memory for past events as a means for formulating abstractions and generalizations. One patient claimed in very general terms that he "liked women" and visited his mistress "on Saturdays," as opposed to singling out a particular woman or talking about a particular Saturday night. On the other hand, patients with only short-term memory are constantly trapped in the specifics of the present. They cannot draw on habitual actions such as seeing their mistress on Saturday nights, which would lead to the generalization of liking women. This inability to have generalized thoughts drastically changes one's consciousness, and, in fact, compromises one's ability to have abstracted views and beliefs.

Rosenfield also cites a patient who could not organize a collection of skeins of wool according to the notion of color. Yet this same patient was able to arrange the skeins according to a highly idiosyncratic and egocentric system, following a pattern similar to one of her dresses. Rosenfield's interpretation of this seeming anomaly of being able to organize the skeins in one way but not another is that the patient could only form views about, and indeed only be conscious of, the present. She was unable to formulate abstract concepts, such as color, but able to relate the skeins to the literal and specific present, the pattern on her dress. When she named ordinary objects, "this usage was not accompanied by any conceptual attitude concerning the objects," her psychiatrist noted. In this case a typical patient with only short-term memory was thus unaware of the meanings of proverbs or metaphors. Only those things pertaining to the patient personally and literally would be part of her conscious experience.

The problem of the other kind of patients, those with only long-term memory, is just the opposite. These patients have full ability to make generalized and abstracted statements, but they are unable to be properly conscious of the present. If a patient has no sense of the present, he has no sense of how to use incoming information from the immediate world around him. Individuals with short-term memory problems, where all information of the present is irrelevant to past knowledge, might feel very strange. Indeed, such patients claim that they "haven't felt alive for a long time." Their world is one of the past, but a past isolated from the specific events of the present. This lack of feeling alive might be easy to understand in a uniform and timeless world of habits and abstractions lacking the technicolored impact of the present. Again, it is not as though these people were in most respects normal, with only memory for the immediate world compromised. Instead, their consciousness is dramatically modified. In general, we can see that our own selves, our bodies, and, in turn, a sense of time passing all might be crucial factors in determining the quality of our consciousness.

It would be no rash claim to say that certain memory impairments give rise to radically modified states of consciousness.

Memory is so interlinked with consciousness that it cannot be regarded as a distinct function and housed in a special place.

In summary, other clues from studies of brain damage examined in this chapter that can be used in a theory of consciousness are that we will need to include some kind of reverberating circuitry among brain regions and that we will have to make provisions for the idea that consciousness is related to the strength (psychological or physical) of the focus of consciousness. Such strength is important in the recruitment of the appropriate neurons for a conscious experience. But how do certain neurons in the brain become "appropriate"? During every waking and dreaming moment consciousness arises from and pervades vast banks of our brain tissue as a single, unique, but elusive sound emerges from a symphony. It is everywhere and nowhere. The time has now come to try to disentangle the basic properties of consciousness from the teeming brain events and behaviors that make up our lives.

chapter five

THE EBB AND FLOW OF CONSCIOUSNESS

The most serious problem of all is where to start. The clues from the previous chapters will be pressed into service for validating a theory of consciousness once we have one. As yet all we have is a collection of disconnected leads that will not spontaneously assemble themselves into a cohesive description any more than a pile of ingredients will assemble, on their own, into a cordon bleu dish. Although we will eventually draw on all of these earlier ideas, we cannot begin with them. We first need to develop the theory, to devise the recipe.

Unconsciousness

Let's start in the most uncontroversial place possible, with nothing. On the face of it, unconsciousness—the complete absence of consciousness—should be much easier to understand than consciousness. To display unconsciousness, an object, such as a stone or a corpse, simply needs to exist in physical space. And yet unconscious is a term we apply only to entities that we assume can be conscious at certain times. Of more interest than unconsciousness itself is the *transition* from having consciousness to losing it, and vice versa.

Let us now concentrate on the normal brain and examine what happens when either anesthesia or sleep blots out awareness. If the activity of neurons is recorded during the unconsciousness state, as was noted earlier, individual neurons do not necessarily shut down. Not only are some neurons active during unconsciousness, but they can be sensitive to changes in the outside world. Certain cells in the visual cortex, for example, increase their discharges during anesthesia in response to a flashing light (Hubel and Wiesel 1962). Similarly, during the sleep-wake cycle, single cells in the cortex are far from quiescent, although the type of electrical discharge generated can change. During deep sleep, the cells are far more synchronous in their activity, with simultaneous bursts of movement against a low background level (Noda and Adey 1970). It is possible, then, in the absence of consciousness, for activation to occur along the incoming neuronal pathways related to the senses and for neurons to remain active. This idea may sometimes be difficult to accept. You could flash a light in front of the eyes of an anesthetized patient or an experimental animal, and the recordings from electrodes in certain brain regions would register that the cells in question had become more active. On the other hand, the patient or the animal would not be *seeing* the flashing light because it was unconscious. Clearly, the step from consciousness to unconsciousness is not controlled at the level of banks of individual neurons independently, yet by chance universally, ceasing to be active.

Thus there is a difference between registering a sensory input in terms of changes in actual behavior of certain neurons and being truly *conscious* of that input. The former does not automatically imply the latter, as we saw in the cases of blindsight. Activation of the sensory organs and their pathways into the brain is an insufficient condition in itself to generate consciousness. Conversely, we must consider apparent consciousness without sensation. During the dreaming phase of sleep, the pattern of electricity generated by way of scalp electrodes is indistinguishable from that recorded when we are awake. This phase is known as rapid eye movement (REM) sleep. The electricity recorded from scalp electrodes during dreamless sleep generates a pattern of slow synchronous waves, whereas when we are fully awake and when we dream, the wave pattern is desynchronized in that it does not follow a repeating, rhythmic pattern at all (Steriade

1984). Ongoing stimulation of the five senses is thus not necessary for consciousness. After all, when we escape to a quiet, darkened room or indulge in the more exotic experience of a flotation tank, we expect to enter a secret world of inner thoughts and fantasies, not to be transformed temporarily into a vegetable. But consideration of unconsciousness enables us to make two preliminary claims: First, consciousness is not a basic attribute of individual neurons, whereby they each generate a small amount of consciousness. Second, consciousness cannot be incurred by merely triggering the incoming sensory pathways to the brain, nor can it be assumed to be absent in the absence of sensory input.

We can go still further by probing more closely into the state of unconsciousness itself. The transition to unconsciousness cannot be summed up by one single change in behavior. There are unequivocal, objective signs that anesthetists rely on to convince themselves beyond any doubt that their patients will know nothing of the ensuing, potentially terrifying course of events (Rang and Dale 1991). These signs mainly involve a change in the rate and depth of breathing, the presence or absence of specific reflexes (such as blinking when the eyes are touched), and the tone of muscle. Contrary to what one might expect, anesthesia is not an all-or-none condition; we are not suddenly thrown into a black state of nothingness but, rather, descend into oblivion in graded stages.

In the first stage, that of analgesia, the patient is still conscious, but sensitivity to pain is reduced. Changes in sensitivity to pain might, therefore, give us some kind of calibration of consciousness. (We return to this idea later.) The next stage of anesthesia is known, paradoxically, as excitement. The patient is no longer conscious but may appear delirious, possibly with involuntary limb movements. He might even urinate, defecate, or vomit before breathing becomes regular and the third stage, surgical anesthesia, is reached. As its name suggests, this is the stage during which the patient is ready for surgery. Reflexes, such as the knee jerk, no longer occur. But even within this stage, different planes can be distinguished, corresponding to the increasing depth of anesthesia, until spontaneous breathing ceases and the fourth and final stage, medullary depression, is reached.

The medulla, situated deep in the most basic part of the brain, the brainstem, serves as the gateway between the sophisticated upper parts of the brain and the rest of the body. Some brainstem neurons send projections down to regulate the nonconscious, mechanical organs of the body, and others reach up to energize the brain by activating a system for arousal (discussed briefly in Chapter 1). All of these primitive but essential medullary neurons are silenced in the final stage of anesthesia so that the patient breathes only with the aid of an artificial respirator. In addition, blood pressure falls. If left untended, coma would ensue if the patient were unconscious for a protracted period of time, and then he or she would eventually die.

Although not all of us have undergone surgery, everyone has experienced sleep. Yet both the conditions of anesthesia and dreamless sleep are comparable, in that respiration and heart rate decrease and normally there is no outward reaction to sensory inputs. Speaking subjectively, we are unaware of our surroundings and hence undoubtedly unconscious. Interestingly enough, a further similarity to anesthesia is that sleep can also be described in stages (Rang and Dale 1991). These stages of sleep can be monitored by recording the electrical patterns of averaged activity in the cortex using electrodes on the scalp. Differences in these patterns characterize four progressive stages in sleep. Also, there is an agreeable preceding zone of relaxation intermediate to sleeping and waking, similar to that attained in meditation, when the waves of activity from the scalp are synchronized into a particular (alpha) rhythm.

The first stage of actually slipping away from consciousness is marked by a sudden convulsion of the body which jolts us back into the world, although not for long. As we drift down through the next three stages, the brain waves become progressively larger and slower. Each stage has a different pattern of electrical activity. Both anesthesia and sleep, then, suggest that there is no distinct barrier between consciousness and unconsciousness across which we clamber every night or before surgery. Rather, there is a progressive shading of one into the other; not a wall but a gentle ramp, a continuum, a dimmer switch.

Few would claim to wake up in the morning immediately fully conscious. We all know only too well that blissful but transient state of semiconsciousness when we cannot name the day of the week or be really sure where we are, particularly in unfamiliar surroundings. This temporary loss of space and time references, as

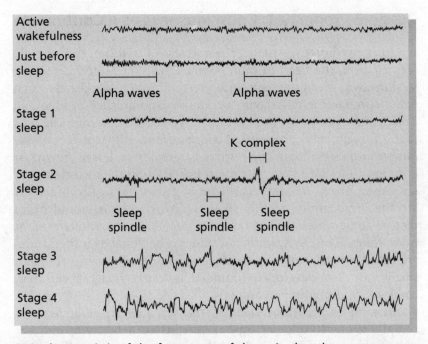

Active wakefulness

Just before sleep

Alpha waves   Alpha waves

Stage 1 sleep

K complex

Stage 2 sleep

Sleep   Sleep   Sleep
spindle   spindle   spindle

Stage 3 sleep

Stage 4 sleep

EEGs characteristic of the four stages of sleep. As sleep becomes progressively deeper, the brain waves as recorded on an electroencephalogram become slower in frequency and greater in amplitude. Stage 2 is characterized by sleep spindles (bursts of 12- to 15-hertz waves) and occasionally a K complex (large biphasic waves). These stages of slow wave sleep do not include REM sleep, when dreaming occurs, and where the EEG resembles the awake state (see the illustration on p. 7). Each trace is 30 seconds in duration. (Modified from J. Pinel, *Biopsychology* [Boston: Allyn and Bacon, 1993]. Copyright by Allyn and Bacon. Adapted by permission.)

well as the fleeting thoughts that wax and wane in our minds as we lie seemingly weightless and immobile in bed, are all evidence of a diminution in, but by no means a total absence of, consciousness. And so if unconsciousness is graded and meshes gradually with consciousness, then it is possible that awareness during the less ambiguous times of day also ebbs and flows. Perhaps consciousness, too, is continuously variable. This concept is the first possible property of consciousness that we can set down. But is it really plausible?

Possible Property 1: Consciousness as a Continuum

In Greek mythology, Athena, the goddess of wisdom, sprang fully formed from the head of omnipotent Zeus, her father. Let us try to shift away from the temptation to think of consciousness as an entity comparable to Athena, a complete and finished product, an object that is or is not there. Rather, we should entertain the idea that a fundamental property of consciousness is that it is *continuously variable* and can thus occur to greater or lesser extents at different times. We have already touched upon the idea that consciousness grows in depth as the brain grows physically, but what are the implications of this view? Quite simply, it would mean that at some times you could be more or less conscious than at other times. This prospect is not quite as heretical as it might first appear if we consider cases of consciousness in creatures with smaller or less developed brains than ours, such as children, embryos, and nonhuman animals.

In simpler creatures such as the sea slug *Aplysia,* there is actually a one-to-one correspondence between behavior and the identifiable neural basis of that behavior, just as we saw (in Chapter 3) that the unconscious conditioned behavior of the nictitating membrane has a one-to-one correspondence with the repetitive modular circuits of neurons in the mammalian cerebellum. Here there is no problem between functioning and function; as in now sadly outdated toys, the unwinding of a spring is *directly* related to clockwork behavior. In creatures such as *Aplysia,* phenomenology translates more readily into physiological events. The behavior of *Aplysia* is not one of complex and subjective emotion, but, rather, its entire observable repertoire is more comparable with the nictitating membrane response.

The particular behavior for which *Aplysia* has become famous demonstrates that a relatively uncomplicated creature can learn to retract its gill because of an outside influence which in itself is neutral and which has no intrinsic significance to the world of the sea slug (Kandel et al. 1987). When a painful stimulus, such as an electric shock, is applied to *Aplysia*'s tail, it responds by retracting its gill. On the other hand, if on a totally separate occasion the stimulus is nonaversive, for example, a gentle touch, *Aplysia* usually does nothing. Nonetheless, if the aversive and nonaversive stimuli are presented simultaneously, *Aplysia* will "remember" the nonaversive stimulus, the gentle touch, as being associated with the painful, aversive stimulus. Presentation of the neutral stimulus alone will subsequently result in retraction of the gill.

Memory for the sea slug is clearly very different from the sophisticated human memory of eating ice cream by a bandstand in a park on a hot summer day while listening to the blare of trombones. But the most important way in which sea slugs differ from more sophisticated animals is that, for them, memory is more immediately and completely translatable into the operations of an identified neuronal circuit. The physical neuronal mechanism has a more ready correspondence with an outside function; the memory of the sea slug is far less of an emergent property. Rather, it is the result of a series of sequential events in a linear relay of neurons. To a certain extent, these events can be traced precisely as to when and where the mechanical stimulus of a gentle touch is transformed, or transduced, into electrical impulses within Aplysia's body and then transformed back again into a mechanical event, the retraction of the gill.

The flavor of an onion is unlike that of a dish of curried shrimp in that it is directly traceable and completely identifiable with the actual onion. Using this analogy, we can regard the memory of Aplysia as more akin to the flavor of an onion: The flavor and the ingredient bear a one-to-one relationship to each other. Mammalian memory, on the other hand, depends far more on a constellation of factors that combine to generate emergent properties, as do myriad spices and other ingredients in a curry dish to produce a final, subtle, and elusive emergent taste. As we saw in Chapter 3, comparable neuronal mechanisms in mammals, such as LTP, are a necessary but not a sufficient component of memory, just like an onion might be to curry. There is more to mammalian memory than a simple adaptation of a small group of brain cells. Memory, in mammals, is intimately connected with consciousness; in fact (as observed in Chapter 4), memory is a facet of consciousness. In more complex animals, both memory and consciousness have so far defied a one-to-one matching of neuron and behavior.

But if simpler nervous systems have more of a one-to-one correspondence between neuron and behavior, where does that leave them regarding consciousness? Let us return again to the transition in and out of unconsciousness. Turbellarian worms and planaria, crabs and lobsters, octupuses and squids, houseflies and butterflies do not sleep as we do. They "rest" for brief periods of time, but this is a very different state from the one we recognize as sleep. Similarly, neither fish nor amphibians display any electrical signs of brain sleep (Hobson 1989). Perhaps in creatures where the unconscious state, the rest period, is not so dramatically different from the awake, moving period, the *degree* of consciousness may not be very developed and extensive. Indeed, the degree of consciousness might be so vestigial that it is as if there were none.

So are animals like *Aplysia* conscious at all? Do we need to decide where in the animal kingdom to draw the line above which animals are conscious and below which they are mere automata? Indeed, the consensus is now that animals are certainly not the input-output automata once imagined by Descartes and then three hundred years later by the behaviorist philosophy of the psychologist B. F. Skinner (1938). As its name suggests, this school of thought placed almost exclusive emphasis on behavior, on the response of the brain to whatever input or stimulus was prevalent at the time. Everything was seen as a result of stimulus-response relations without any need for intervening thought processes (cognition). Following this line of reasoning, then, it might seem unnecessary for nonprimates to be conscious. Yet a variety of experiments demonstrate quite clearly that Descartes was wrong, that animals that have no language (in our human sense) are far from furry machines and are conscious of what is happening around them. The biologist Gerald Edelman asserts that animals such as the lobster are not conscious, and that even conscious animals have only primary consciousness which "does not afford to model the past or future as part of a correlated scene" (1992). On the face of it, however, the proposition that animals effectively just live for the moment and do not make use of past experiences seems improbable.

Edelman sees a liberation from the present as a higher order consciousness. This condition encompasses an ability for internal representations, which Edelman refers to as the "conceptual symbolic." It is clear that only with higher order consciousness would we be able to daydream, reminisce, or speculate; only with the ability to form subtle concepts would we be able to be aware of ourselves. Although Edelman concedes that higher order consciousness might have some existence in chimpanzees, the operational definition of this type of consciousness raises nagging questions concerning animal consciousness in general. Do other animals not have any memory beyond a covert system of values? Can they not form internal representations that have been allocated to higher order consciousness?

Over twenty years ago an ingenious experiment was designed to test whether or not animals were aware of what they were doing (Beninger et al. 1974). Rats were allowed to engage in one of four activities forming part of their natural repertoire: face washing, rearing up, walking, and remaining immobile. In each cage were four levers, corresponding to one of these activities. If a rat pressed the right lever after performing the appropriate act, it received a food reward. The rats were able to perform this task successfully, thus demonstrating that they were aware of what they had been doing.

Subsequently, the psychologist David Olton has shown that rats can remember the location of food in a radial maze, a maze which is like a wheel with spokelike alleys emanating from the center (Olton and Samuelson 1976). Rats could only develop this strategy based on memory if they had some type of internal representation concerning the correct position. Another example comes from an experiment involving a rat's views on whether or not to drink a solution of sugar (Premack 1976). The experiment starts off traditionally with training rats to pull a chain for a sugar solution. However, the next step is quite unusual. The rats are given the sugar solution without having to pull the chain, but they are then injected with lithium so that the once pleasant-tasting sugar water is now aversive. Not surprisingly, the rats now refuse to drink the sugar solution. The critical step occurs in the final stage. If the rats were unable to think about the water and its newfound aversive significance when they were placed in front of the chain, then they would pull the chain. This would be the prediction of behaviorists who consider that the animals' behavior is primarily dictated by locked-in pairings of a particular response to a particular stimulus, in this case chain-chain pull-good water. However, if the animals were able to think about the water, even when the water was not present, and, furthermore, if the animals, in the light of recent experience, could then break the association between chain pull-good water, they would no longer pull the chain. It turned out that the rats did *not* pull the chain, thus showing that they could think, could form internal representations not only of the water but also of their now changed attitudes toward it. Thus we can see that rats possess views independent of the immediate physical appearance of an object.

It would appear, then, that animals can not only be conscious, but that they can think beyond the sensory snapshot of the immediate world about them. Hence rigid distinctions among higher order consciousness, primary consciousness, and no consciousness are not very helpful. Similarly, were this type of distinction to hold within our own development, there would one day presumably have to be a Paul of Tarsus–like experience, where sometime in our infancy or even in the womb, consciousness suddenly came to us in a blinding flash. On the other hand, if we accept that consciousness can be variable, it is far more plausible, and far less arbitrary, to maintain that consciousness deepens gradually as animal brains of all types grow. We could then say that some animals were more conscious than others according to the relative sophistication of their brains. Animals such as *Aplysia* would have very little consciousness, none that really counted, but enough for it to represent the lowest end of a continuum.

Furthermore, if consciousness is truly variable, there is no reason why we should assume that variations in degrees of consciousness do not continue for the rest of our lives, or that we are more or less conscious compared with other people and more or less conscious than we were moments ago. There are times—when we are tired or have the flu or have overindulged in wine—when our consciousness will be blunted. During such periods we are not capable of abstract inner thoughts on a consistent theme; disconnected images and propositions flit incoherently, uncohesively, and dreamlike in and out of our minds in a blur. We seem remote from the world and uninvolved in it, as though peering at distant scenes through a mist. Conversely, there are other times—such as when we have just fallen in love or are on an isolated beach or listening to Mozart—when we have never felt more alive, when our consciousness seems heightened. Gustave Flaubert captures vividly this increase in consciousness when he describes the start of the love affair between Emma and Léon in *Madame Bovary* (1857):

> *It was not the first time they had seen trees, blue sky, green grass, not the first time they had heard running water and the*

wind blowing through the leaves; but certainly they had never yet admired it all as though nature had only just come into existence, or only begun to be beautiful since the gratification of their desires.

We spend most of our lives neither bogged down with flu nor at the beginning of love affairs. Yet we fluctuate in our states of awareness, albeit in far less obvious and contrived ways. Staring out the window into a blanket of solid sky on a long airplane journey can be a far more numbing, consciousness-shrinking experience than skiing down a mountain or climbing up one. The idea of an expanding and contracting consciousness is alien to the consistency we like to attribute to ourselves and to how we like to see the world. In Chapter 1 we saw that a changeable consciousness was the centerpiece of the theories of consciousness offered by Dennett and Parfit, each of whom was happy to relinquish any claims to an enduring personality or mind. Here, however, there is a different claim: Consciousness does not simply change in *quality* from one unconnected state to the next, but it can change in *degree*. For the time being, let us put aside questions relating to changes in the *quality* of consciousness and focus instead on the continuum, the possible changes in the *quantity* of consciousness.

If we were to become increasingly more conscious in our early years, could we then claim that the degree of consciousness was simply related to the number of neurons—the more the better—as our brains develop? Immediately this idea seems wrong; we actually lose neurons as we mature. Moreover, it seems that sheer numbers of neurons are not as important as the connections among them. If rats, even as mature adults, are exposed to an environment that is enriched with numerous intriguing objects to investigate, their brains change dramatically compared to those of rats living in a more normal laboratory situation (Greenough 1988). The brains of the rats from the enriched environment do not have more brain cells, but more connections among the brain cells. It could be that the brain would possess a greater capacity for consciousness as the numbers of operational neuronal connections increased.

In the human cortex there is an awesome number of neurons, approximately ten billion. But the astonishing figure is the number of connections in the cortex, about one million billion. To count one of these connections each second would take thirty-two million years (Edelman 1992). Even more stunning than the number of connections is the way the connections can be combined. The number of combinations that can be formed from the number of connections in the cortex is many times greater than the number of positively charged particles in the known universe, a number so great that we cannot give it a meaningful name. Nonetheless, it is clear that if you are an organism with relatively few neurons to start with, the number of connections that can be formed is obviously limited. It is the number of connections, not just the number of neurons, that most likely give the growing brain the power for increasing consciousness.

Associations occur as our neurons form connections in certain ways as the results of exposure to particular environments, utilizing pretty much the same mechanisms that we explored in Chapter 3, namely, Hebbian weighting. One might suppose that as we grow up more neuronal associations would be formed and we would actually become, by some special means we have still to discover, more conscious.

In Chapter 3 we also saw that connections among neurons are highly plastic and capable of great change. Even in the mature brain, the continuing ability to learn and remember is most readily explained by the fact that these neuronal connections retain the ability to adapt to inputs as we go through life. Moreover, if we consider how such changing connections can be used in all manner of combinations, then we can start to see how we might have a basis for an ever changing consciousness, even when our brains have ceased to grow any further in three dimensions. If it is true that consciousness emerges in relation to the complexity of neuronal interactions, and if these interactions are constantly changing, then consciousness has to change as the pattern of these interactions changes, all the time.

The value of this view of consciousness is that it allows us to have a dynamic consciousness even in maturity. We are not restricted to relating consciousness to the static properties of neurons, and we are once again eased away from the idea that, even in the mature human adult, consciousness has congealed into a solid and unchangeable state.

The Story So Far

It might be a good idea at this stage to recapitulate what we have learned that can contribute to the construction of a theory for the physical basis of consciousness. We cannot equate any aspect of our outward behavior with a specific function actually within our brains, any more than we can say the firing of a spark plug is the same as the acceleration of a car (Chapter 3). There is no simple matching of the activity of certain neurons with certain conscious behaviors. We have seen the importance of what our senses relay into our brains, in particular that the degree of sensory intensity (whether literally in physical terms or in psychological impact) can influence consciousness (Chapter 4). We have also seen the astonishingly sensitive and dynamic interaction among neurons as they become weighted (Chapter 3), as well as the importance of memory to type of consciousness (Chapter 4).

These basic facts point to more generalized ideas, notably that there is no consciousness center or uniform distribution of consciousness in every neuron (Chapters 1 and 2). Rather, it is far more plausible to consider different groups of noncommitted brain cells each taking over the job temporarily from one moment to the next (Chapter 2). These groups of brain cells might organize themselves in some way interactively with the external environment (Chapter 3) and might be connected to one another in an incessant reverberating dialogue (Chapter 4). In this chapter we entertained the idea that consciousness might be variable in depth, in both the development of the individual and in evolution.

If consciousness is a potential property of many transient groupings of neurons and if consciousness is variable, it is easy to regard our brains as a restless grouping and regrouping of temporarily relevant neurons with greater and lesser connectivity, like blobs of mercury of varying size. In this way there would not only be a *qualitative* change but a *quantitative* one in depth, too. But how might such a scenario actually be achieved?

chapter six

A THEORY
OF CONSCIOUSNESS

A conscious experience may involve memories, hormonal drives, and sensory inputs, but it is experienced as a seemingly harmonious and unified piece, like a symphony. In this chapter we shall see how this effect might be achieved not only for a second but for a lifetime, despite the fact that there is no single center in the brain, no committed set of neurons acting as a central headquarters.

If consciousness were generated across nonspecialized aggregations of neurons, we would have to imagine diverse, multiple groups of neurons subserving different consciousnesses to different extents at different times, no less than multiple consciousnesses. As early as Chapter 1 we met the "bundles" of Parfit and the "multiple drafts" of Dennett. But is there any actual evidence for multiple consciousnesses? Perhaps one of the most pertinent observations comes from the split-brain patient mentioned in Chapter 4. This patient had a sense of being one single entity ("Are you guys trying to make two people out of me?"). Of course most people claim a certain oneness when talking about themselves. Indeed, it would be hard to provide evidence that we normally think of ourselves as many people. A further clue, then, is of a seemingly *single* consciousness; but it complicates the issue because it leads to a paradox. How can we have multiple potential consciousnesses with only one salient conscious state at any one time?

This riddle can be solved by remembering that just because something is unique in time does not mean it has to be unique in space: Many different people can stand on the same spot, but only one person at any one time. The idea of a consciousness center is a *spatial* concept, whereas the unitary nature of subjective conscious experience could be essentially *temporal*. This distinction of space from time makes it possible to imagine the following scheme without contradicting any of our previous conclusions: If the single nature of consciousness is temporal, the earlier statement can be modified by saying you can only have consciousness at any one time, but that other potential consciousnesses could be generated in space, in other parts of the brain. This *spatial multiplicity* combined with *temporal unity* can be regarded as the second property of consciousness.

Possible Property 2: Consciousness Is Multiple in Space but Unitary in Time

If consciousness has an ultimate physical basis but is neither homogeneously distributed in every neuron nor specifically localized in a special region, then where is it generated? We have seen that this apparent paradox can only be solved by viewing consciousness as an emergent property of aggregations of neurons in some part of the brain. But, to avoid the enticing and beckoning entrance of the Cartesian theater, we have to show that this scheme is crucially different from a single center. Aggregations of neurons must not be committed full time and irrevocably to consciousness; they should have no special feature. If such groups of neurons are not exclusively special for consciousness, then they need not be responsible for consciousness all the time, nor need they be a unique population within the brain. Thus consciousness may be generated at different times by shifting populations composed of different groups of neurons.

The reasoning behind this second property poses a problem. If consciousness is spatially multiple, why should we assume it will *always* be temporally unitary? What would be the underlying principle to ensure that only one consciousness ever prevailed? Surely the possibility remains that there might be two assemblies of neurons forming simultaneously in the brain: Would we not, then, have two consciousnesses? The argument in Chapter 5 ran that the more neuronal associations in the brain, the more consciousness. It follows that the fewer neurons recruited, the less consciousness. Small neuronal assemblies would generate negligible consciousness, akin to that of insects. It is likely that consciousness is only appreciable as a large number of neurons is recruited. Since the pool of appropriate neurons from which consciousness is formed would be vast but nevertheless finite, the formation of a neuronal group large enough for consciousness at any moment might preclude the formation of any equally large second assembly at that particular time. If in a group of fifteen people, eleven are recruited for a football team, there are not enough to make up a second team simultaneously.

If we accept that different, nonspecialized groups of cells are distributed throughout the brain, and that these groups are constantly re-forming their connections and thus changing their size and pattern, then we can easily perceive that such groups of cells would be the appropriate physical bases for multiple potential consciousnesses, only one of which is realized at any one time. To this end we have concentrated on the varying sizes of any one neuronal assembly and any one moment of consciousness, and the latter's place on a continuum of degrees of consciousness. This is the *quantitative* factor, the particular depth of consciousness at any one time. But how do we normally make the transition from one train of consciousness to another, to a consciousness mediated by an entirely different assembly of neurons, one that is *qualitatively* different?

Imagine living in a world where everything has significance. In a sense the schizophrenic has this problem. Compared to those of normal people, the schizophrenic's trains of consciousness can impinge too rapidly upon one another so that one line of thought cannot be sustained but is sidetracked by extraneous and irrelevant associations. "I feel so bad even the picture has a headache," claimed one patient who had caught sight of a picture on the wall as he was talking; he was unable to disregard whatever invaded his senses. The same happens, in a more general way, to the schizophrenic's attitude toward the outside world. The patient is fleetingly but irredeemably conscious of passing elements of the environment so that they constitute ready sources of distraction and even alternative trains of consciousness (McGhie and Chapman 1961). For example, perception of a simple object such as a flower is more likely to trigger a bigger train of consciousness than normally might have been expected.

The effects of hallucinogenic drugs have often been compared with the symptoms of schizophrenia. Essentially the central problem with hallucinogenic drugs is that either the person is overly obsessed with an object or thought or is too readily distracted along some tangential and idiosyncratic pathway. As Aldous Huxley noted in *Doors of Perception* (1954), the mescaline taker is not someone who wants to be in control of life, but one who is at the mercy of his or her unfettered and unmarshalled multiple consciousnesses, all vying for a moment of domination.

Consideration of the consciousness-changing effects of hallucinogenic drugs and schizophrenia can help us to define further not only whether there are multiple consciousnesses but also the elusive factor or factors that would control which consciousness prevailed. The critical issue for resolving this problem is that we need a means of apportioning significance to some objects at the expense of others. So how and by what agent could a particular potential consciousness be selected to become the prevailing conscious state for that moment?

What object, then, can act as the focus of our thoughts? We have explored the nature of the salient conscious state at any one time, and I have suggested that it is a continuum—the quantitative factor. We now have to turn to the qualitative aspects of consciousness, how one state or one train of consciousness differs in content from the next. We need to think not of depth of consciousness (the quantitative factor) but, rather, of the transition from one train of consciousness to the next. What defines the qualitative factor of a state of consciousness?

Imagine that you are looking at an orange. It might engender not merely thoughts of eating or of slaking your thirst but also of a holiday in Morocco, balls, the sun, an orange dress, or even an allergy to citrus fruit. The degree of consciousness triggered by the orange would depend not only on how many associations are recruited, that is, the *significance* of the orange to you in particular, but also on your current circumstances, such as whether or not you are thirsty, or hot, or nauseous, or how long you have to contemplate the orange before a new trigger generates a new conscious state. This new stimulus could be either a very strong association, perhaps initially triggered by the orange, which then eclipses it in importance—for example, a plan to return to Morocco—or some unrelated but strong stimulus in the environment, such as a loud noise or the sudden appearance of an old friend. It is in this way that our consciousness of some event, object, or idea shrinks or expands, continues or is cut off as it is sequentially defined by a series of epicenters of varying idiosyncratic significance to ourselves. This triggering of associations is no plodding series of algorithms but is more analogous to a raindrop hitting the surface of a puddle and creating ever widening concentric ripples. Consciousness draws on associations as a poet does on images.

Although we might not have our entire awareness centered on an orange, we are always aware of something at any one time. After all, it is a contradiction to be conscious of nothing. Of course, it does not have to be a purely incoming sensory signal that we are homing in on, at least not in our more sophisticated brains. It can well be a psychological or cognitive, internalized representation, such as a hope or a memory. Usually, however, we are receptive to both our inner thoughts and the outside world; hence our consciousness is the product of an interaction of sensory and cognitive factors. Perceptions and reactions to different objects are colored to greater or lesser extents by idiosyncratic associations and an ongoing physiological state. Perhaps, then, different experiences of consciousness can be defined and selected in terms of their focus. This is the third important step toward trying to define consciousness in terms of its basic properties. This third property is that a moment of consciousness always entails a stimulus or focus; it develops from a kind of epicenter.

Possible Property 3: Consciousness Develops from Epicenters

Let us now look at the idea that consciousness devolves from some sort of triggering epicenter. We'll worry about what an epicenter actually is, in physicochemical terms, in Chapters 7 and 8.

For the time being, let's treat the term not as a literal element of the brain but as a metaphor analogous to the center of an earthquake. For the purposes of this chapter, our working understanding of the term epicenter is simply that it is the central focus of that which you are conscious at any one time.

We can now use one of the clues discovered in Chapter 4 from observations reported in patients with disorders of recognition. Remember, we saw that if a stimulus of which a patient was oblivious was made physically or psychologically stronger, the patient became aware of that stimulus. Hence, in blindsight, an increase in the degree of movement enabled the patient to see the previously unperceived objects. Similarly, in prosopagnosia, recognition was more likely to occur by placing the face into a familiar category, making it psychologically stronger. Strength of stimulus somehow elicits a greater degree of consciousness. To understand how this effect could be achieved in the brain, let us relate this phenomenon to more everyday situations.

One focus of consciousness that everyone has experienced is pain. If you are in extreme pain, that pain is the center of your whole world. But pain is so subjective that we have no objective terms to describe it. Rather, metaphorical adjectives are borrowed from the actual cause of the pain, for example, burning, stabbing, pricking. Notwithstanding such subjective descriptions, two different types of pain are objectively recognized. *Fast pain* is transmitted to the brain quickly by way of large nerves and is relatively easy to localize. The other sort of pain is *slow pain,* a far more unpleasant experience. It is called slow simply because a special thinner, uninsulated type of nerve is used to conduct the electrical impulses more slowly. This pain differs from fast pain in two important qualitative ways: First, it is much harder to localize within the body; and second, only slow pain is effectively combated with morphine.

For current purposes we will discover more by studying slow pain because it is more sensitive to subjective factors (Ottoson 1983). It was one of the great discoveries of modern neuroscience that sensation and suppression of pain are linked to a naturally occurring morphine in the nervous system, enkephalin (Snyder 1986). In chronic pain conditions, the levels of enkephalin decrease in body fluids; conversely, agents that block the working of enkephalin concomitantly reduce pain relief from acupuncture

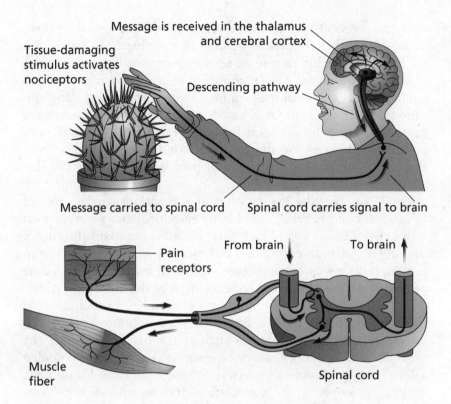

Message is received in the thalamus and cerebral cortex

Tissue-damaging stimulus activates nociceptors

Descending pathway

Message carried to spinal cord   Spinal cord carries signal to brain

Pain receptors

From brain   To brain

Muscle fiber

Spinal cord

How pain is transmitted to the brain. Chemical messages from damaged tissue are converted by free nerve endings in the skin, nociceptors, into electrical signals. These signals, or impulses, are conducted to the spinal cord and carried first to the most basic part of the brain, the brainstem, and then to the thalamus and cortex (see arrows), where they are perceived as pain. These messages can be suppressed by a system of neurons descending from the brain to the spinal cord that originates in the midbrain (see arrow). Some of these descending pathways contain a natural pain reliever called enkephalin, which is similar to morphine. (Modified from J. Carey, ed., *Facts: A Primer on the Brain and Nervous System* [Washington, D.C.: Society for Neuroscience, 1990].)

and actually increase the perceived unpleasantness of pain following dental procedures.

We all know that pain can be sensed in the most primitive of ways. If you pick up a hot plate, you will automatically drop the plate without having to think about it. After all, sensation of pain is one of the vital keys to the survival of animals; it enables them to withdraw their bodies as quickly as possible from harm. But we have seen earlier that mere sensation cannot be equated with conscious awareness. The responses of neurons to such treatment could be recorded even if the animal were anesthetized. Our sensation of pain is invariant. The nerves that conduct the impulses caused by a painful stimulus into the brain do not change their physical properties of diameter or conduction velocity, even though our conscious perception of pain is both variant and dissociable from the painful event.

For example, the degree of pain perception can be affected by attitudes and beliefs, as well as by emotional and psychological states (Bates et al. 1993) Not only do individual pain thresholds (the degree of pain considered unbearable) vary from person to person, but they can change even within an individual. The same person may have a different consciousness of the same pain stimulus, depending on circumstances such as mood and anticipation of pain, in which case it will be experienced as more severe. The reverse can occur in situations such as the battlefield where the ongoing state of affairs can be so riveting that a badly wounded soldier may be completely unaware of any pain from his injuries. Another example of the dissociation and manipulation of consciousness comes from the reported effects of morphine. Patients taking morphine have claimed that they can still sense the pain, but it is no longer relevant or significant—that is, it does not dominate their consciousness (Bowman and Rand 1984). Finally, when consciousness starts to shrink in the first stage of anesthesia, remember that there is also analgesia, reduced awareness of pain.

What can we deduce from these examples? Consciousness of the same noxious stimulus can certainly vary according to circumstance. The phenomenon would correspond to the idea of a variable, waxing or waning consciousness devolving around a particular epicenter—in this case, the pain. If the pain was intensely burning or psychologically associated with certain events, then the degree of consciousness, its depth, would be greater. The more powerful or stronger the epicenter, whatever it may be in either physical properties or psychological terms, the deeper the consciousness at that particular moment.

There is, however, a potential snag here. If we consider pain again, we can imagine that a very intense pain might be overwhelming. On the other hand, it seems counterintuitive to believe that total obsession with a terrible pain means we are more conscious. After all, in such situations all we know is the pain; we become oblivious to any purported associations. The important point here is not to confuse the idea that a large number of neuronal associations causes a deep consciousness with the actual experience of being *aware* of every single one of those individual associations. Degree of consciousness can be the product of the extent of associations triggered by an epicenter, and indeed the power of the epicenter can be defined in terms of the number of neuronal associations recruited. But these associations serve as the ingredients that give rise to the emergent yet elusive flavor; we are not necessarily aware of them individually and piecemeal in their own right.

Consider this example: Although I am British, I dislike tea. Moreover, for some reason unknown to me, and much to the mystification and irritation of my friends, I always leave a small amount of any hot drink at the bottom of the cup. Perhaps when small I swallowed a mouthful of tea leaves—hence a complete aversion to tea and the redundant but persistent caution of leaving enough liquid at the bottom of the cup in case, contrary to all expectations, the coffee or hot chocolate somehow magically contains tea leaves. I have no awareness of the actual associations that modify my consciousness of tea and resultant behavior, but whatever they are, they make a powerful contribution to my net state of awareness. The reason I find the taste and even the mere smell of tea unpleasant is not because of clear associations vividly recalled in some piecemeal fashion. Instead, there is simply an all-embracing, unified consciousness of subjective unpleasantness associated with tea that is impossible to convey or understand.

We have already seen that these types of cognitive associations, such as anticipating a pain, will make the pain worse and our consciousness of the pain more extensive. We do not have to be aware of all the associations, including the anticipation, while we are actually experiencing the particular consciousness. A single unified conscious experience would not really be an emergent property any more than a curry would be a curry if we were conscious of each separate component. Instead, it would be a combination of onion, coriander, turmeric, and so on. If we were always aware of why we experienced things in a certain way, why our consciousness at particular times was as it was, then "priming" would not have proven so valuable and psychoanalysis would never have furnished its amazing revelations. Perhaps it is the identification of associations normally covert and constituting the quality of a moment of consciousness that makes passages such as the following from James Joyce's *Ulysses* (1922) so remarkable.

> *The sister of the wife of the wild man of Borneo has just come to town. Imagine that in the early morning at close range. Everyone to his taste as Morris said when he kissed the cow. But Dignam's puts the boots on it. Houses of mourning so depressing because you never know. Anyhow she wants the money. Must call to those Scottish Widows as I promised. Strange name. Takes it for granted we're going to pop off first.*

Consciousness, then, can be viewed *qualitatively*, in terms of different neuronal assemblies, and *quantitatively*, in terms of the size of the neuronal assembly and the extent of its interconnections. This assembly is, in turn, recruited by a triggering epicenter. At any one time one assembly will predominate, only to give way to a new grouping of a greater or smaller size, which in turn will be superseded by a third, and so on, just as each raindrop falling in a puddle dominates for one moment the surface of the water as its ripples emanate in concentric circles. But if these are the basic properties of consciousness, how might they be fitted together to form a cohesive description?

Descriptions of pain are metaphorical, always couched in terms of a nonliteral source—for example, "stabbing," "pricking," "burning." Our consciousness of pain, thus, is usually described in terms of association. It is possible that the degree of consciousness we experience at a given time is high or low on a scale according to the *number of associations* triggered by a particular epicenter. We could start to build a description of consciousness, with the operational definition that it is a variable, analog process the extent of which is determined by a stimulus epicenter.

If consciousness really is a continuum such that it can vary at any one time, then the *degree* of consciousness would be directly proportional to the extent of the objects or concepts entailed and the number of diverse and idiosyncratic associations triggered.

Because these associations would be many, disparate, and partly influenced by other transient but prevailing factors (such as hunger, fatigue, temperature, or hormones), there would *not* be a predictable, linear, and completely reproducible evocation of subsequent conscious states from one individual to the next, or even from one moment to the next. Rather, we might envision temporary, highly individual, illogical associations spreading out ever more tangentially from the original cause.

It is now possible to make some tentative steps toward describing consciousness. This concentric description of consciousness at the phenomenological level is *based on a triggering epicenter (albeit a sensory input or an internal cognitive factor or both) which sets in motion nonlinear, concentric associations. The more extensive or sustained they are, the more consciousness will be experienced at that particular time. We need not actually be conscious of each of these associations as separate components. Rather, they conspire together to give a single experience at a specific moment in time.* Meanwhile, at the physiological level of brain events, the same concentric description can be translated into more scientific terminology such that consciousness is *spatially multiple yet effectively single at any one time. It is an emergent property of noncommitted and divergent groups of neurons that is continuously variable with respect to and always entailing a stimulus epicenter.*

Thus we have one description that can be applied equally to the physiology and the psychology of consciousness. Before we see just how successful we might be in applying this description of consciousness in terms of both brain events and behavior, let us first savor its fuller implications.

Neuronal Gestalts

If consciousness is an emergent property, it means that the whole is more than the sum of its parts, just as an oval, two dots, and a straight line in a certain configuration give a crude schema for a face. Such a schema could never be derived from the dots, oval, or line individually, nor arranged in just any way; the simple elements have to form a certain overall pattern. The importance of the *relationship* among components in giving rise to a higher order of product was introduced in 1912 by a group of German psychologists—Max Wertheimer, Wolfgang Kohler, and Kurt Koffka—who called their philosophy *Gestalt* (pattern) (Rock and Palmer 1990).

The idea behind the gestalt school of thought is that perception is global, not local; objects or features are perceived in relation to one another, giving a final holistic view that cannot be inferred from the individual components alone. One of the biggest ramifications of this philosophy, which can be applied beyond the

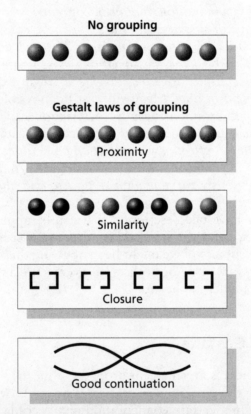

Gestalt philosophy of relationships. In contrast to the behaviorist school of thought, Gestalt theory asserts that we automatically arrange patterns from a range of smaller components. (Adapted from I. Rock and S. Palmer, "The Legacy of Gestalt Psychology," *Scientific American*, December 1990, pp. 84–90.)

process of visual perception to thinking, is that it offers an alternative to the behaviorist school of thought popularized later by B. F. Skinner (see Chapter 3). Whereas the behaviorists maintain that we make responses to immediate local stimuli, such as invariantly stretching out our arms toward a fire, gestalt philosophy argues that the whole situation of fire and its significance should be considered together; consequent behavior is chosen as that which is seen as the most appropriate. At a very formal gathering, for example, it would be socially unacceptable to rush through a crowd of dignitaries to warm oneself by the fire; or if the fire was a barbecue on a midsummer day, one's reaction would be different compared to that when standing in front of a living-room fireplace in December. Thus gestalt philosophy is wide ranging in that it encapsulates the basic idea that the whole is more than the sum of its parts in whatever system is under consideration, whether a symphony or a football game.

The hypothetical groups of neurons envisaged so far work well with gestalt philosophy in that their whole is more than the sum of their parts. Moreover, it is very important to realize that both space and time are important in the formation of these key aggregations of neurons. If we were to speak of a combination or assembly of neurons, we would be using a purely spatial concept, with no reference to the dynamic nature, the temporal element which is important in their assembly. Conversely, to describe the working of the assembly as merely contingent on synchronous activity neglects the importance of the spatial extent of interconnections among neurons. A more embracing term is needed that encompasses the idea of a combined spatiotemporal emergent property: "neuronal gestalts." In spatial terms, multiple consciousnesses, as outlined in Chapter 5, would be accounted for by the constant forming and re-forming of multiple gestalts with sufficient *potential* complexity for appreciable consciousness. The definition of a neuronal gestalt would be: a highly variable aggregation of neurons which is temporarily recruited around a triggering epicenter. The actual size of the gestalt corresponds directly and simultaneously to the degree of consciousness at a given time. By emphasizing the size of a neuronal gestalt, we have a neater way of referring quantitatively to the depth of consciousness regulated by a stimulus epicenter according to the concentric theory.

Formation of neuronal gestalts and subsequent generation of consciousness are influenced by factors in the external environment; conversely, the size of an existing gestalt, the depth of our current consciousness, influences how we interpret sensory inputs as they bombard us from the outside world. For example, if I am facing a pile of oranges in the supermarket, my consciousness at that moment will be to a greater or lesser extent colored by the external and immediate presence of the oranges; the virtual saturation of my retina by a wall of orange spheres will have some sort of impact on my visual awareness. If I am a very young child who does not yet know that one can eat these orange balls, or if I am preoccupied with some inner anxiety about the cost of a car repair, or if I am very thirsty, then the actual impact of the oranges will vary according to each of these different types of prevailing awarenesses. The oranges will impinge on my consciousness to greater or lesser extents, and my prevailing consciousness will influence how I process the sight of the oranges. The environment of oranges and my consciousness will, therefore, be mutually interactive.

But surely there is more to consciousness than these temporary aggregates of neurons, these neuronal gestalts. For multiple neuronal gestalts to match a particular conscious experience, there must be a means whereby they can be assembled and then sequenced in a flash of time so that one experience gives way seamlessly to the next. We also need a plausible means for that dominant gestalt to work almost instantaneously in some way differently from "normal" groups of neurons elsewhere. We will have to consider an additional factor in the formation of a neuronal gestalt large enough for appreciable consciousness.

We saw in Chapter 1 that arousal is a powerful factor in determining the final quality of consciousness, although it is not the same as consciousness. Arousal can be described as a generalized degree of alertness: It is low when we are relaxed and high when we are frightened or angry. This state can be measured in two ways. One method (the electroencephalogram, EEG) uses electrodes on the scalp to record the combined output of neurons in the cortex. When they create low-frequency, large-amplitude waves, where the neurons work together in slow and steady unison, then arousal is low. Hence, in normal sleep, the EEG gives a characteristic waveform that is very different from that when we dream. During dreaming, the EEG pattern becomes "desynchronized": The neurons are more active, each appears to work more individually, and the pattern recorded is far more scrambled, resembling that when we are awake and alert. Another accurate method for measuring the degree of arousal is by electrodes attached to the skin where the sweat glands are the most sensitive to emotional stimuli: palms of the hands, feet, armpits, and forehead. When we are excited and highly aroused, we start to sweat in these places, and this increases the ability of the skin to conduct electricity. Hence electrodermal activity gives a good measure of the degree of arousal.

When arousal is high, we find it hard to sit still and concentrate on any one issue. Attention itself has been referred to as focused arousal. William James defined attention as "the taking possession by the mind, in clear and vivid form, of one out of what seems several simultaneously possible objects or trains of thought." In "normal" people, normal behavior can be viewed as a compromise between arousal and attention. As we move around in the world, we become excited by new and different features, but at the same time we try to make sense of them. We are constantly balancing a tendency for distraction with a need to pay attention. If we manipulate the attention-arousal axis, how might we influence gestalt formation and thus consciousness?

Arousal and Consciousness

Let us start with an example of fragmented consciousness. When we dream we are more aroused than when we are simply sleeping, but we are, nonetheless, in a state of relatively low arousal compared to moments of high excitement when we are awake. Our skin conductance just before an interview or a speech probably indicates a far greater arousal than when we roll around in our dream world. Unlike when we are awake, there are in the dream world rapid shifts of scene and highly idiosyncratic associations that, in retrospect, defy logic and common sense. This mental inconsistency is consistent with the idea of multiple potential consciousnesses, all jockeying for dominance. Since there is no guiding, constraining, or overriding sensory input, no neuronal population is sufficiently extensive in its recruited associations to last very long or to ensure a smooth continuity of awareness. Hence, a friend is transformed into a relative who becomes oneself while the scene shifts without apparent reason from inside a house to outside, from city street to open field, and so on. Although such experiences may be vivid in quality, they are usually very fleeting—a little like, but not quite as brash as, the mercurial, almost subliminal, string of disparate images sequenced in rapid succession in some TV advertisements or music videos. Dream states, then, could be generated by relatively modest neuronal aggregations, where ripples from the epicenter are weak in the absence of ongoing external sensory priming. The depth of consciousness is at any one time slight and the gestalts are small.

By contrast, consider the situation where we are not only awake but are very excited or highly aroused. In such conditions it is hard to stay still and concentrate on any one idea; our consciousness is a disconnected jumble of impressions, reactions, and surprises at each new sight. Like a child in a candy store, as soon as we have one thing we want another. Consciousness in such circumstances can also be interpreted as one of small gestalts. When we are dreaming we can scarcely be said to be highly aroused; in fact, we are asleep and it is that critical condition of being asleep—insensitive to our immediate sensory world—that distinguishes it from normal consciousness. It is possible, then, that very low arousal levels (dreaming), like very high ones (excited), have the *same* result, small gestalt formation. But were that the case, why do these two states differ? What is the critical difference in the consciousness experienced (if we accept that both are small gestalt states) when we are unable to sit still and when we are floating in a dream world impervious to the alarm clock?

The critical difference this time is the *recruiting power* or the *strength of the epicenter.* When awake and highly aroused, the sensory epicenter is very powerful: External objects are strong stimulants with the *potential* for recruiting large numbers of neurons. But due to constant distractions from new epicenters available as well as ongoing movement affording the opportunity of still more novel sensory experiences, such epicenters recur in rapid succession. Each gestalt does not have the time to grow, but is jostled out of place while it is still small. By contrast, when we sleep, the memories that constitute the fragile epicenters of the scraps of consciousness of our dreams are relatively weak. The gestalts in this case *do* have the time to grow, but the epicenter is not sufficiently strong to maintain such growth. Hence a rival, highly transient, and only tenuously associated gestalt glides into place, and you are suddenly transposed from a house in England to an African beach.

Nonetheless the fragile epicenter of a neuronal gestalt in our dreaming consciousness is still more powerful than no consciousness, no gestalt at all. Remember it is *harder* to wake someone in REM sleep who is *relatively more aroused* than someone in normal sleep. When we are asleep and not dreaming, there is no competition for the formation of the first gestalt that will comprise our waking consciousness of an alarm bell or whatever has dragged us back into awareness. On the other hand, if we are dreaming, then a gestalt has been formed, however fragile. The scrap of ensuing consciousness subsequently serves as the modest, initial form of competition to the external, powerful alarm bell. It is the subtle *interaction* between arousal and gestalt size that dictates our prevailing consciousness.

Strength (recruiting power) of the epicenter might interact with arousal to generate three different situations. For gestalt formation and for consciousness, it is very important if arousal is low, medium, or high. When arousal is high and the epicenter strong, then only small gestalts are formed because of the rapid imposition of new epicenters bombarding our senses due to high arousal and the constant exposure to new aspects of the external world, themselves due to the attendant high degree of restlessness and movement. Now imagine a situation where the converse applies. We are less readily distracted, less aroused, but the focus of our consciousness is still strong. In such cases, when arousal levels are more moderate, gestalt formation is larger because the epicenter acts as a raindrop in a puddle where the ripples are unopposed. We are paying attention, deeply conscious of a specific object. In the third situation arousal is low. Because we are asleep and the epicenters are completely internally driven, and thus weak, gestalts are again small. Consciousness is composed of mere fragments: We are dreaming.

Of course it is quite unlikely that the body has three discrete types of arousal, like settings on a microwave oven—low, medium, and high. Rather, arousal is a continuously variable factor. This idea is far from new. For a long time psychologists have plotted levels of arousal against performance in certain tasks and have shown a curve shaped like an inverted U (Yerkes and Dodson 1980). Efficiency at a task is optimal in the *middle* range of arousal; if we are too relaxed or too distracted, then performance declines. Hence maximal efficiency corresponds to the situation of large gestalt formation. There is a possible balancing act between attention and arousal. It would follow that there is a trade-off in terms of survival value between being able to concentrate and being aware of change. Thus we can see that arousal is an interactive factor, along with the strength of epicenter, in determining the final size of gestalt formation and hence consciousness. High and low degrees of arousal can both be associated with the formation of small gestalts, namely, rapidly shifting states of shallow consciousness, whereas an intermediate level of arousal favors the formation of fewer, longer lasting, and larger gestalts, amounting to promoting a deeper consciousness, attention.

It has been clear from as early as Chapter 1 that there is more to consciousness than arousal and that the two do not go hand in hand. If you have more of one, you do not necessarily have more of the other. According to the description developed in this chapter, we can see how arousal could be linked to consciousness but not yet equated with it.

From Metaphor to Reality

Before we can examine the success of the concentric description as it currently stands, let's look at it in full: *Consciousness is spatially multiple yet effectively single at any one time. It is an emergent property of nonspecialized and divergent groups of neurons (gestalts) that is continuously variable with respect to, and always entailing, a stimulus epicenter. The size of the gestalt, and hence the depth of prevailing consciousness, is a product of the interaction between the recruiting strength of epicenter and the degree of arousal.*

To be acceptable as a theory, any new description should have the promise, at least, of being able to accommodate a scheme more organized and deterministic than the happenstance one by which unmarshalled, multiple potential consciousnesses surface randomly for domination in a kind of neuro-lottery. The concentric theory should now provide some means for accounting for an enduring, idiosyncratic theme for individuals as our consciousness shifts, shrinks, or expands. Such a scheme might account not only for consciousness but mind as well.

The concentric theory can embrace potential multiple consciousnesses of the type proposed by Dennett and Parfit, where only one consciousness is realized at one time. But can we go further and offer an alternative to a system wherein consciousness has a continuity and consistency that is unique for each brain? By introducing the concept of neuronal gestalts, we can say that the repertoire of potential connections among neurons, and also the size and shape of particular gestalts, are specific to each individual brain. These idiosyncratic connections have been formed not just as a result of one's genes, but, more significantly, as the brain interacts with the environment. Hence the transition from one conscious state to the next is unique for any individual, as the ripples emanating from the epicenter recruit a particular pattern of neurons. Our continuity of consciousness, then, occurs as a chain of associations devolved around an epicenter.

In the example of the orange used earlier in this chapter, we saw that we might finally think of an old friend, which might next act as a trigger for further associations, so that it effectively becomes a new epicenter. It is similar to raindrops falling in a puddle. As soon as one set of ripples is set in motion, a nearby drop overrides the previous ripples with its own, just like a new pattern of neuronal connections. This new epicenter may be cognitive or externally derived. For example, while thinking of an old friend, I might see a pile of oranges, which I then look at in a certain way colored by past associations of a time that friend and I had together. On the other hand, all this reverie could be disrupted by a car screaming around the corner. In this second scenario, there would be no continuity of consciousness at all, but a new and rival epicenter imposed by the outside world. We frequently have these ruptured states of consciousness, especially as children, but mostly, as adults, we interact with our environment in a smooth, nonemergency fashion. As varying degrees of new sensory information come in, as our internal body environment fluctuates in its levels of glucose, hormones, and so on, and as the ripples of one gestalt spread out to ever more remote associations, so a new epicenter starts to recruit neurons into a gestalt. This new gestalt supplants the original, and our consciousness subtly shifts.

This continuity, where one gestalt triggers the next, offers a much more attractive alternative than the random selection of gestalts through a neuro-lottery. And that very continuity provides at the same time a basis for a more enduring and individualized mind beyond the quick fix of a kaleidoscopic, ready-made, instant consciousness. The individual size and shape of gestalts, and the particular *transition* from one to the next, might actually be a plausible basis for an enduring individuality. Of course, we are not necessarily aware that our consciousness is shifting from one focus to another, nor are we aware of the depth of consciousness at any given time, and we are certainly not aware of all the associations that might be contributing to a specific state of awareness. Normally, as we saw earlier in the case of my dislike for tea, a moment of consciousness *just is*.

To sum up, it seems that the concentric theory can actually accommodate some of the clues collected earlier regarding consciousness. These include the importance of the intensity of the focus or epicenter of consciousness, the importance of previous associations (memory), the presence of a consciousness in animals and children that is different from our own, and the elimination of a fixed consciousness center. On the other hand, we are now committing the very error that has hampered other models of consciousness, where an explanation is little more than a metaphor. After all, it is one thing to offer a cohesive account in terms of gestalts, epicenters, and arousal. But however tidy it is, we are still left with only speculative word spinning that is no help unless we see such terminology put into practice.

In the course of developing the concentric theory, there has been blatant pilfering from both physiological and phenomenological scenarios. The critical issue now is whether or not we have a description of consciousness that can eventually transcend these scenarios. Of course neuron is a physiological term, but we are speaking of large groups of neurons defined in time as well as space, and giving them a special name (gestalts). As such, we need to see if the idea of a gestalt, as used here, can be readily applied to psychological as well as physiological phenomena. Epicenter is a term used by neither psychologists nor physiologists; it is simply a metaphor. The question now focuses on whether the epicenter can be identified at both the phenomenological and physical levels. Finally, we have seen very early on that arousal has a significance in both psychological and physiological terms. As such, it is a term that we can accept as ambidextrous without further worry. It is time, then, to put these concepts and terms to work and look for a *real* physical basis for the formation of neuronal gestalts (Chapters 7 and 8) and hence of consciousness (Chapter 9).

chapter seven

THE REALITY
OF CONSCIOUSNESS

The consciousness you are currently experiencing is the result of neurons generating electricity and squirting chemicals around inside your head. No product is being exported for appreciation elsewhere; nothing is being translated back into the color red or the sound of a bird chirping. Everything happening in the outside world is reduced to the diffusion of free-floating molecules and the banal fluxes of ions, and stays that way. What happens next? Can the concentric theory formulated in the previous chapter now be transformed into actual events in the real brain?

From the outset it has been clear that we would not have any success looking at any one brain area as a mini-brain in isolation; rather, it is much more realistic to consider the brain as an integrated, holistic entity. There is a big difference between *homogeneous* and *holistic* functioning: Our description of consciousness will have to refute the former, which regards the brain as merely a global clump of generic brain cells, but embrace the latter, which sees different brain regions each making an integral contribution to the final net output. In short, we need to think simultaneously of individual brain regions and of those regions working as a coordinated whole. But the webs of enigmatically ordered brain cells are only of use to us after we have a dynamic scheme to impose on them; the physical mass of heterogeneous tissue can effectively be a back-drop, not a springboard.

Since we are now finally dealing with real physicochemical events, it would be tempting to start again in true reductionist fashion with the most obvious building blocks of the brain, single brain cells. But we have already seen that this strategy is unlikely to get us very far: A neuron in isolation does not contain any ethereal element of consciousness. Furthermore, we have seen that once we venture beyond animals such as the sea slug *Aplysia,* we do not have the one-to-one matching of physiology with psychology, that easy correspondence of neuronal and behavioral events comparable with the winding of a spring and the resultant clocklike behavior.

This discrepancy between what neurons *do* (generate action potentials) and what they can *accomplish* (contribute to the generation of consciousness) needs emphasizing. It is very enticing, at least for a scientist, to postulate that the most basic elements of the brain must somehow be the most basic elements of consciousness. For example, in a recent article, Francis Crick and Christof Koch (1993) have seized upon the neurons that are organized into the six layers of the outer rim of the brain (the cortex) as the source of consciousness. They suggest that "the activities in the upper layers of the cortex are largely unconscious ones, whereas the activities in the lower layers (layers 5 and 6) mostly correlate with consciousness." They go on to claim that "the idea that the layer 5 neurons directly symbolize consciousness is attractive, but it is still too early to tell whether there is anything in it." Surely this line of reasoning is problematic. How could anything, least of all consciousness, be symbolized in the brain? How can a neuron, or group of neurons, stand as a symbol, and what would there be in the brain to appreciate the symbolism? We are back to the problem encountered in Chapter 1, that of starting to think of a vivid metaphor as a literal reality.

Since we cannot start off by applying the concentric theory to a physical lump of brain, nor to its smallest components, we need a scheme whereby neurons can somehow generate consciousness at a level that lies *between* the single cell and the unified brain. At the heart of the description developed in Chapter 6 is the transient teaming up of neurons into a gestalt. We will need to see how aggregations of neurons might operate, and investigate whether or not they can function in both time and space like these theoretical gestalts. But we must be careful that these gestalts do not have a rigid, fixed anatomy and that they are not localized in one brain area. Indeed, we need a scheme whereby transient aggregations of neurons are forming, operating, and re-forming all the time in multiple areas of the brain, such that at any moment one particular group somehow generates consciousness.

So what clues have we discovered? Two basic factors are central to the implementation of the concentric theory: neuronal gestalts, which are in turn influenced by arousal. Both of these concepts are promising ones for us to use as a bridge between phenomenology and physiology, as both force us to think of large groupings of neurons, intermediate between the whole brain and the single neuron. At the same time, the basic ideas of arousal and neuronal gestalts are not anatomically restricted to a specific brain area and could thus be viewed more broadly as pivotal factors in integrated brain function. We are going to journey into the brain using the following route: First, explore the physicochemical bases of gestalt and arousal independently, and second, develop a physicochemical description of the interaction whereby levels of arousal and gestalt formation act in concert to generate consciousness.

Neuronal Gestalts: From Theory to Reality?

Neurons are the most basic element of the brain, yet it has been repeatedly suggested for a hundred years that they do not work in isolation; and thus the concept of neuronal assemblies has haunted brain research. One of the founders of modern neurophysiology, Charles Sherrington, spoke at the beginning of the century of "neuronal pools," aggregates of brain cells projecting toward the same target. In the 1940s Donald Hebb gave his name to an "assembly" of neurons defined as a network of connections between neurons where communication was made easier or strengthened by experience. This is the concept of weighting. More recently, the term correlational assemblies has crept into the vocabulary of neuroscientists as they have grappled with the realization that the brain operates by parallel processes. These correlational assemblies can be defined, crudely, as groups of neurons active to the same extent in the same way at the same time (Gerstein et al. 1989).

Despite the familiarity of the concept of neuronal assemblies, the sheer difficulty combined with the utter beauty of recording the electrical activity of a single brain cell has captured the imagination and monopolized the efforts of many scientists over the years. Indeed, the march of technology has been ever more reductionist as scientists have learned first to record the subtle fluxes of ions inside a cell and then focus on those isolated fluxes in a tiny segment of the wall of the neuron. We have already seen how hard it is to regard the isolated neuron as a faithful index of global brain events, just as it would be hazardous to infer the progress of a football game by observing a single player. Clearly we need a way of studying how brain cells work together and the types of groups they form.

The most basic property of neuronal gestalts, that they are a type of neuronal assembly, is therefore neither original nor heretical. On the contrary, it is timely and inevitable. This progress toward a more integrated strategy in brain research represents a shift from analysis to synthesis. The earlier reductionism of neuroscience research, which has dominated experiments if not theories, is probably one of the strongest reasons why empirical neuroscience has not added much to the debate on the physical basis of the mind. By changing direction from taking things apart to bringing them together, neuroscience might eventually make a real contribution toward a fuller understanding of the brain events underlying consciousness.

The current momentum for exploring functional groups of neurons in general has provided fertile ground for collecting exciting evidence that neuronal gestalts exist. In the previous chapter a gestalt was defined as *a highly variable aggregation of neurons that is temporarily recruited around a triggering epicenter.* Not all neuronal assemblies are gestalts, but all gestalts are neuronal assemblies. Gestalts are assemblies that are as transient and unique as clouds but spinning out from an epicenter like concentric ripples in a puddle. In order to get used to the idea of brain cells working in assemblies, let us look briefly at some simple examples. These examples focus on more modest groups of neurons that are neither transient nor subtle in their functioning but, rather, are fixed, and with operations that are easy to understand.

A good place to begin is with a short excursion out of the brain and into the unlikely arena of the lobster stomach (Marder et al. 1987). This circuitry is relatively simple to understand because the activity of the nerves in question corresponds directly to mechanical actions. The lobster stomach carries out the digestion of food by the movement of muscles similar to those in the leg. These muscles grind up food in an appropriately dubbed "gastric mill." As might be imagined, the grinding motion requires a lot of coordination of the muscles but need not be constant. Rather, the overall movement can vary from time to time, just as walking can vary. The muscles, which contract rhythmically, are controlled by a total of twenty neurons grouped together in a hard-wired assembly, that is to say, the connections among them are fixed and unchanging. It is an intriguing fact, however, that the output of this group of neurons is not fixed and invariant; the rhythms of contraction of the stomach muscles that they produce are enormously versatile. The reason for this variation lies in the emergent properties generated by a group of individually simple elements which can produce complex effects when they act together. Only five neurons in the lobster stomach directly affect the muscles and they are connected by seventeen crisscrossing pathways. Nonetheless, the possible combinations of these seventeen elements at any one time are 6,188 (or $17!/5! \times 12!$).

Such combinations would be several orders of magnitude higher if we also consider that each neuron is not like a digital switch on a computer (either on or off) but is generating an analog, graded signal. This difference from the typical computer is achieved by the way in which the connections are *biased* over periods of time ranging from a second to minutes and even longer. Such biasing, referred to by neuroscientists as "neuromodulation," occurs when certain neurochemicals do not necessarily participate in direct signaling but, rather, reduce or enhance the excitability of a neuron in response to a signal coming in at another time. Neuronal groups, even of the simplest, hard-wired, and smallest kind, are capable of giving rise to highly versatile emergent properties that depend on how the cells have been biased. Perhaps not surprisingly, this situation is rampant among the more complex neuronal interconnections and sophisticated functions of the brain.

Let us return to the brain for a closer look at cooperativity among neurons. Neurons are often organized into discernible assemblies that are repeatedly lined up next to each other throughout certain brain regions like cookies cut from the same cookie cutter. Each of these identical yet independent units is a module, like cookies systematically laid out in a box in organized rows and piles. A good illustration of this modular arrangement of neurons is in the cerebellum, the structure that appears to ride piggyback on the main brain and that is associated with unconscious behavior. The modular arrangement of the cerebellum is straightforward: In its simplest form it consists of two inputs converging on an output cell. Even this elementary arrangement allows for a simple form of automatic motor learning. As we saw in Chapter 3, the final response to a simple stimulus is determined by whether or not conditioning had taken place, which in turn depends on the activity of one neuron in the circuit being paired with another. In reality, no cells have been added or taken away, nor have any of the participating neurons undergone any conspicuous alterations in shape. Since there has been no dramatic change in the neuronal group, the change must be a subtle chemical one.

Like the cerebellum, the outer layer of the brain—the sophisticated cortex—also resembles a box of cookies in that it, too, is organized into modules (Thach et al. 1992). There are six anatomically distinguishable layers parallel to the surface of the brain. Neurons in each layer reach up and down, at right angles, to the brain's surface, to connect in vertical columns. These columns are the basic modules of the functionally complex cortex. As the cortex becomes increasingly dominant in animals that are more developed, the critical factor that changes is not the number of layers and not necessarily the number of cells, but the distance and hence the potential complexity of connections among these cells. Imagine how the potential for communication is increased dramatically by increasing the number of telephone lines among individuals in a large office building.

This is a very important point because in the cortex the functional groups participate in working conversations with one another. They need not be locked into a perpetual dialogue, and the relevant connections need not be *functionally* fixed and predetermined. Neuronal gestalts, we have seen, would be essentially *transient* groupings of neurons where the connections among them are only temporarily functional. Therefore, the corresponding real groups of neurons would have to be highly labile, occurring in a flash in a particular space and time frame. They would need to be fleeting, but while they existed, they would have a conspicuous profile and identity. In short, they would be like clouds.

Clouds in the Brain

It is now established that groups of neurons in the brain do not have to be irrevocably hard-wired, destined forever to communicate with a rigidly fixed set of neighbors. During development, for example, dramatic occurrences in the outside environment can change the internal arrangement of brain cells. In research on mice it was discovered that the whiskers are connected to neurons in the brain that monitor the pressure on the whiskers when the mouse passes through a narrow gap. The neurons representing each individual whisker team up in the cortex, so that when examined on a stained histological section of brain tissue, the shape of the neuronal cluster resembles that of a barrel (Cowan 1990). If a line of whiskers is removed, then the neighboring barrels—the neuronal groups representing the still intact nearby whiskers—expand so that *all* the original area in the cortex still contains barrels of neurons, albeit fewer and larger ones. Denied the opportunity to work in the original group, where they can no longer register signals from a recently extirpated whisker, the dispossessed neurons team up with neighboring groups, thus forming the larger barrels representing the extant whiskers.

We can infer, then, that there must be active competition for survival among groups of neurons, even in such hard-wired circuits. Neuronal groupings such as these barrels are essentially maps of properties in the outside world: There is a point-to-point correspondence between the space occupied externally by the whiskers and the space occupied in the cortex by the respective neurons. This example of the mouse snout shows us that during development there is clearly a dynamic process whereby the brain is interacting with the environment. But the notion of neuronal gestalts demands much faster changes in neuronal groupings, occurring within fractions of a second, where clusters of neurons are incessantly re-forming, accumulating, and breaking up. Furthermore, such changes would have to operate all the time, right up to old age.

So what happens to the barrels of neurons in a much faster time frame? Harry Orbach and his colleagues (1985) made use of special dyes sensitive to voltage which fluoresce when neurons become active as the voltage across their membrane reaches a level of depolarization for which the dye is selectively sensitive. Barrels of neurons can actually be visualized in the area of the cortex concerned with touch (somatosensory cortex) of the living rat brain. If two separate whiskers are touched, two separate amorphous blobs in the brain transiently light up. It is not possible to see the precise geometry or orientation of the individual neurons but, rather, an area of light corresponding to the total perimeter of a group of cells. It is a fascinating feature of this type of study that whereas the barrels seen using conventional staining on dead brains show an area of about six hundred microns across, the functional area that lights up in the living brain is much greater, some thirteen hundred microns in width. Hence the degree of neuronal communication, the size of a functional assembly, is far more extensive than we would have been led to believe by looking at the anatomy alone. Such direct visualizations of dynamic neuronal groupings are our first real evidence that gestalts might exist.

But that is not all. If two whiskers are touched simultaneously, the areas of fluorescence overlap, forming, as we might say, one gestalt. And if two such events occur more or less simultaneously, the events will apparently be classed by the brain as one and registered by one correspondingly larger neuronal grouping. The size of the fluorescent blob appears to be in no way predetermined, as one would expect of a fixed group of cells performing a fixed function. Rather, a host of factors seems to determine the final size of the net working assembly.

However, when one whisker is touched more than twenty milliseconds after the other, the second assembly does not form; there is no fluorescent blob because the relevant neurons are not active. This is evidence of overt competition in the transient assembling of these primitive gestalts. The idea that gestalts compete with one another to develop explains why it is harder to be awakened during dream sleep (even though we are more aroused) than during nondream sleep. In dream sleep there is already an existing consciousness; fragile and fragmented gestalts causing our consciousness during dreaming act as rivals, however puny, to the alarm bell.

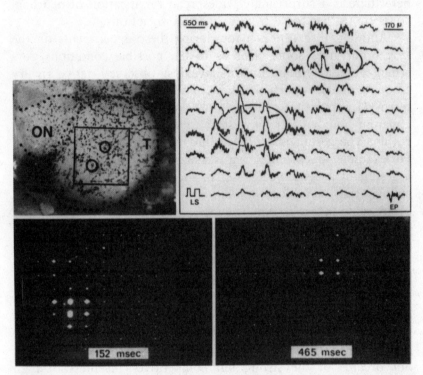

Optical imaging of neuronal groups. *Top panel, left:* These patterns in neuronal activity in the frog's brain were evoked by spots of light. *Top panel, right:* Responses from a 9 × 9 photodetector. Two loci of activity could be resolved, corresponding to two different light spots presented one after the other to the opposite eye (40 trials were averaged). (EP, evoked potential; LS, timing of the light stimuli.) *Bottom panels:* Visualization of spatial patterns of activity at two different times depicting two loci of activity. Note that the response to the second stimulus (465 milliseconds) was inhibited by the first response (152 milliseconds). (From R. D. Frostig, E. E. Lieke, A. Arieli, D. Y. T'so, R. Hildesheim, and A. Grinvald, "Optical Imaging of Neuronal Activity in the Living Brain," in *Neuronal Cooperativity,* ed. J. Kruger [New York: Springer-Verlag, 1991], pp. 52–67. Reprinted by permission.)

In the much simpler situation of the frog brain, R. Frostig has shown that a sensory input, such as a flash of light, recruits a group of neurons around a central focus of excitation or, as we would say, an epicenter (see Frostig et al. 1991). This central zone is surrounded by an area of cortical activity larger than might have been predicted from recording the activity of single, isolated cells. Again we have the basis for a primitive gestalt, and even here there is a surprisingly widespread ramification of neuronal connections that could trigger diverse associations.

Another observation made during these experiments on the frog brain gives some clues as to the possible conditions governing gestalt formation. We have just observed active rivalry among gestalts. A particularly fascinating aspect of the size of the recruited population of neurons is that the neurons beyond the apparent boundary of the gestalt are *actively inhibiting* the ones within: The gestalt is actually inhibited around its very borders. For example, an epicenter that is a simple spot of light may recruit a gestalt of a certain size. But in the presence of a drug (bicuculline) that can block inhibition among neurons, the gestalt becomes ten times as big. The size of a gestalt is determined not only by the recruiting strength of the epicenter but also by its power to sustain a large group of interactive, cooperative neurons. Strength can be viewed as the extent in both time and space by which the cohesiveness of the transient group is maintained in the face of opposition from counteractive influences pressing at its boundaries. In a way this balance of power in gestalt formation is like arm wrestling: If you weaken, you immediately lose territory. As we saw in the previous chapter, the easily displaced gestalts of our dreams or the strong but competitive epicenters of high arousal states will in both cases result in the formation of only small gestalts.

Ad Aertsen and George Gerstein (1991) have developed a series of computational methods for classifying the simultaneous multiple recordings of electrical output of individual neurons into working assemblies, this time in the cat visual cortex. Their most significant finding is that these groups are highly dynamic, forming and re-forming over a period of ten milliseconds to ten seconds. Moreover, individual cells might participate in one assembly on one occasion and in another group on a subsequent occasion. Perhaps most important for the theory of neuronal gestalts, however, is their finding that the neuronal groups are also context dependent. Such groups differ in their connectivity, for example, if a visual stimulus (a moving bar of light at different orientations) presented is the *same as* or *different from* previous presentations.

In this way we can see that the momentary context, the associations linked to a particular stimulus, is important. In our own brains associations would accrue as we grow up and our consciousness expands as objects acquire significance. Context-dependent neuronal assemblies in the cat brain are possibly a physical basis for such a scheme, albeit on a more modest scale. Such experimental observations mesh well with the concept of neuronal gestalts. But it is not enough to know that they might exist. If the concept of gestalts is truly pivotal to understanding consciousness at the physiological level, then we need to address two critical questions: How do such groups work, and how are they formed?

Creating Neuronal Gestalts

So-called correlational assemblies of neurons, comparable to the gestalts described in the previous chapter, can be detected by a common spatiotemporal pattern of electrical discharge from each member neuron, a little like synchronized swimming. When two brain regions, the thalamus and the cortex, are active in unison, there is evidence for focused arousal (Pinault and Deschenes 1992; Sheer 1989; Murthy and Fetz 1992; Tütinen et al. 1993). In addition, perhaps under direction from the thalamus (Crick 1994), a similar synchrony may occur among subsets of neurons in the cortex itself, where members of transient groups can be recruited over relatively large distances, up to seven millimeters apart (Gray et al. 1989).

In a normal situation, the nearer one neuron is to another, the more likely they are to be excited by each other, since any chemical messenger released locally within a group will not have far to diffuse. Are gestalts, then, determined passively by the simple diffusion of transmitters? The type of synchronous signaling, where a particular kind of electrical activity can act as the credential for membership of a gestalt, means that recruitment is *not* on the grounds of mere proximity, which would thus automatically limit our consciousness. Rather, it would be far more flexible to be able to generate an extensive gestalt of neurons spanning a larger area from which they were selectively recruited by their electrical discharge, diffusion of chemicals, or even a frequency of oscillation. Wolf Singer (1990) has shown that disparate neurons large distances apart in the area of the cortex associated with vision can actually oscillate in their excitability in a synchronous fashion, if they are processing respective parts of a pattern with a common feature. This feature might be a similar orientation of a visual stimulus, such as a bar. It is suggestive of people in a search party spread out over a field so they cannot shout to one another easily. Instead, they wave to one another as they perform different aspects of the same job, each contributing to the global function of a search but each in his or her own territory.

Another feature of gestalts suggested by experimental data is that they are ceaselessly at work, shuffling and reorganizing their internal communications. The oscillations of a specific group have been shown by Reinhard Eckhorn (Eckhorn et al. 1990) to have a momentary frequency, that is, they do not only oscillate at a fixed rate under a particular condition all the time. Rather, the oscillations can vary from one moment to the next, presumably because of changes in the interactions within the network—a subtle interplay of as yet unknown events as in the lobster stomach but a lot more complicated. In more complex situations, where a gestalt may be generating consciousness, we might expect shifting changes *within* a gestalt at any one time as further associations are triggered and new associations made. Effectively, this process might constitute the behavior or the phenomenon of thinking.

Another determining feature of the size of gestalts is the relative strength of the epicenter. We have seen earlier that the stimulus epicenter could be strong not only in correspondence to an external stimulus that was conspicuous in physical terms (loud, bright, big, moving, and so on), but strong in cognitive terms (having associations with reward or pain, or being made special or significant by an experimental protocol or by a past individual history). There is considerable empirical support for the idea that the stronger and more powerful the epicenter, the more neurons recruited in an assembly. If a light is presented to both eyes of an awake cat rather than to just one eye, the transient group of neurons recruited in the visual cortex is *six* times greater (Eckhorn 1991). Since large numbers of neurons seem able to be readily recruited in this way, into whatever gestalts are produced during an experiment, it suggests again that one neuron need not be committed to just one gestalt. After all, even though there are an astronomical but finite number of neurons in the human cortex, the number of possible conscious experiences is infinite.

Hence, one might expect that neurons would be recruited into different groups. Eilon Vaadia (Vaadia et al. 1991) has recorded from different parts of the monkey cortex and has shown that a single neuron can participate in more than one group. Furthermore he has demonstrated that neuronal groups can organize to perform specific tasks and then reorganize to form new groups serving new functions. For example, neurons in the auditory cortex can be involved in responding purely to a tone and on other occasions to a tone followed by a specific motor response. But how is such mercurial flexibility possible?

Neurons could be active in synchrony if they were close enough together to make direct contact with one another. But if they *always* excited one another, they would be effectively hardwired, which would make the scenario of rapidly *shifting* gestalts impossible. The problem, then, is not so much how such cooperativity could happen but, rather, how it could *not* happen, how the synchronous activity could be achieved among a group of neurons in one area on some occasions but not on others. The establishment of the physical connections among neurons, where one is juxtaposed to another across a narrow gap (a synapse), is not a brief encounter. We saw in Chapter 3 that the plasticity needed for learning and memory takes much longer than hundredths of a second and entails changes that occur over hours or days and that, once established, have a degree of permanence. So it is truly puzzling how functional groups of neurons can form and re-form in fractions of a second. This point is critical to the search for the physical basis of consciousness because a rapid and dynamic time frame is essential to accommodate our restless awareness.

Vaadia suggests that the answer lies not in the physical connections among neurons but in how those connections are used. If the connections existed among vast arrays of neurons but were inefficient in their operations—were in Hebb's terms *weakly* weighted—then it would be unlikely that electrical messages sent along them would ever have an effect on target neurons. A gentle push may have no effect on you whatsoever. On the other hand, if a target neuron received a number of weak signals simultaneously, then it could activate that cell. If many people push you gently at the same time, you might fall over. Hence synchronicity of firing is important in selectively recruiting a neuron. Only cells receiving a specific degree of activation are recruited.

So far we have seen how simultaneous activation of inputs can gang up to recruit a cell into synchronous activity with its neighbors to form a gestalt. But this process in itself is still insufficient to trigger the aggregation of the very large numbers of neurons that are needed in the type of gestalt we have been envisaging that could be associated with appreciable consciousness. In the previous chapter we noted that gestalt formation *on its own* is a necessary but not a sufficient factor for appreciable consciousness. At any given time the brain is full of multiple *potential* consciousnesses, gestalts of different sizes and durations. It is this quantitative aspect of a gestalt—its actual extent in both time and space—that is a vital consideration for lifting us above the vestigial consciousness of the most basic animal and determining the depth of consciousness that we experience. We cannot assume that any dynamic neuronal group, a gestalt of just any size, will invariably generate consciousness as we know it. It is time, then, to look at what else happens when the gestalt, beyond merely existing, causes appreciable consciousness. Until now we have assumed that the transient neuronal groupings correspond to potential gestalts. But let us examine a neuronal group that really does seem to be in some way connected with consciousness and that can be a basic, first example of what we have been speculating would be needed for conscious states.

This simple model of consciousness concerns the registration of the significance of a smell to a rabbit. Walter Freeman (1991) has shown that a very large group of neurons in an entire brain region is involved by his derivation of a characteristic "phase portrait" from EEGs of the activity of neurons in the olfactory bulb, the first relay station in the rabbit's brain that processes smells. This EEG pattern changes if the significance of a certain odor changes, as, for example, whether or not it becomes associated with something pleasurable such as food. Such immediate and simultaneous mass activation is not made possible by the mere presence of local one-to-one connections alone. The time taken for a transmitter to diffuse across a synapse is at least five-thousandths of a second. If the neuronal assembly consisted of a linear relay of approximately ten thousand neurons (a colossal underestimate), it would take at least fifty seconds for a signal to be passed through a gestalt in a linear relay—almost a minute! Rather, the neurons in such a large group have to be *globally* alerted, primed in some way so that they can all become active simultaneously.

According to Freeman, the priming can be accomplished in three ways. First, it can occur through the Hebbian, or neuronal, system whereby, through use, a neuronal contact becomes strengthened. As a starting point we can assume so far that there are vast assemblies of neurons connected to one another anatomically but with poor communication at the points of contact, the synapses. It is like two people standing next to each other. One person is hard of hearing and the other has laryngitis and cannot speak above a whisper: Despite the proximity, oral communication is ineffective. One way, as we have seen, of ensuring that neuronal contacts become more efficient is by Hebbian strengthening. We know that this type of modification really occurs because of the well-established phenomenon explored in Chapter 3, long-term potentiation. Neuronal strengthening, then, is very useful for establishing associations among neurons as an infrastructure for learning. But as we all know, learning takes some time and once achieved is, we hope, far from transitory, as it forms the basis of our memory.

The time frame of Hebbian strengthening over hours, then, is not quite right for our purposes here of providing a physical description of consciousness. After all, what is needed is a method of ensuring a corralling of cells achieved in fractions of a second and equally rapidly disbanded. The ideal would *not* be a rearrangement of the hardwiring. Another problem is that if we place the emphasis on an enduring association among specific neurons, as we would for some detailed, learned association, we fall short of what we need for a gestalt. What is necessary for the formation of a large neuronal group is some nonlocal means of activating not specific contacts among neurons but vast aggregations of cells. If you want to inform crowds of people of the results of an election, it is not very efficient to rely on word of mouth from one individual to the next; it is far more practical to make the announcement to everyone simultaneously. In just such a way, in both time and space, we are looking for far more ambitious and sweeping actions than could be achieved alone by Hebbian strengthening.

The second means of increasing cell receptivity is to exploit a property of neurons: Their sensitivity to respond to an input increases as that input is maintained. More specifically, if a neuron is excited by an input, it becomes still more excited as that input remains. Hence a neuron that is not initially active is not at its most sensitive. It is like the increasing irritation we might have toward someone coughing in a concert hall. Initially, we are relatively insensitive to the intrusion, but if the coughing continues, we wait anxiously for the next cough to occur. When it does, we may overreact; we have become far more sensitive to the stimulus. The enhanced sensitivity of a group of cells to a persistent epicenter can fuel the recruiting power of an already existing epicenter in fighting off a rival gestalt, a consciousness of something else. On the other hand, such a mechanism might only account for the maintenance and even expanding cohesion of a gestalt; it would not be sufficient to account for the facilitated aggregation of cells in the first place.

Rapid changes in the activity of very large groups of neurons acting in concert cannot be achieved with just a strong epicenter sending out passport signals for recruitment of vast banks of remote neurons, nor indeed can it be achieved by a time-consuming, progressive change in each local contact according to Hebb's principles. We need to turn to a third factor that can prime the formation of very large gestalts. It is third and last in the list because it *actually provides the basis for the link between the two vital factors in consciousness, strength of epicenter and size of gestalt.* It is arousal. Remember that, according to the concentric theory, gestalts will only generate appreciable consciousness when they are sufficiently large. Their existence, for which we now have some real physical evidence, in itself will not testify to consciousness any more than, as we saw in Chapters 1 and 6, arousal itself will. Consciousness, as described in the previous chapter, is a product of at least both of these factors. The way in which arousal might prime the formation of transient neuronal groups is thus central to the realization of the physical basis of consciousness according to the concentric theory. But first we need to see exactly what arousal is.

The Biology of Arousal

Arousal for a physiologist occurs when electrical activity in the cortex of the brain, as recorded by surface electrodes on the scalp, reveals that the active neurons are not in synchrony, but are each active in different ways and times, producing a desynchronized EEG. The ultimate source of this increased activity is about as far away from the cortex as possible, deep down in the brain, serving as a gateway between the spinal cord and all the higher centers. Evolutionarily, this is the most basic part of the brain; it swells out just above the top of the spinal cord and is called the brainstem (Steriade 1991). It is in this very primitive region, which we looked at in the previous chapter, where the incessant and automatic control of heart rate and respiration operates from birth to death.

But neurons in the brainstem do not just influence nerves descending from the brain and entering the rest of the body. The brainstem, which sticks into the brain like the core of an apple, is also the first stage of a pathway of neurons reaching upward and forward into sophisticated brain regions, toward that large area nestling deep within the brain which is important in biological models of consciousness, the thalamus. From the thalamus the pathway pushes upward as extensive, multiplying branches pervade the outermost layer of the cortex, the most complex and, evolutionarily, the newest of all. Hence in two crude stages we can reach from the oldest and most basic part to the newest and most sophisticated. It is perhaps not surprising that neuronal connections among brain areas have long been seen by scientists as a key factor in consciousness. We have already seen a specific example of a reverberating loop in the visual system used to explain blindsight (Chapter 4). It might be helpful now to look at previous biological accounts of neuronal loops such as these, to see how they have been used to account for consciousness.

Reverberating Neuronal Loops

In order to prevent matters from becoming unnecessarily and prematurely complicated, let us stay for the moment with the basic type of consciousness that we can think of as a crude snapshot of consciousness of the immediate world and that Gerald Edelman dubs primary consciousness, a frozen moment in our awareness. Presumably different groups of neurons conspire to present a scene such as a hot summer day by the seaside. This supposition is redolent of Dennett's use of memes to build up a kind of neuro-ecosphere where *just for that moment* different factors in the brain produce a kaleidoscopic scenario never again exactly the same. According to Edelman this primary consciousness requires three properties of the brain: first, a cortex (the outer rim of brain); second, a memory linking the cortex with the deeper and more primitive limbic system; and third, a new reentrant circuit for consciousness. Let us look at each item on this list in turn.

The significance of the cortex is that it gets larger as animals become more sophisticated and seems to be the seat of the higher brain functions. On the other hand, it may be a bit hasty to assume that all simpler animals with little or no cortex (Edelman singles out the lobster) are not conscious at all. As to the second prerequisite, the link between two major brain regions is an attempt to connect internal hedonism, which Edelman localizes in subcortical brain regions, with external perception, which he places in the cortex. This second property enables us to interpret what we perceive in some sort of internal value system.

While it makes perfect sense to suggest, as in the previous chapter, that we interpret what we experience in the outside world in terms of past experiences, the postulated link between a subcortical area responsible for the internal associations and another for ongoing perceptions is a colossal simplification of what we know of the physiology of the brain. As we have already seen (Chapter 1), we cannot localize functions in specific brain regions with any great accuracy, and it is erroneous, according to what we do know, to suggest that the cortex plays no part in previous associations or that the limbic system plays no part in processing incoming information. We have just seen, for example, in Chapter 3 that long-term potentiation, which occurs in part of the limbic system (the hippocampus), is an important part of the process for consolidating memory. Conversely, there are areas of association in the cortex that are in some way related to making use of previous experiences (thinking) and that are not just incoming perceptual ones or outgoing, ongoing movements. Hence the second item on the list, the "link" between subcortical areas and the cortex, offers no new insights.

The third requisite is a tautology. In order to have consciousness it is hardly surprising that you have to have some means for consciousness. Surely this is the very mystery that we need to solve! Moreover, it is not immediately obvious what is meant by "a new reentrant circuit." Edelman uses a term associated with space travel (reentry) in an unusual way. It seems that reentry is a kind of feedback whereby the output of a group of neurons doubles back to become an input and then contributes to modifying the activity of the group. Recall that computationalists frequently incorporate this property into models of neuronal networks to increase the chances of neurons adapting appropriately to constantly changing circumstances. Reentry also conveys the idea of reciprocal connections among separate groups of neurons such that selection of particular groups also entails the recruitment of other associated groups. In Chapter 4 we saw that Zeki made use of this idea of Edelman's to give a physiological explanation of blindsight. The idea of reverberating loops within the brain, among groups of neurons, might be useful as a clue to the physical basis of consciousness, although we need not refer to them by using extraneous terminology such as reentrant.

But Edelman goes further and suggests that by way of reentrant circuits, diverse permutations and combinations of neuronal groups are selected in a coordinated fashion at any one time. Although no one would dispute that groups of neurons in the brain might be interconnected in a subtle and complex way, it is hard to see how reentry is, as Edelman claims, the "main basis for a bridge between physiology and psychology" (1992). We have seen in Chapters 1 and 3 just how difficult it is to relate neuronal activity in a system of one-to-one matching with ongoing behavior. Reentry appears to be a resolutely physiological concept that, by influencing the state of neuronal groups, obviously influences behavior. But how the former is actually underscored by the latter—the real nature of this bridge—remains as elusive as ever.

Reentrant circuitry is all very well when used for a specific phenomenon such as blindsight where it can be applied, as it was by Zeki, to a specific neuronal circuit. But one of the huge problems that remains totally unanswered concerns the application of this concept to the general holistic functioning of the brain. How would reentrant circuits be coordinated across sensory modalities? Would all these neuronal loops finally feed into a master loop? And, if so, where is it, and exactly how does it actually correlate with consciousness? The problem is that "a reentrant circuit," when couched in such general terms, is really just a metaphor with no obvious relation or any sort of correlation to conscious states.

However, in as many as three recently published biological descriptions of consciousness—from the physicist Eric Harth (1993), the biologist Francis Crick (1994), and the physiologist Rodolfo Llinás (Llinás and Pare 1991)—attention focuses on a *particular* loop, that between the cortex and the thalamus. What has excited these three scientists of very different expertises is that not only does the thalamus project into the cortex but, in turn, the cortex projects back into the thalamus.

When the electrical activity of neurons in both the thalamus and the cortex is monitored, the activity of neurons in one area influences that in the other area. The cortex and the thalamus are in constant conversation (Steriade et al. 1991). This interplay among the outer layer, the cortex, and the intermediate thalamus is very important. Certain groups of neurons within each region generate similar patterns of electrical activity. It is as though in two adjacent swimming pools some of the bathers in each pool are performing the same synchronized swimming movements simultaneously. We would immediately suspect some sort of collusion or rapport between such individuals acting in unison, albeit in different locations. In all three investigations, consciousness is regarded as some sort of effect of a vigorous dialogue between the two brain areas.

In Harth's model the centerpiece is a particular section of the thalamus, the lateral geniculate nucleus, which plays a part in the processing of visual inputs by relaying signals from the retina to a specific area of the visual cortex. Equally important to this model is that the cortex sends a connection back into the thalamus. Hence there is a shuttlecocklike interchange between the two regions. But Harth envisages the game as not necessarily even. If the input from the thalamus is stronger, then consciousness is flavored by direct visual images of the external world transmitted from the retina. The more dominant the other part of the loop, the input back into the thalamus from the cortex, the more consciousness is liberated from the sobering input of the retina and the more we are at the mercy of cognitive processes in the cortex—our dreams, fantasies, and delusions.

One problem with this account is that it does not help us understand consciousness beyond eidetic awareness or vivid pictures in the head. We have little idea how consciousness of other sensory modalities might be brought about and still less about consciousness of abstract ideas or emotions, or multimodal scenarios, real or imagined. Another problem is that we again run into a difficulty similar to that encountered with Dennett's model of multiple drafts (Chapters 1 and 2): Just how is the relationship controlled between the external world and our internal consciousness? Harth speaks briefly of an internal logician, but that, again, is just a metaphor that does not explain, at a biological level, how the domination of one side of a loop over another, and the extent of that domination, are decided. Because so much emphasis is placed on the loop between the cortex and the thalamus, we end up almost regarding the loop as the center of consciousness.

Francis Crick (1994), on the other hand, manages to circumvent this problem while retaining the idea of a reverberating loop as the central, all-important neuronal mechanism. Crick (1984) has suggested that this system of mass interchange acts as a searchlight to recruit all the neurons in the cortex connected in some way with the object under scrutiny. We can imagine a type of subconscious mental activity which, when lit up by the searchlight of attention, enters our actual awareness.

There is burgeoning empirical evidence that attention in cats, monkeys, and humans is associated with a synchronous discharge (oscillations in potential with an average of a forty-hertz frequency) of neurons in thalamocortical assemblies. Crick later refined his views. He subsequently suggested that there are many thalamocortical loops with the potential for generating consciousness, with the exception, interestingly enough, of Harth's particular cortex-thalamus loop. In experiments on monkeys Crick and Christof Koch found that the activity of the neurons in

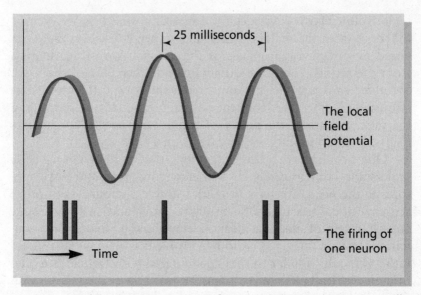

A scheme showing how neurons can fire together to generate an oscillation, for example, with 40–hertz frequency. (A 40–hertz oscillation repeats every 25 milliseconds.) The smooth curve represents the average activity of many cells in a particular neighborhood, the field potential. The short vertical lines show the activity of just one single typical cell. Note that when the single cell generates an action potential, it does so on the beat of its neighbors. (From F. Crick, *The Astonishing Hypothesis* [New York: Charles Scribner's Sons, 1994].)

this particular circuit did not appear to be affected by changes in the animal's attention and hence presumably in its consciousness. Crick looked instead beyond the lateral geniculate nucleus and its projection into a relatively primitive part of the cortex, to other parts of the pulvinar thalamus and its projections into parts of the visual cortex with allegedly more sophisticated functions. Each of these circuits, or projection units, was envisaged by Crick as being capable of a range of different functions, some of them to underscore consciousness. However, he suggested that consciousness only occurs some of the time under special conditions. The characteristic mode of functioning for a projection unit would be for the relevant group of thalamic cells to act as a conductor, with the target population of cortex as an orchestra. The precise role of this neuronal conductor would be to entrain the cortical neurons, for a time, to be active in synchrony.

We know that this synchronous firing is important for the brain to register patterns, since it only occurs when patterns of objects, as opposed to randomized dots, are presented to experimental animals. On the other hand, we have no clear proof that such synchronous firing would occur *only* if the animal was conscious of the pattern, but not otherwise. Then, again, when conscious is abolished with deep anesthesia, so is the synchronous neuronal response to the presentation of that pattern. The real problem lies, however, in establishing the *sufficiency* of neuronal synchrony as a basis of consciousness. According to the concentric theory, it would simply be a necessary but still insufficient requirement. Crick claims that the all-important factor is the degree of reverberation in the thalamocortical loop. There must be a high degree of traffic, dialogue, shuttlecock, or whatever metaphor you like between the respective portions of the thalamus and the cortex. In this respect, Crick's idea is similar to Edelman's in that the emphasis is placed on vigor of communication between two regions in the brain, what Edelman refers to as reentry. In a similar vein Llinás has gone so far as to suggest that "it is the dialogue between the thalamus and the cortex that generates subjectivity" (Llinás and Pare 1991).

We can see the appeal of this loop system for physiologists in trying to find the physical basis of consciousness. There is a clear physical pathway linking two major regions of the brain and there is evidence from electrical recordings that this pathway is in some way at work during attention. A particular strength of this type of scheme, at least in the view of Llinás, is that emphasis is shifted away from the purported dependency of consciousness on just the external sensory world in favor of the internally generated cognitive states such as memories or dreams. It is important to note that another difference between the models of Crick and Llinás is that Crick deals mainly with visual awareness, whereas Llinás is expressly concerned with consciousness that is independent of sensory inputs. Hence, he focuses on another part of the thalamus, the nucleus reticularis, which seems to be involved with more generalized states of arousal during sleep and waking.

In the case of Llinás's model, emphasis is placed not on the fact that there is a loop, as does Harth, or the degree of reverberation, as does Crick, but rather that the synchronous firing of the relevant groups of thalamic and cortical cells can oscillate in their activity in synchrony, in a fashion not requiring any other type of input. Since the brain is capable of such autonomous rhythmicity, Llinás reasons, which can occur independently of sensory inputs, then sensory inputs are merely incidental, an optional extra in consciousness. Llinás's line of argument is consistent with the conclusions reached earlier that sensory inputs are insufficient in themselves to generate consciousness and that consciousness can occur without sensory inputs. But there are also several difficulties with attributing the entire conscious condition to this neuronal loop.

A first problem is the activation of this circuit, which appears to be all-or-none; either it is on or it is not. Were this the case, we would have to accept that a sudden transformation occurs at some stage in our early development when a second or two before we had been, as fetuses or even as babies, nothing more than vegetables. A switch is thrown, and suddenly the whole concert hall of consciousness lights up. This idea runs counter to the scheme, sketched out in Chapter 1 and developed in Chapter 6, where it seemed that a more plausible description of consciousness was to say that it was graded, like turning up a dimmer switch, and grew as the brain did in terms of both evolution and individual development.

Were consciousness just to depend on large groups of neurons in the thalamus engaging a target population of neurons in the cortex in a reverberating chorus, then some of the features of consciousness we have deduced so far would remain unaccounted for. In order to accommodate the variability of consciousness, we would have to postulate that in different animals, as we trace the progress of evolution, the thalamocortical loop itself gradually becomes more active for more of the time. But there is currently no evidence at all for this idea. Because primates have a much larger cortex, we have the potential for the buildup of more associations. These associations, as we have seen in Chapter 3, are not on their own synonymous with consciousness. Apart from the difficulty of explaining the apparently plausible phylogenetic variability in consciousness, it would be even harder to explain in terms of our own brain states how we might change the degree of consciousness from one moment to the next in terms of the thalamocortical loop engaged in an all-or-none manner.

Second, just because consciousness and synchronized activity between the thalamus and the cortex can both occur in the absence of sensory stimulation does not mean that one causes the other, that consciousness arises wholly from that synchronized activity. The attention mediated by assemblies of neurons firing at high rates in synchrony could well *contribute* to consciousness without *being* consciousness.

Hypotheses such as those of Harth, Crick, and Llinás seem to be not so much wrong as lopsided in that they minimize other vital factors that must be contributing to consciousness. What, precisely, would the searchlight be focusing on? Crick claims that it is the main projection neurons in a certain layer of the cortex that express consciousness, whereas Llinás refers to cognitive states, without saying what such states are in physicochemical terms. This point is more than just a quibble, since we need to know how such states or targets of the searchlight would be assembled and subsequently selected. By emphasizing the search-light or degree of interaction while minimizing the shifting target of that light or the actual participants in the interaction, the thala-mocortical loop insidiously starts to take on the appearance of a center of consciousness, a more than half-built Cartesian theater!

The Significance of Focused Arousal

In any event, this relay of the thalamus is highly significant for distinguishing a refinement in the *type* of arousal that eventually prevails, as we can see from the consequences of very severe brain injury. A frequent result of head injury, whether from an internal stroke or an external force, is coma (Plum 1991). Contrary to popular belief, no one who survives such vicissitudes is ever in a true coma for very long. To be in a coma means that the brain is not working at all. If this state continues without outside inter-vention for a few weeks, the comatose patient dies. The reason a coma is so life-threatening is that the mechanisms in the primitive brainstem, which control basic life processes, cease to function. Although the control of respiration can be taken over by a machine, and the heart has its own internal autorhythmicity, there are still the less obvious problems of maintaining body temperature and controlling the hormones that circulate in the body and are essential for life. If these processes are shut down for very long, survival is impossible.

We are all familiar with reports of patients who have been in what is loosely termed a coma indefinitely. What has really happened is that such people have come out of their coma but have entered a clinically distinguishable condition where they are still unconscious, called a persistent vegetative state. Patients in this condition regain sleep-wake cycles and are able to regulate body temperature and successfully fight infection. They can breathe, as well as chew, swallow, and digest food. Usually the eyes retain a parallel, conjugate gaze, with the pupils responding partially to light. In addition, patients have reflex responses whereby they withdraw from painful stimuli, and they may even smile or scream occasionally. But none of these behaviors appears to bear any relation to the outside world or to any changes in internal body function; these patients are deemed not conscious. They have suffered "cognitive death." This fate can await not only those who suffer head injuries, but frequently it is the final stage of degenerative disorders such as Alzheimer's disease, and can lead ultimately to a virtual abolition of consciousness.

Understanding persistent vegetative state is important for understanding the nature of consciousness, since it is a clear situation where there is *arousal without consciousness*. For the generation of consciousness some additional ingredients are necessary. One such ingredient appears to be the more refined type of arousal frequently called "focused arousal," or attention. Focused arousal requires the integrity of the second stage in the ascending path. We saw in the previous chapter that arousal and attention counterbalance each other and that the relation between the two determines the degree of gestalt formation and our eventual consciousness. But when there is extensive damage to these more sophisticated regions of the brain, arousal may continue in a primitive cycling of sleep and wakefulness, and nothing else. There is no means of focusing attention to any degree on an epicenter; the patient is conscious of nothing, unconsciousness.

Focused arousal might be a valuable concept for us. Both its localization within the brain and its very name suggest that it is a component vital to consciousness. But what would be the target?

According to the concentric theory, the target of focused arousal is the epicenter of a gestalt.

Although we have already examined in this chapter the physical bases for gestalts, the following statement on neuronal assemblies by Ad Aersten and George Gerstein (1991) is particularly apt:

> *Instead, we should distinguish between* structural *(or anatomical) connectivity on the one hand, and* functional *(or effective) connectivity on the other. The former can be described as (quasi) stationary, whereas the latter may be highly dynamic, with time constants of modulation in the range of tens to hundreds of milliseconds. It appears that dynamic cooperativity is an emergent property of neuronal assembly organisation in the brain, which could not be inferred from single neuron observations.*

According to the concentric theory, the two major components that would be sufficient for the generation of consciousness—arousal and gestalts—do indeed have clear physicochemical bases. And so we now have in place the basic building blocks for developing a neuroscientific model for the generation of consciousness.

chapter eight

A MODEL
FOR THE MIND

L et us stay in the world of real neurons. The concentric theory suggests that consciousness is composed of two principal components: arousal and the formation of transient neuronal assemblies, gestalts. We have seen that both concepts can be translated independently into real events in the brain. The aim of this chapter is to see how arousal and gestalt formation actually relate to each other. This step is the linchpin in a model of consciousness, since the way these two distinct events influence each other is critical for determining the type of consciousness generated at any moment and, indeed, whether or not consciousness will occur at all.

It might be a good idea to have the theory formulated in Chapter 6 fairly accessible, so here it is again: *Consciousness is spatially multiple yet effectively single at any one time. It is an emergent property of nonspecialized and divergent groups of neurons (gestalts) that is continuously variable with respect to, and always entailing, a stimulus epicenter. The size of the gestalt, and hence the depth of prevailing consciousness, is a product of the interaction between the recruiting strength of the epicenter and the degree of arousal.*

There is already experimental evidence that arousal plays a clear part in the formation of transient neuronal groups. Walter Freeman (1991) has shown that if an animal is hungry, thirsty, sexually aroused, or threatened, groups of neurons fire in synchrony much more easily than when the animal is presented with, for example, a smell under more normal, relaxed conditions. Similarly, when Wolf Singer (1990) mimics an aroused condition by electrically stimulating the primitive brainstem directly, the probability of transient neuronal cooperativity is enhanced. So what actually happens in arousal and focused arousal at the level of the neurons? How can arousal act to bind a group of neurons temporarily and rapidly into a single team?

The brainstem, which is the origin of the basic arousing system, is the site of very discrete clumps of neurons that contain a class of chemicals (amines) that act as messengers or transmitters among cells. These brainstem neurons do not make short-distance one-to-one contacts, but send their outreaching branches (axons) over long distances into the center of the brain and beyond into the cortex. It is a fascinating feature of the brain that these clumps of neurons are relatively small but nonetheless send out projections that make wide-ranging contacts with vast banks of neurons in the more sophisticated areas toward the front and top of the brain (Cooper et al. 1991; Saper 1985). This conspicuous divergence in the pathways, by which the oldest part of the brain in evolutionary terms influences the newest, suggests a very diffuse and generalized form of communication.

The way in which the neurons present themselves at the receiving end, in the target regions of the cortex, also suggests that the amine chemicals are not necessarily working for the precise transmission of signals from one individual neuron to the next. Frequently the receptor protein which acts as a target for the amines is not situated on the narrowest part of the gap (synapse) between one specific neuron and another, but in a place that would make it more accessible to amines released from many different nerves (Beaudet and Descarries 1978). Moreover, in key regions such as the cortex, the anatomical arrangement of nerve contacts suggests that the amines will be in a good position to intercept and interfere with, bias, any ongoing local communication. But what does a bias in neuronal communication actually mean?

The Concept of Neuromodulation

Over the last fifteen years there has been a change in the way neuroscientists think of neurons communicating. Researchers into the brain are gradually realizing that neurons do not just transmit short-lasting, specific messages to one another. Instead, much of the signaling among neurons takes the form of *biasing* the target neuron so that it responds in a different way to an on-off signal that may or may not be generated at some future stage. This form of communication, which itself might not produce dramatic effects but might change how a cell reacts subsequently, is known as neuromodulation (Kaczmarek and Levitan 1987).

Neuromodulation should not be confused with the long-term, less reversible neuronal adaptation underlying the Hebbian strengthening of neuronal contacts that is thought to enable learning. Rather, it is a process for biasing the response of a neuron for relatively short periods of time ranging from seconds to hours without changing the response of that neuron permanently. For a while after eating a big meal, we might refuse a slice of cake which at other times would be devoured with varying degrees of gusto, depending on whether we had just been to the dentist or were half asleep or had not eaten all day. So it is with neuromodulation. Neuromodulation gives a neuron a recent history, a working past; without it, all neurons in a certain brain area would respond in an invariant and predictable way. Hence we can catch a glimpse of how certain events in the brain are subtly contingent on previous ones. We are using a video recorder instead of taking a snapshot of the brain at work. Neuromodulation is effectively neuronal time.

The positioning of amine chemicals in the brain is exactly what we would expect if they were working not as classical on-off transmitters but as a means of bias. As neuromodulators they are in a perfect position to influence large populations of cortical cells rather than transmit highly specific signals across discrete contacts. They all emanate from relatively small cell groups in the brainstem, yet push outward and upward into the front of the brain in a diffuse manner, like fountains. These modulatory fountains are of critical importance to brain function in that they are perfectly positioned to influence formation of large enough gestalts for the generation of consciousness. Thus the next step is to work out exactly how arousal might have a modulatory role in the release of these amines and then how such modulation might favor gestalt formation and hence consciousness.

Fountains in the Brain

There are as many as five distinct amine chemicals associated with the central ascending pathway and the states of arousal it generates: serotonin, acetylcholine, dopamine, norepinephrine, and histamine. From this list, less is known about the modulatory actions of histamine, so although it may well turn out to have important functions, we shall focus on the other four substances. Serotonin is very important in sleep (Aghajanian et al. 1987). When it is introduced into the fluid that bathes the brain and spinal cord, dreamless sleep ensues. Conversely, if the discrete clump of neurons in the brainstem from which serotonin emanates is destroyed, the result is complete insomnia for three to four days. The drug LSD is a blocker of serotonin and it is also well known to cause hallucinations. Hallucinations also occur if we are deprived of sleep, when presumably serotonin is less available. Thus there seems to be a relationship of some sort between consciousness, both in terms of its absence (sleep) and its distortion (hallucinations), and the availability of serotonin.

Acetylcholine is also linked to sleep, but in the opposite way (Jasper and Tessier 1971). This time the chemical contributes to the transition to and from dreaming states. Release of acetylcholine into the cortex is clearly correlated with consciousness since it is decreased in dreamless sleep. We can see, then, a balance of chemicals engaged in the changes into and out of consciousness: Increases in serotonin are associated with a release *away from* consciousness, whereas acetylcholine is in some way linked to the time when we return *back* to awareness. The other two transmitters, dopamine and norepinephrine, also play a role, but less is known of their action. Dopamine may be associated with *enhanced* general (as opposed to focused) arousal, a distracted state where it is hard to settle on any one project and hard to sit still. Drugs such as amphetamine, which increase the availability of dopamine, also cause restlessness. Because of such an increase

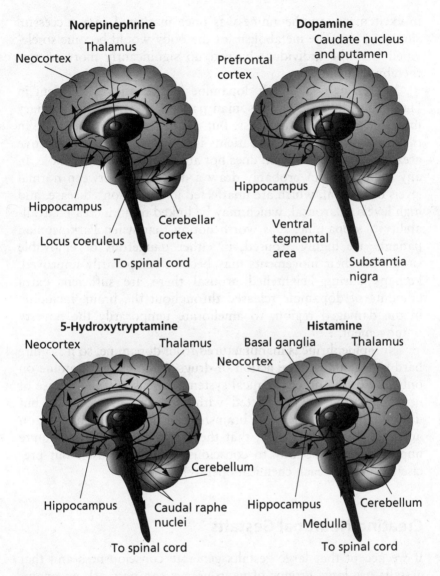

Norepinephrine

Neocortex

Thalamus

Hippocampus

Locus coeruleus

Cerebellar cortex

To spinal cord

Dopamine

Caudate nucleus and putamen

Prefrontal cortex

Hippocampus

Ventral tegmental area

Substantia nigra

5-Hydroxytryptamine

Neocortex

Thalamus

Hippocampus

Caudal raphe nuclei

Cerebellum

To spinal cord

Histamine

Basal ganglia

Thalamus

Neocortex

Hippocampus

Medulla

Cerebellum

To spinal cord

Fountains in the brain. Shown here are the central pathways for four amines: norepinephrine, dopamine, 5–hydroxytryptamine, and histamine, in the human brain. In all cases the neuronal pathways originate from relatively discrete groups of neurons in the most basic parts of the brain and then "fountain" upward and outward into the more sophisticated regions. (Adapted from J. Nicholls, A. R. Martin, and B. G. Wallace, *From Neuron to Brain*, 3rd ed. [Sunderland, Mass.: Sinauer Associates, 1992]. Reprinted with permission.)

in excitement, amphetamine was once marketed as a successful slimming aid. The metabolism of the body would become so elevated that the individual burned up significantly more energy, thereby reducing fat.

Interestingly, although dopamine is dramatically deficient in Parkinson's disease, Parkinsonian patients do *not* suffer primary impairments in consciousness. But the deficiency in dopamine in the brain of Parkinsonian patients is restricted to a very selective area below the cortex and does not affect the brain as a whole. In any event, we can probably draw a distinction between normal levels of arousal, which are unaffected in Parkinson's disease, and high levels of arousal, which may be linked to an increased availability of dopamine. It is worth noting that when Parkinsonian patients are highly aroused, in either dangerous or enjoyable situations, their movements may become temporarily improved. Perhaps during heightened arousal there are sufficient extra amounts of dopamine released throughout the brain, including in the damaged region, to ameliorate temporarily the poverty of movement.

Norepinephrine is manufactured from dopamine, so it is quite hard to disentangle the action of drugs such as amphetamine on only one or the other chemical system. Increases in the release of norepinephrine are associated with increases in alertness, but destroying the source in the brainstem has no long-term effect on arousal. We can see, then, that these amine fountains are quite important in some way to consciousness and arousal. But precisely how does each chemical operate?

Creating Neuronal Gestalts

If we accept that large gestalts generate consciousness and that gestalts are large groups of neurons, we can now ask an unambiguous question about consciousness: How does arousal influence or actually trigger the formation of gestalts and, thus, the generation of consciousness? At the same time this very question can be translated into neuroscientific terms: How can amines, released in different states of arousal, modulate large interconnections of neurons to be more sensitive to the activity of one another so that they form a working group, a gestalt?

The very fountainlike arrangement of the pervasive pathways of nerves releasing amines does not necessarily respect the precision and specificity of normal neuronal contacts, so that the modulating chemical is already poised to flood onto large arrays of cells. What we need is an actual mechanism for each of these amines, when they are unleashed under diverse states of arousal, to bias the cell in some way so that it has the *potential* to be temporarily more excitable, more sensitive to a signal from another member of the aspiring neuronal group.

There are actually many examples of how the amine chemicals can make a target cell potentially more excitable or sensitive to future inputs. We will look at several typical cases in order to appreciate just how diverse the modulatory effects of amines can be. What we need is a means whereby neurons can be made more sensitive to signals from one another on a very rapid yet temporary basis. We need a way whereby the amines are able to make a neuron potentially more excitable without necessarily having any overt effect on its own.

A brain cell is said to be excited or active when there is a transient change in potential difference—the voltage measured across the membrane. This change (an action potential) is caused by sodium ions rushing into the neuron by way of a special channel in the membrane wall. This custom-made route, with a special condition for opening, prevents haphazard admission into the cell by the sodium ions at just any moment. The sodium channel only opens when the potential difference across the cell wall is reduced (depolarized), when the inside of the cell becomes less negative than usual with respect to the outside. If the potential difference reaches a certain level (voltage threshold), the channel opens and so much sodium pours into the cell that it generates an unambiguous electrical signal which signifies neuronal excitation (the action potential). The neuron is then ready for communication.

Although the action potential is an all-or-none event, the voltage threshold necessary for the channel to open can be reached more readily if the inside of the cell is not so negative with respect to the outside, if the potential difference is not so great. After all, it is easier to climb over a wall (an all-or-none event) if you start by standing on a box. If the cell is modulated so that the potential difference across the membrane is *slightly* reduced (depolarized), this new potential would not be sufficient in itself to cause the sodium ions to flood in and create an action potential. On the other hand, in this modulated condition, the equivalent of standing on a box to climb over a wall, it would be *easier* for the channels for sodium to open in response to any further normal input to the cell.

Even when a neuron is not active it is rather leaky, which is to say that ions dribble across the membrane one way or the other all the time. One ion particularly prone to leaking is the potassium ion that is normally inside the cell. The more the positively charged potassium ions leak out, the more negative the cell becomes on the inside with respect to the outside. It will have a larger potential difference (hyperpolarized). But if in some way the potassium ions are prevented from leaking out, the cell would have a smaller potential difference (be more depolarized). Once depolarized, it would be more readily excited, more sensitive to an input for generating an action potential. If we could now show that the chemicals pulsing into the top of the brain were able, somehow, to prevent the efflux of potassium ions, then we would have a good basis for the amines to act as modulators. Such an action by these chemicals in modulating a transient excitability and hence a fleeting, functional neuronal connectivity would provide us with a key for understanding how gestalt formation and, hence, consciousness could be controlled under different states of arousal when the amines are released.

Let us start with serotonin. The modulatory power of this particular amine was first revealed in the basic nervous system of the sea slug *Aplysia*. Serotonin released on the outside of the cell wall can activate its particular receptor protein to set in motion a cascade of chemical events inside the neuron, to have the very effect we just noted that would modulate the cell to be more easily excited, the temporary closure of potassium channels (Kandel et al. 1987). In mammalian brain, too, serotonin acts in a modulatory way. In cortical neurons it has no effects on its own. On the other hand, it can amplify the excitatory actions of a completely different chemical transmitter (glutamate) used widely in the cortex (Nedergaard et al. 1987).

This modulatory action of closing potassium channels is not restricted to serotonin. In a similar way acetylcholine can shut down a potassium channel in mammalian brain (Cole and Nicoll 1983). A particularly elegant feature of this acetylcholine action is that it only works once the cell is already excited. Normally, excitement (the discharge of action potentials) in particular groups of neurons is curtailed by a special type of potassium efflux designed to make the cell have a greater potential difference, so that the sodium ions cannot enter so easily (like trying to climb a wall from the bottom of a ditch). The effect of this efflux of potassium ions acts just like a brake might on a car; it slows down the electrical activity of the cell. In this instance of modulation, however, acetylcholine counteracts this brake on neuronal excitability by blocking the efflux of the compensating potassium ions. The result of this effective double negative, the blockade of a blocking mechanism, is to cause a net *increase* in the extent to which the cell can be excited. The degree of excitement of the neuron determines whether or not it will generate action potentials as neighboring neurons attempt to establish temporary lines of communication.

Remember that all a cell needs to be more excitable is for the inside to have less negative charge than normal with respect to the outside—namely, to have a reduction in potential difference, to be depolarized. If all that matters is the net difference in charge, there might be other ways of bringing about this situation. Instead of stopping positively charged ions (such as potassium) from leaving, a cell could become *potentially* more excitable if more positively charged ions were encouraged to enter. Instead of plugging up a leaky tank, an alternative is to keep filling the tank. The net result would be the same.

The positively charged ions that are amassed in the fluid in the spaces around brain cells, compelled by both electrical and chemical forces to enter the neuron as soon as the way is clear, are sodium ions, which, we have seen, constitute the action potential. There is, however, another positively charged ion that would enter the neuron if it could penetrate the membrane wall: calcium. Calcium ions on their own do not constitute the full-blown action potential. Rather, the sustained flow of this doubly positively charged ion into the interior of the cell will make the inside more positive and thereby reduce the potential difference so that the cell is *potentially* more excitable. Under such depolarized conditions, sodium channels can subsequently open up more readily and the cell will thus be more sensitive to future inputs or signals from other cells. In this case calcium entry would be an alternative surefire way of modulating the cell to be more sensitive to the attempted formation of a gestalt.

Just as we saw that there are different channels for potassium and sodium ions, there are also special entries for calcium. As with the other channels, these calcium channels are usually closed and only open under special conditions. For the purposes of our current discussion, two calcium channels are particularly important. Both of these channels are very fussy over the conditions that must prevail in order for them to open and let the calcium ions in.

The first channel will only open to an incoming signal when the potential difference across the membrane is abnormally and somewhat paradoxically great. This prerequisite of an initially higher voltage acts a bit like a bolt being drawn back from a door; we do not necessarily open the door but now, compared to before, it is at least possible (McCormick and Pronce 1986). The opening of the door would be analogous to a signal coming into the neuron. We can see that any agent which increases the potential difference would be acting in a modulatory capacity to bias the cell to let calcium in were a subsequent signal to arrive. Interestingly enough, both acetylcholine and dopamine can have this action on certain brain cells. They can make the potential difference greater (by *opening* a potassium channel) and thereby create the prerequisite condition, the drawing back of the bolt, for a calcium channel to open and for the cell to be eventually depolarized. If the signal arrives while the cell is modulated in this fashion, the calcium channels will open and the cell will be much more excitable than otherwise. In this sense we can say that acetylcholine and dopamine can enhance the sensitivity of the neuron to the signal, which is precisely what would be required for a large-scale priming of a gestalt.

The second type of calcium channel functions in a reverse way, in that it is only open when the potential difference is abnormally small, when the neuron is depolarized. This channel is referred to by neuroscientists as the NMDA channel, after the substance N-methyl-d-aspartate, which activates it. It is the channel we have already met in Chapter 3 (Watkins 1989). In this case, a sustained excitation, a *reduced* potential difference, makes this certain type of fussy target (receptor) become unclogged so that it is free to be excited by a chemical and consequently allow into the

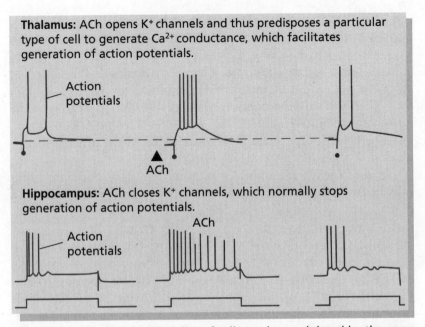

Thalamus: ACh opens K⁺ channels and thus predisposes a particular type of cell to generate Ca²⁺ conductance, which facilitates generation of action potentials.

Action potentials

ACh

Hippocampus: ACh closes K⁺ channels, which normally stops generation of action potentials.

ACh

Action potentials

Two ways in which the excitability of cells can be modulated by the same chemical. The traces show the potential difference across the membranes of two different neurons in the thalamus and the hippocampus, respectively. In both cases the neurons have been stimulated electrically (dot in upper record, step in lower trace) to generate action potentials. When acetylcholine (ACh) is added, it has *opposite* effects but produces the same net result. In the case of the thalamic neuron, ACh makes the potential difference more negative (center). This more negative potential is a prerequisite for activation of calcium entry into the neuron, which in turn causes the neuron to generate more action potentials. In the case of the hippocampus, however, the ACh has stopped positively charged potassium ions from leaving the cell. Because potassium does not leave the cell, the potential difference remains more positive than when ACh is absent (see record on left), so that more action potentials are generated. In both cases ACh has increased the number of action potentials generated but by different mechanisms: predisposing a calcium channel to open in one case and closing a potassium channel in the other. When ACh is washed off (right), note that in both cases the neurons revert to their original responses. There has been no long-term change. (Based on data from D. A. McCormick and D. A. Prince, "Acetylcholine Induces Burst Firing in Thalamic Reticular Neurons by Activating a Potassium Conductance," *Nature* [1986], 319, 402–405; and from A. E. Cole and R. A. Nicoll, "Acetylcholine Mediates a Slow Synaptic Potential in Hippocampal Pyramidal Cells," *Nature* [1983], 221, 1299–1301. Adapted with permission.)

cell large amounts of calcium ions. Here, again, acetylcholine plays a critical role. We have seen that it can prolong excitation by negating the blocking effects of a compensating potassium efflux when a cell is stimulated. Hence, by means of this action of *blocking* potassium channels, acetylcholine can act to maintain the cell in a state of excitation that favors the unplugging of the powerful calcium channel. The net effect would again be an increased possibility of excitation occurring in the attempted formation of a gestalt.

In these ways fountains of transmitters can modulate brain cells to be more excitable and thus more prone to the formation of transient, working groups. These groups are formed more readily once the relevant cells are more easily excited. Broadly speaking, amine chemicals either reverse the braking actions of potassium efflux or encourage the animating calcium ions to enter the cell by precipitating conditions favorable to the opening of calcium channels. By opening or shutting different potassium channels to create the appropriate voltage conditions, the amine chemicals will subsequently make it possible for the calcium channels to open if one neuron in a potential gestalt signals to another.

The most happy aspect of this modulation is that it has the same space and time frame needed for gestalts. First, the squirting of the amines within the cortex could be fairly widespread and pervasive, and second, these substances have immediate modulatory effects that can last for varying periods, yet need not last indefinitely. The neuron that had been modulated would at some future stage be free to be recruited into some other gestalt by being modulated all over again. Thus the regulation of the spatial and temporal aspects of amine invasion of the cortex would ultimately determine the nature of your consciousness from one moment to the next.

A model for the physical basis of consciousness might run something like this. A stimulus, in the simplest case an object in the outside world such as an orange, triggers a series of diverse, idiosyncratic connections in the cortex—for example, eat, seeds, diarrhea, first peel. The strength and extent of these connections depend on experience (as outlined in earlier chapters). Such connections are long-lasting and not very flexible. Thus there would be a reasonable infrastructure for learning certain associations, the basis for an *enduring* significance of objects around us—for example, the intrinsic properties relating to the taste or the method and consequences of eating oranges. In addition, whatever degree of arousal happens to be prevalent at the time will ensure that a certain amount of particular amines is released within the cortex and that the amines modulate very large groups of neurons to be *potentially* more excitable by means of the type of ionic mechanisms we have just been discussing. Wherever neurons are modulated, for a temporary period, to respond easily and sensitively to the corralling signals from the group of associated neurons, a gestalt forms, and a unique consciousness is generated for that moment.

If arousal is high, the gestalts forming will be small due to a rapid turnover. They will be readily formed but also easily displaced by the formation of new competing assemblies, which are themselves quickly displaced in rapid succession. Earlier news of a promotion might make me so excited that I would be barely aware of oranges in a shop window before being distracted by the sight of pineapples. On the other hand, if arousal is more moderate, a stronger epicenter, due to a louder or brighter external stimulus (a screeching cat) or a cognitive trigger (the prospect of promotion), will be needed for a gestalt to be established at all. The orange will be an effective epicenter *only* if it happens to have temporary significance, perhaps caused by my hormones signaling that I am thirsty, in conjunction with no competition plus time to recruit an increasing number of associations which would become stronger, like a flame burning out along a network of fuses. These types of associations could include a trip to Morocco, my mother's tales of the lack of oranges during World War II, and so on. They would deepen my consciousness of the orange as I stared at it in the window. Anyone seeing me would conclude that I was concentrating on the orange.

Normally such concentration for a protracted period is only sustained by the most powerful of epicenters, such as the all-consuming worry about a loved one late coming home, or a very intense sensory input, such as a brass band in the street or a car accident. In most of our daily lives, there is a plethora of potential epicenters all jostling to recruit ever more neurons into a temporary assembly, a new gestalt, a new consciousness. On some occasions, however, there is a paucity of such epicenters. As we fidget on a hard chair in the doctor's waiting room, the most banal objects, such as the faded posters on the wall or the notice of the office's hours, hold our attention far more than usual. Since competing gestalts are less readily formed, since there are fewer candidate epicenters, there is less scope for distraction through competition with new gestalts, and the original gestalt grows unrivaled to become larger than it would have been in a more normal situation and stretching the preexisting hard-wired associations to the limit. Functionally, we are brooding or we are bored.

This, then, in crude outline, is how arousal and gestalt formation could interact to give rise to consciousness, at the actual physicochemical level of the neuron. But there are still some critical questions to be addressed before we can be sure we have made any progress.

Some Critical Questions

The first issue is how the many amines released from the pathway into the cortex vary in the effects they have on arousal and consciousness. Why, so far, have only four or five different chemicals been determined? It is most likely that there are many other chemicals used and the scenario sketched out above is just the tip of the iceberg. In addition, any one chemical might have more than one effect.

For example, serotonin might not only modulate the neurons to be more sensitive for a brief period, but might also make it easier for more permanent associative synaptic strengthening to occur. It has been shown, at least in the sea slug, that serotonin can encourage a neuron to digest certain large molecules (Bailey et al. 1992). These molecules, on the outside of the cell, normally have the job of stabilizing contacts among nerve cells, of making the connections among neurons more hard-wired. It might be that the neuron is like a wax model: When cold it has a rigid shape, but the release of serotonin is analogous to applying a flame to the wax. It would become more malleable and thus able to be reshaped according to any new outside influence. If an incoming nerve was very active and released serotonin, it would be effectively signaling to the target neuron that it should absorb the stabilizing molecule. The nerve would then become less hard-wired and flexible enough to arrange a different, better facilitated (adapted) type of contact with its target. The effectiveness of such connections would thus be proportional to activity of the inputs, a true weighting.

Serotonin can induce dreamless sleep and appears to block the dreaming REM phase (Kelly 1991). One of the functions of sleep is thought to be consolidation and reconciliation of experiences from the previous day. Were this the case, the serotonin released during dreamless sleep would help fuel the process of reorganizing neuronal contacts. It is important to note that we are speaking of the state where there is *no consciousness*. Even though there may be multiple potential gestalts, arousal is too low. Less serotonin is probably released during dreamless sleep than when we are awake, because the relevant neurons are less active. Nevertheless more of the transmitter is still released during normal sleep than during dreams when the relevant cells are quiescent. Perhaps during normal wakening, serotonin makes a major contribution to consciousness by facilitating the formation of long-term associations, more "hard-wired" neuronal connections, as well as contributing to the generation of arousal. During sleep, however, the reduced but persistent levels of serotonin might be used for the restructuring of long-term neuronal connections in the absence of any immediate consciousness.

Whereas an amine such as serotonin may, under certain conditions, be restricted to establishing hard-wired neuronal connectivity rather than arousal, other amines might be released relative to *different types* of arousal. We have already seen that different chemicals are involved in the induction of sleep and dreams, and that arousal can be variable. Perhaps such amines are released primarily in these conditions. Serotonin may be released during sleep, where arousal is very low so that gestalt formation is insufficient to generate even the scraps of consciousness of our dreams. When we dream, it is acetylcholine that predominates. During sleep, acetylcholine elevates the level of arousal that would then be enhanced enough for the formation of gestalts large enough for fleeting consciousness or dreams. Once we are awake, an increased release of acetylcholine could trigger sufficient but not excessive increases in arousal to enable us to experience focused arousal. Consistent with this idea are a variety of findings that link acetylcholine systems with learning and memory (Vogt 1991). Presumably, attention is a prerequisite. In a similar vein it has also been suggested that only when both of the two main acetyl-choline-containing inputs to the cortex (directly from the basal forebrain and indirectly by way of the thalamus) are active is the brain in a mode whereby it is interactive with the environment effectively on a standby mode for the efficient processing of information, which would include paying attention (Steriade and Buzsaki 1990).

Let us turn to dopamine and norepinephrine. These substances may be involved in less focused arousal, such as seen in extreme cases where large amounts of these substances are liberated in the brain by amphetamines or cocaine. In both cases, the individual becomes very restless, distracted, and easily agitated. We can imagine that when we are highly excited, more dopamine and norepinephrine are released. It is known that the cells of origin for norepinephrine (locus coeruleus) are maximally active during wakefulness but quiescent during dreaming. The effects of these substances might be not so much to favor a situation where a gestalt might form but, rather, to induce a situation where there might be many rival gestalts and, hence, the opportunity for only a rapid succession of only small gestalts to ever predominate at any one time.

We can envisage, though not at this stage in any detail, a symphony of chemicals released to different extents under different prevailing conditions, both in the external world and in the internal environment of the body. Serotonin would facilitate the formation of gestalts without much influence on arousal; acetylcholine would generate moderate levels of arousal. Together these two substances would enable the formation of gestalts large enough for consciousness in dreaming states, as well as when moderately aroused and paying attention while awake. Dopamine and norepinephrine would counteract these tendencies, during conditions of higher arousal, by restricting the size of gestalt formation in that they would provide conditions favoring the generation of rival gestalts. All amines would be working in conjunction, in different cocktails and balancing acts, to give rise to the varying quality and quantity of consciousness from one moment to the next, both night and day.

Another important question about the physical basis of consciousness concerns its location. After all, consciousness must be generated somewhere in the brain, but at the same time there seems to be no obvious single area, no Cartesian theater.

Undoubtedly we cannot treat all areas of the brain the same. As we have seen from patients in a persistent vegetative state, the brainstem has very different functions from the cortex. And it is to the cortex that we have been turning because it increases disproportionately in size as the brain becomes more sophisticated and consciousness grows greater. Also, the cortex is the most frequently studied area for the formation of the labile aggregations of neuronal gestalts. Although we cannot preclude other areas where aggregations take place, it is simply that the cortex has been by far the best documented.

Interestingly enough, although many parts of the cortex have been conceptually divided into zones called visual, auditory, and so on, there are vast parts of it with no clear function in either pure sensory processing or pure movement generation. These areas of the brain, which seem in some elusive way to be associated with the thinking that accompanies moving and processing sensory inputs, are referred to as the association cortex. Lesions in these areas lead to subtle changes in behavior which might be the faint echoes of aspects of a consciousness subtly impaired (Goldman-Rakic 1987). The inability to assign clear functions to these regions can be explained if we accept that by lesioning parts of the association cortex, we are really tampering with the dynamic process of the formation of transient gestalts. As neurons form and re-form in a kaleidoscope of responses to each moment, the damaged region might understandably distort normal cognitive processes. Ultimately this would be reflected in a subtly aberrant behavior. But to infer what is happening within the brain by examining the behavioral responses in experiments is to be like those persons in Plato's *Republic* who were forever chained to the walls of a cave, so that their whole impression of the real world was based on the shadows that flitted across the wall in front of them. Many experimentally contrived behavioral responses are merely the shadows of assemblies of neurons and chemicals thronging the brain. There are no fixed functions in these brain regions, no little creatures, no rigid and direct relation from neuron to behavior. The more sophisticated a brain function, the more it is intimately linked to consciousness. It is scarcely surprising, therefore, that we cannot pin down different fixed anatomical bits of cortex as mediating different bits of consciousness.

Most likely, when we are conscious, most of the cortex is active for different reasons. Some parts pertain directly to our ongoing awareness, others indirectly by idiosyncratic association, and still others by the encroaching formation of a potentially new consciousness due to rival gestalts. In addition, active participation of the thalamocortical loop (that centerpiece of earlier biological theories of consciousness) is needed, as is a functioning brainstem.

We have seen that different thalamocortical inputs are associated with either nonspecific or focused arousal (Roland 1993), whereas others, such as the lateral geniculate nucleus (Crick 1994), are related to purely sensory processing, irrespective of the attentional state. But at this stage of neuroscientific knowledge, it would be misleading to attempt to specify in any detail thalamocortical interactions in terms of the interactions of amines. First, the amines can send projections to the cortex along routes that do not pass through the thalamus. Second, the neurons deep in the brain using acetylcholine and dopamine (which directly and indirectly influence the thalamus) have indirect effects on the cortex that are hard to trace with any precision. Nonetheless, it is quite within our grasp to understand one day not only the anatomical circuits that connect brainstem, thalamus, and regions of the cortex but also to be able to identify the transmitter substance in each case and the action of that transmitter, modulatory or otherwise, on different target regions. For the time being we can be reassured that we are not guilty of knocking at the door of the Cartesian theater, since no particular region has been designated as special.

Principles of Gestalt Formation

What are the actual principles of gestalt formation? Until now we have used the term epicenter as a metaphor almost identical with a raindrop falling on the surface of a puddle without actually probing into what this vitally important component might be in real, neuronal terms. We have already seen that it is unlikely that a single neuron could be activated by a grandmother or a yellow Volkswagen, and we can therefore eliminate the possibility that a gestalt would form around a single neuron. So what are the alternatives? Clearly the very idea of gestalts is one where certain groups of brain cells are linked and become active at the expense of others. Thus we can make the rather unremarkable deduction that an epicenter must be some small aggregation of neurons. This idea is borne out by imaging studies (discussed in Chapter 7) wherein the center of the neuronal assembly emitted the strongest signal. The particular combination of connections within this more hard-wired hub of cells acts to trigger the ripples that encompass wider and wider populations of cells.

The strength of the epicenter can be reflected in the degree of vigor, the amount of intrinsic electrical activity, and/or its size, as well as the actual number of working interconnections entailed. In any case, when the epicenter is strong, because of either the strong physical qualities of a particular external object that impinges on the senses or that that object triggers certain extensive idiosyncratic associations, we can imagine that a group of neurons would be either highly active and/or had already developed extensive interconnections. Such a highly active group of cells with a large number of connections would have a higher probability of recruiting into a gestalt still more neurons, by way of a greater number of signals and a greater number of potential connections, than a potential gestalt with only a weak epicenter, where the signaling was more intermittent and by way of fewer neurons. After all, the greater the initial number of neurons, the greater the potential number of working connections to other cells.

Moreover, we saw earlier that once a cell is active, subsequent transmission is facilitated, as is the likelihood of shouting at someone who coughs repeatedly at a concert. We might view this enhanced sensitivity of neurons to a persistent stimulus as further evidence of the accuracy of predictions regarding neuronal gestalts. Once conscious of something, it is harder to become conscious of something else. Hence the synchronous cooperativity or ripples emanating from a particular epicenter and the gestalt consequently created both make it harder to establish a rival gestalt. This is why it is harder to be wakened from dreams than from normal sleep.

How might a gestalt organize itself, considering its myriad neuronal connections? We have seen in Chapter 3 that algorithmic computation might not be the most appropriate description of operations in the brain leading to consciousness. An alternative system would be for the neuronal gestalt to be established or, rather, organize itself following the principles of quantum mechanics, where changes are *nonlocal* and where alternative combinations could coexist until the successful combination emerged.

The Uncertainty of Brain Processes

Quantum is Latin for "amount" and refers to an area of physical science where we are dealing with very small amounts, or packets, of energy. Once we enter the arena of quantum physics, where we want to describe subatomic particles, we have to make a decision: Either the position of the particle can be described or its momentum (mass times velocity), but never both. In this regard, quantum physics diverges from the classical physics developed by Isaac Newton (1642–1727) in that the latter can specify both the position and the momentum of an object in space. This exclusivity of description, either position or momentum, is the essence of the uncertainty principle (Von Neumann 1955).

It is important to grasp at this stage that both ways of describing the particle can be equally valid but mutually exclusive once one option is chosen—as though we had an initial choice of describing an event in either French or English but not in a mixture of the two languages. It might not be immediately obvious why these types of events on the smallest possible scale could be of any relevance to brain function, and in particular why quantum mechanics could be a more attractive alternative than algorithmic processing. The critical factor is *predictability*. Neuroscientists tend to be a bit coy in predicting the outcome of a simple process, such as whether or not a particular cell will be active. In general it is actually more appropriate to speak of neuronal events, such as the discharge of a cell, in terms of probability. This kind of uncertainty is best modeled by quantum physics.

The idea that quantum events are unpredictable has had far-reaching implications, not least for studies of the brain. If there is no single predictable outcome of a system, then there must be alternative possible outcomes. In complex situations such as the trajectory of a ball in a pinball machine, there must be an almost infinite number of outcomes, although some are clearly more probable than others. While all of these outcomes are possible, one interpretation of quantum theory holds that all actually occur but belong to separate, parallel scenarios, or "many worlds" (Everett 1957). If there truly are many versions of an outcome in many worlds, we could go beyond describing events as unpredictable and say that they are also indeterministic. Determinism crops up in the very different but more easily comprehensible context of ancient Greek tragedy. In the plays of Aeschylus, Sophocles, and Euripides, we can see grand themes, such as revenge and blood lust, unfolding over generations where the individuals involved appear to be just pawns of the Fates, who sit weaving the fabric of each person's destiny. Determinism occurs when there is some sort of preordained scheme. The plan might be so complex that it is unpredictable and incomprehensible, as it was to the hapless victims caught up in the weaving of the Fates, but the scenario is most emphatically not random.

If the many-worlds scenario is true, there is no single plan and it would be indeterministic or random as to which one we finally encountered. The idea of many worlds, even if founded on unjustified premises, might nevertheless be quite an interesting idea when applied to consciousness. Both Dennett's multiple draft theory and the Buddhist bundle theory (see Chapter 1) are founded on the idea of multiple consciousnesses. But the corollary of the many-worlds scenario is the uneasy prospect that brain states are actually randomly ordered, jostling with one another until one surfaces as dominant by chance. This idea was eliminated, however, in Chapter 1 when we considered Dennett's description with regard to the unlikelihood of a neuro-lottery. On the other hand, the many-worlds scenario is not a cornerstone of quantum theory; it is just one of many interpretations and is far from widely accepted.

When we put the many-worlds scheme aside, we can say that if brain processes behaved according to quantum theory they would be unpredictable yet reassuringly still deterministic, obeying known equations yet part of a symphony so intricate in its composition that we are unable to encompass all of it. Ants and bees may generate such life symphonies of behavior but on a far more modest scale than what occurs within our own brains. Quantum theory, then, would be appropriate for accounting for the seemingly paradoxical properties of the brain—that there is some overall organization but one that is so complex that it *looks* random.

Roger Penrose (1989) has made progress by suggesting how quantum mechanical processing could be used in descriptions not necessarily of consciousness itself, but of the presumably prerequisite physical event, adaptation in and plasticity of the brain. He takes as a starting point the fact that crystals and quasi-crystals are formed by atoms settling into states of lowest energy, not by some preordained algorithm but by a sequential trial-and-error process. This process involves cooperation among atoms that interact with one another in a way that can be described using quantum mechanics. Penrose suggests that connections in the brain are like atoms in crystals and quasi-crystals in that they are in a constant state of change. Hence they, too, might organize themselves according to quantum mechanics, and "the action of conscious thinking might be the resolving out of alternatives." In other words, the essence of thinking, of consciousness, might be an incessant quantum mechanical reorganization of neuronal connections. But before we become complete converts to quantum theory, there are still several anxieties to be dealt with from a neuroscientific perspective.

The first issue is exemplified by the party game known as "In the Manner of the Verb" (which is actually a lot more fun than its academic-sounding title suggests). There are two teams. Team A beats Team B if Team B cannot guess a word that Team A has chosen. This word has to be an *adverb*. Members of Team B go out of the room, leaving behind one of their number. This unfortunate is told the adverb that the others on the team will have to guess. When the other Team B members reappear, ignorant of everything apart from the fact that the mystery word is an adverb, they ask the individual to enact various behaviors "in the manner of the verb." Depending on the skills and ingenuity of the chosen individual, Team B might finally work out the adverb as they shout, "Walk across the room in the manner of the verb" or "Pour a glass of wine in the manner of the verb." Obviously, the skill required from Team A is to select an adverb that tests one's theatrical and intellectual skills a lot more than do common but vague words like "slowly."

So what has this all to do with the drawbacks of applying quantum theory to a description of consciousness? The point is that even if we were to arrive at describing the exact way in which neurons interact in ever larger groups, we would, in a sense, only have sight of the manner of the verb, the adverb "quantum mechanically." We would have a generic principle of neuronal behavior but not an identification of the behavior itself. We would be in the opposite position to Team B; we would know the adverb but not what process it described.

A second issue is that of temperature. Until 1987 the upper limit for the detection of quantum events was twenty degrees. This value might not seem worth mentioning until we learn that it is not twenty degrees centigrade or Fahrenheit but twenty degrees Kelvin, relatively near absolute zero where no molecules are in motion. The change that came in 1987 was the introduction of a new class of high-temperature compounds (superconductors) where quantum events were detectable at the much higher temperature of two hundred degrees Kelvin (–73 degrees centigrade) (Hazen 1988). Superconductors, however, presented a very special case. The temperature of the brain is about three hundred and ten degrees Kelvin (37 degrees centigrade). Thus there is an enormous amount of thermal motion. In our hot brains it is hard to imagine how reliably quantal phenomena might occur above the background random noise. However the answer is embedded in the problem: It might just be that this is the very state of affairs, of poor signal to noise ratio and high instability, that we need in a physical description of consciousness.

Walter Freeman (1991) has shown that large neuronal assemblies, or as they would be called here, gestalts, can change remarkably rapidly. Indeed we all know that consciousness can shift instantaneously. A car screeching around a corner would make even me come out of my reverie during my evening walk back to the college. In the simple example of a rabbit gestalt large enough for consciousness, there is one waveform characteristic of a certain state, and then suddenly another signifying a new state entirely—hence a switch in consciousness. We can easily accept that such abrupt changes occur. But how?

This rapid change in state is typical of chaotic systems where there is a systematic order that is nonetheless so complex that it defies analysis (Gleick 1987). In systems as elaborate as gestalts, where there are many influences all interacting to produce a certain outcome, a seemingly minor change could have large-scale consequences. A change in consciousness might arise if two potential gestalts (newly formed neuronal groupings gradually expanding around two separate epicenters) were arising simultaneously. The resultant instability would lead to three possible outcomes: first, a rapid shift from one gestalt to the other; second, an increased sensitivity to incoming (weak) stimuli; and third, possible novel patterns of activation or a new gestalt that has never been formed before. In this way it could be possible for a rival gestalt (as already hypothesized) to curtail an existing gestalt. There would be a shift in the object of consciousness with the increased likelihood of noticing something of which we had previously been unaware, such as the weak incoming stimulus.

The precise principles governing and regulating gestalt formation are of course still in the realm of speculation. Nonetheless, we can see that we should not be thinking in consecutive, algorithmic, computational steps unfolding in accordance with set rules, but in terms of rapid and sensitive global changes where new formations of neurons can occur as a result of competing systems—hence the genesis of new states of consciousness, of original ideas, of insights and imagination. In addition, we have here the physical basis for generating false beliefs. If new gestalts can be generated independently of the outside world through internal competition, they no longer have to have an indirect correspondence and faithfulness to the outside world, to reality.

But there is still the nagging question of how the combination of connections within a neuronal group (its epicenter) really *is* the equivalent of, for example, our consciousness of an orange. The answer is that there is no real, empirically proven answer. Instead, we can imagine that the relays of signals coming in parallel from the relevant peripheral sense organ (where color, shape, smell, touch, and so forth are converted into nerve impulses and transmitted to certain regions of the brain) mean that presentation of an orange in the outside world favors the hard-wired formation of certain connections among networks of neurons that are different from those caused by a pear and certainly different from the taste of curry, a pinch on the arm, or a baby crying. The actual physical nature of an epicenter is really a straightforward concept, but then it is most important to bear in mind that an epicenter in itself is merely a necessary, *but not sufficient,* condition for consciousness.

And so what is the magic step that makes the quantitative feature of a group of neurons (the large size) have a qualitative special property (appreciable consciousness)? Although we can say that consciousness is a product of arousal levels and gestalt size, we could not from this description actually create consciousness any more than we could create life. We can envisage how life evolved from hydrogen, water vapor, methane, and ammonia to sulfur-based compounds and on to RNA and DNA. Although the description of this chemical chain is lacking in continuity, it seems plausible, at least in principle, that life could have begun spontaneously from nonliving forms some three and a half billion years ago. Thereafter, however, all life as we know it has come from living organisms. We know that biological life is dependent on DNA activity, such that molecular biologists can manipulate all number of physical characteristics, including the mutations manifest as diseases, by tampering with DNA. But we cannot say what life actually *is* in physical terms; we would surely not attempt to describe it in terms of sequencing, splicing, and base pairs. We are nowhere near being able to create life from components that were not themselves formed from the living parts of other living cells.

And so it is with consciousness. If we cannot create consciousness, then we might aim to do the next best thing and manipulate it as precisely as possible, rather as molecular biologists are starting to manipulate DNA. Just as molecular biologists need to understand the molecular basis of genes, we need to know exactly the conditions for the formation of different types of gestalts. Unlike the actual creation of consciousness, or indeed of biological life, this more modest goal may actually be within our eventual grasp.

At this stage it might be a good idea to look again at the description of consciousness (developed in Chapter 6 from the concentric theory) to see just how successful we have been. We claimed that *consciousness is spatially multiple yet effectively single at any one time. It is an emergent property of nonspecialized and divergent groups of neurons (gestalts) that is continuously variable with respect to, and always entailing, a stimulus epicenter. The size of the gestalt, and hence the depth of prevailing consciousness, is a product of the interaction between the recruiting strength of the epicenter and the degree of arousal.*

There is good evidence, as we saw in Chapter 7, that *nonspecialized and divergent groups of neurons,* which we call gestalts, actually exist. These assemblies have many of the properties that our theory requires: highly dynamic and transient; size dependent on strength of the epicenter; size dependent on strength of rival gestalts; active selection of neurons according to their functional state rather than passive recruitment of any nearby cells; context-dependent formation. Furthermore, we have discussed here a plausible physical basis for a *stimulus epicenter* and have seen how it could vary in its actual features according to its *strength*. Finally, in this chapter it has been possible to develop a means at the physiological level whereby the *interaction between the recruiting strength of the epicenter and the degree of arousal* could determine the quality and quantity of consciousness we are experiencing at any one time.

By describing what exactly gestalts are and how they are formed, we thus have a means of substantiating the idea that *consciousness is spatially multiple but continuously variable*. However, the one part of the formal description that we have been unable to justify in physical terms is that consciousness is an *emergent property*. This shortcoming is scarcely surprising inasmuch as if we could explain consciousness as the mere aggregation of its constituent parts—arousal and gestalts—it would not be an emergent property after all.

The best possible way, at least within the scope of present knowledge and technology, to show that consciousness is truly an emergent property of the physical scenario we have just described is to switch back to phenomenology, the actual experiences of consciousness. Then we will be able to see if exactly the same formal description we have put together here on the physical level can also be understood in accordance with diverse psychological and psychiatric phenomena. Let us turn, finally, to see the concentric theory at work.

chapter nine

IDEA AND REALITY

Between the idea
And the reality
Between the motion
And the act
Falls the shadow

   —from "The Hollow Men,"
    T. S. Eliot

he ultimate task of brain research is to understand how our behavior is translated into and out of the incessant trafficking of ions and molecules within our brains. These cellular events have a terminology, principles of action, and outcomes that are all their own, and which remain restricted to the inner world within our heads. In the previous two chapters we stepped into that world and saw how the concentric theory of consciousness could be couched in terms of real interactions among real neurons. But in itself, the fact that large banks of neurons can ceaselessly form and re-form like clouds in the sky or blobs of mercury tells us little about the shifting, subjective states of consciousness that might ensue. Therefore we now switch from the physiological level, where consciousness is generated by real neurons, to phenomenological scenarios, where we shall assume it is already in existence. Can we interpret the actual subjective *experience* of consciousness in terms of the cycle of formation, dissolution, and re-formation of fleeting neuronal gestalts?

The Phenomenology of Neuronal Gestalts

Some remarkable observations made by the neurosurgeon Wilder Penfield over thirty years ago can be interpreted as a direct demonstration of neuronal gestalts being forced unnaturally into operation (Penfield and Perot 1963). Penfield studied patients who were undergoing brain surgery. Since there are no sensors for pain in the brain, it is a seemingly macabre but actually painless and feasible procedure for the patient to remain conscious while the operation is being performed. With the brain exposed in conscious patients, Penfield stimulated parts of the outer layer (cortex) and reported the resultant effects on apparent awareness. Quite often the stimulation had no obvious effect at all, but sometimes there was a clear and fascinating response: The stimulation appeared to evoke vivid memories. These memories were not abstract concepts like the translation of a French word but specific multisensory sensations of complex events.

These reports generated much excitement for those scientists in search of memory traces, but from the outset there were seemingly insurmountable difficulties in interpreting Penfield's work. Subsequent stimulation of the same site did not necessarily promote the same memory, and stimulation of some other site in the brain could evoke the original memory. It is unlikely, then, that there is any discrete storage of memory traces in the brain, as if they were records systematically stored and filed in an archive. A further worry was that the memories evoked were often not like real memories at all. Sometimes the patient was not sure if the events had actually happened. In addition, it was impossible to highlight the experiences as single, individual events in that they frequently had a more generic, routine quality, such as a dog chasing a cat or a son speaking. Moreover, the experiences evoked by stimulation of the naked surface of the brain were often not so much like actual memories but like those in dreams. The stimulated experiences lacked specific space-time reference points and were actually reported as seeming dreamlike. What follows are some direct quotations from different patients during the stimulation process, as documented by Larry Squire (1987):

Now I hear them. . . . A little like in a dream; I keep having dreams. . . . I keep seeing things. . . . I keep dreaming of things; A dream is starting. There are a lot of people.

We have seen in Chapters 6 and 7 that dreams could be described (in terms of the concentric theory) as the formation of modest neuronal aggregations, like the effects of a gentle pattering of raindrops onto a large puddle. The ripples that result spread only a small distance. Dreams were thus postulated to be the result of minimal gestalts. Similarly, the demonstrations of Penfield could be explained as the stimulation of minimal gestalts where, as in dreams, there is no clear logic, no continuity, but, rather, a disembodied scene. The failure of the stimulation most frequently to produce any effects at all might simply be that not enough neurons were recruited and/or that the stimulating electrode was in a poor site to trigger an appropriate epicenter.

The finding that stimulation of the same site could give different results suggests that other factors were at play that had changed between the first stimulation and the second, and that influenced how a gestalt was formed. These changes might be in the patient's environment, including the words he or she heard spoken by the surgeon and members of the surgical team which could trigger different images and which could be different each time. In addition there would be changes in the internal states of the body chemistry, such as decreases in glucose levels, which would make the patient feel hungry, or changes in sex hormones or levels of a substance, such as in the epinephrine that circulates in the body and feeds back to the brain when we become aroused. Furthermore, the fact that the same memory could be generated from different stimulation sites could be viewed as ripples, albeit extending from different initial epicenters, that incorporated common, overlapping neuronal connections or involved a common gestalt. These small, minimal gestalts, then, produced artificially by Penfield but more normally during the dreaming state, could be regarded as scraps of consciousness torn from the seemingly cohesive fabric of our awareness. But when the brain is not stimulated and has no artificial trigger imposed on it, what might serve as the normal epicenter?

Phenomenology of the Epicenter

A good starting point is with newborn babies. A newborn, on seeing a dog, will not be able to relate the dog to anything else for the simple reason that the baby has not been exposed to any previous experience with dogs. The dog in itself will have no significance. The baby's awareness of the dog would be at the lower end of the continuum of the infant's consciousness. As the child develops, however, and is exposed to pictures of dogs, toy dogs, and, of course, real dogs, the sight of a dog will trigger more associations. The child will then start to view a dog in terms of the associations it evokes: Its awareness of the dog and its *depth of consciousness* on seeing the animal will increase.

This scenario suggests that as children develop they have a *gradually growing* consciousness of the physical world around them. The "booming, buzzing confusion" with which the psychologist William James vividly summed up a baby's circumstance gradually gives way to a world that is cohesive in both time and space, where colors, shapes, and sounds are transformed into mother, food, trees, and cars, which in turn acquire names and are ultimately recalled and mentioned when they are not even physically present. In this way, the gestalts in our brain acquire the potential to become progressively larger around the epicenters that correspond to objects populating the external world.

But our consciousness, as we have seen, is not a cybernetic pairing, a mere chart of physical associations and labels. Instead, never more so than as children, we are on a roller coaster of exhilaration, misery, hunger, and contentment. Slowly we make the transition from reacting without thought to the outside world, with our emotions at the mercy of external objects, to generating, seemingly spontaneously, particular feelings all on our own.

Developmental psychologists regard the child's use of language as indicative of three critical stages of consciousness (Perner 1991). In primary representation words are mere labels of objects in the immediate world, where the child lives effectively in the present. After the age of about two years, the child is able to establish relations among objects—secondary representation—and start to anticipate the future and refer to the past. Around the age of four years, the child finally becomes liberated entirely from the immediate environment and attains free recall.

Free recall, according to the developmental psychologist Josef Perner (1991), means that a child can spontaneously generate an idea without any external clues. For example, a child before this age might be able to say yes or no to the question (asked inside the house) "Is Daddy's car red?" But only at the age of four will that child be able to volunteer the answer to the simple question "What color is Daddy's car?" It is at this final stage of metarepresentation that a child's memory improves dramatically, clearly because the child has a means for internalizing more efficiently events in the surrounding world. Words are no longer simply labels, but symbols. This important stage of metarepresentation also heralds the ability to divorce ideas from reality and to recognize false or imaginary beliefs—in short, to indulge in the full range of human thought.

Perhaps the most exciting aspect of this stage is that it is at this time that a child begins to attribute thoughts to others. This ability is shown very clearly in the Smarties test (Frith 1992). Smarties are chocolate drops coated with different colored candy, roughly the equivalent in popularity in Britain as M & M's are in the United States. Children of different ages are shown a box of Smarties, which has a distinctive cylindrical shape and cover design, and are asked to guess the contents. Not surprisingly, the child, as probably any British adult would, hazards the most obvious reply, "Smarties." The experimenter then shows the child that he is actually wrong because the box turns out to contain a pencil. Now comes the critical question. The child is asked to imagine that a friend is going to come into the room. What will this friend say is in the box? Children under four cannot imagine anyone knowing anything different from themselves, and reply, "A pencil." However, once they have reached the final stage of metarepresentation, they are able to imagine the friend's less informed situation, and reply, "Smarties."

In contrast, Robert Seyfarth and Dorothy Cheney (1992) have shown that vervet monkeys can communicate but are unable to imagine another monkey less informed. Vervets make different alarm calls for different predators, such as one call for snakes and another for eagles. This behavior is beneficial for the vervet community because, when informed that there is a particular type of predator, the monkeys can adjust their escape strategy accordingly. Indeed, vervets seem to understand what the different vocalizations stand for. But these vocalizations are not used in the same way as humans use language. It seems immaterial to the vervet that is making the vocalizations whether or not it is understood; it does not communicate to change the state of mind or the beliefs of other vervets. Frequently, a vervet will continue to give a predator alarm even when its companions have already fled. Similarly, macaque monkey mothers that have been allowed to see a hidden apple or a hidden predator behave no differently in the way they communicate with their offspring, irrespective of whether or not the offspring have shared their mother's experience.

Very young children and monkeys, then, are capable of communication, of having beliefs about objects in the external world, and of recognizing them on repeated sightings. But these talents on their own do not necessarily entail ability to attribute to others independent minds or to conjure up a spontaneous thought *in the absence of a sensory cue* (free recall). One gradually becomes aware that one has a separate mental state. It would seem that only human beings, finally privileged with language and an ability for handling the abstract, enter at this stage into this final zone of the continuum, that of being self-conscious. This process covers the transition to maturity and stamps each of our tickets to being a unique human being. These more sophisticated processes do not appear until relatively late in development, at about the age of four years (Perner 1991).

This apparent tardiness might be due to the fact that a nonsensory (cognitive) stimulus which is generated internally with negligible sensory cues (for example, the free recall of an anxiety that mother might not come home that evening) can only be generated as a result of complex and idiosyncratic concentric associations, potentially large gestalts, which had not developed sufficiently in earlier years. As children grow older they are no longer bribed with a bar of chocolate to stop crying. Their initially fragile cognitive epicenters are no longer so easily overwhelmed by the immediate sensory environment that they readily abandon a worry, a hope, or a question. Such nonsensory cognitive factors come to rival the outside world of chocolate bars, to act as the epicenter, the raindrop on the puddle.

It is possible that cognitive associations could be traced back to diverse, external sensory stimuli, which might in themselves seem remote and unconnected. The more the brain is steeped in experience, the more secondary, tertiary, and so forth associations will be in place, so that thought will increasingly be free recall as the original triggers are buried deeper in more obscure and indirect links. "Worry about mother not coming home" will be able to act as an idiosyncratic epicenter to promote consciousness by way of related associations only in a relatively mature system. In this system, with more extensive neuronal connections, there is the potential for a wider range of associations: stronger and more extensive ripples. Hence, there will be more scope for a much earlier and more tangential sensory epicenter of consciousness, such as the smell of cooking, to trigger an idiosyncratic link (that mother frequently cooks) to the absent and therefore free recall of mother, as further associations are in turn triggered of previous times when mother was late coming home. Such memories, associative links, woud act in turn as the drop in the puddle for "worry about mother not coming home." As the brain becomes more developed, the wider the associations and the more chance for a physical stimulus to set in motion a series of associations for triggering a seemingly unassociated worry, the thought of an event that has not yet happened, or even a false belief.

There is, however, a basic objection to the idea that consciousness is driven by an internal cognitive factor, just as there is with how the probe works in Dennett's multiple drafts model of consciousness. After all, we cannot evoke an executive brain region to act as the boss. How, then, could some cognitive factor arise as predominant to be the triggering epicenter? Why suddenly should "worry about mother not coming home" surface as the prevailing epicenter? Most of the time consciousness is triggered by a combination of sensory inputs in full spate, in addition to other factors in our internal environment, such as arousal, levels of hormones, glucose, and salt (which contribute to sensations of hunger and thirst), as well as past associations (memories) and anticipated associations (worries and hopes). The richer the connections established in the brain, the more scope there is for some remote epicenter, itself indirectly caused by a sensory stimulus, to act in turn eventually as a nonsensory epicenter for a purely cognitive consciousness.

We can imagine a sequence of epicenters, each strongly or loosely associated with the one before, depending on what other internal or external factors intervene. No boss decides our state of consciousness, but, rather, it is the result of living and moving about in the world. Usually we maintain at least a passing awareness of what is happening around us, although the *degree* to which we interpret the world in terms of our own idiosyncratic associations (namely, our depth of consciousness) from one moment to the next varies according to age, mood, environment, and so on. This uniquely individual linking of epicenters enables us to maintain a continuity of consciousness, so that we do not lurch randomly from one state of consciousness to another. There is no need for a neuro-lottery if we imagine that the ripples from one gestalt trigger the epicenter of the next, that our consciousness is controlled at least in part by the particular associations that have evolved in our own brains (our minds) and in part by the unexpected and uncontrollable thrills and spills of the outside world. There is no inflexible or intransigent boss because we are in constant dialogue with our environment. The world about us continues to flavor the way we think, and the way we think colors our idiosyncratic view of the world. Nonetheless, we can conceive examples where the dialogue is quite one-sided.

In the case of young children, the dominating factor is the external sensory one, the bar of chocolate that banishes all fears and memories. On the other hand, as adults we have all experienced times when the outside world seems very remote, such as when we walk home from work reliving a scene far more vivid than the external reality—perhaps some harrowing confrontation that we embellish with imaginary outcomes ever more favorable to ourselves. People in the street pass unnoticed as we embroider the memory of the confrontation with the crushing retort that we were not quick enough to make at the time. Daydreaming is an extreme example of consciousness at the mercy of such highly complex cognitive epicenters when the influence of sensory input is minimal. How easy it is to walk home unaware of the route, so involved in our own inner fantasies that we are effectively blind and deaf to all around us. It is worth noting that children rarely behave in this way for sustained periods of time without props from the outside world. To generate a deep or heightened (the two adjectives are actually synonymous in this context) consciousness, we need a powerful epicenter. A powerful epicenter could be cognitive, such as an all-pervading worry, or it could be external and strong, due to an intrinsic brightness or loudness of an outside object or to heightened arousal (the case with Madame Bovary when, as we saw earlier, she was in the first flush of love).

But surely there is a problem here. We are frequently *highly* conscious of very *minimal* stimuli, such as a whisper or a light touch on the skin. The concentric theory could account for these observations in two ways, both of which endow the stimulus with more significance than might be imagined from the actual weak intensity. First, the weakness of a stimulus, in physical terms, should not be assessed on its own but, rather, in the light of the signal-to-noise ratio. If someone whispers in a library, we are immediately aware of it because there is no other sound, as compared with a whisper at a cocktail party. Hence if there is a situation relatively devoid of powerful incoming sensory stimulus, such as being alone in a house at night, then even the smallest creak on the stairs may dominate our consciousness.

The other way in which a physically weak stimulus could be powerful is if it triggers a large gestalt either because it has strong *cognitive* associations and/or because arousal is high. At a party, the whisper or small gesture of a lover may have immediate significance (trigger many associations) even in a crowd of people. Conversely, if we hear a creak on the stairs when alone in a house at night, the disproportionate size of the gestalt recruited, to which our consciousness corresponds, would be in part attributable to our high arousal level (because we are frightened). Effective strength of stimulus and the degree of consciousness it subsequently triggers are highly variable. They depend on the time of the competing stimuli, the cognitive significance, and arousal levels.

Another completely different example of how the concentric theory could account for the phenomenology of consciousness also comes from a consideration of pain, particularly from migraine. Awareness of pain, which we saw in Chapter 6 is both highly variable and metaphorical in the way we describe it, could correspondingly be attributable to different degrees and manners of subconscious associations generating gestalts of varying sizes.

The greater the gestalt, the greater the pain might be perceived. If this were so, the potent painkiller morphine and the brain's own equivalent enkephalin might be involved in restricting the formation of gestalts. Indeed, reports of the analgesic effect of morphine are that the pain is still present, but that it no longer matters to the patient; it no longer has significance. In terms of the concentric theory, we might say that the pain no longer triggers extensive associations, as it would in normal-sized gestalts. Conversely, we might think that for someone experiencing pain, the brain would be dominated by larger than usual gestalts. As the gestalts start to grow larger than normal prior to an attack, the sufferer might be more deeply conscious than otherwise. In migraine this is exactly what happens: There is indeed *hypersensitivity,* an increased consciousness not only eventually to pain but initially to all the sensations of the external world (Blau 1986, 1990).

So far we have seen how the concentric theory can be used to interpret a range of anecdotal and known phenomena post hoc. But now we can actually use neuronal gestalts to make some predictions. The basic idea we are about to test is that size of gestalt has a direct relation to depth of consciousness. Remember that a gestalt has both time and space dimensions, so a large gestalt would imply a sustained period of deep consciousness around a particular epicenter that triggered many associations, whereas a small gestalt would imply a shallow consciousness of short duration centered around an epicenter where associations were sparse or where there was insufficient time for many associations to be made.

We shall see whether different pathologies have a common problem of neuronal gestalts that are, for whatever reason, of an abnormal size. A caution, however, is that we should really speak of *factors* rather than *causes* in these examples of pathological consciousness because the formation of gestalts is an *interactive* process with the environment.

Living in the Present

Imagine a person with a brain where neuronal gestalts, *for whatever reason,* were incapable of proliferating beyond a certain size.

How would the consciousness of such a person differ from that of normal people with larger gestalts? The concentric theory argues that small gestalts occur either in the case of a weak epicenter (as in dreams) or where too many gestalts compete (as in over-arousal). In both cases there are no strong, continuous, associative links from one small gestalt to the next; the ripples never extend far enough to recruit another epicenter cognitively by previous, abstracted associations. Hence, when awake, a person who, for whatever reason, had only small gestalts, would experience an abrupt shift in his consciousness governed by the caprices of the external sensory world as it flooded the brain.

Alternatively, the gestalts might just overlap enough to cause tenuous connections in the flow of consciousness. Compared to normal consciousness, these connections might be sparser, more obscure, less obvious, and highly individualistic, appearing to out-siders as trains of thought that were illogical, just like dreams. Since the gestalts would be small in size, we might also predict that this hypothetical person felt less concerned with pain. After all, the argument developed in Chapters 6 and 7 stated that the subjective sensation of pain is metaphorical, depending on the variable number of associations the painful stimulus triggers. If these associations were sparse, we would predict a reaction to pain similar to that of the morphine taker, for whom pain is no longer significant and for whom consciousness is, incidentally, often reported as dreamlike. Another corollary of small gestalts where the associations arising from an epicenter are limited would be that memory for past events was not strong.

Would these abnormally small gestalts be reflected in outward behavior? Let us consider an epicenter which was primarily sen-sory. If a sensory epicenter had only a tenuous or limited signifi-cance, then there would be abrupt shifts to another focus. Our hypothetical person might seem more readily distracted than oth-erwise. We could take this idea still further: If the individual is unable to form large gestalts, the chances of forming a new gestalt by focusing on a new epicenter would be maximized if he moved about, thereby increasing the variety of novel sensory cues. Of course cause and effect are interchangeable here, and we could quite as easily devise a reverse sequence of events. It might be the case that someone who was restless and moving around exces-sively, due to drugs, sport, or whatever, was thus bombarding his brain with strong sensory cues, and hence imposing the formation of only small gestalts since new epicenters intervened as the movements continued. In either case small gestalts and excessive movement would be correlated.

A profile of someone with small gestalts might be as follows: restless, incessant movement combined with an inability to concentrate, think logically, or form abstract concepts. Such people could also have poor long-term memory. They would also have an active interest in their surroundings and a breezy attitude toward pain. Life would be lived in the present as a continuous reaction to the outside world.

Schizophrenia is not the dual personality of popular imagination. True, "schizo" in Greek means split, but the split is not into two personalities. Rather, it is a split between what an individual perceives and what he or she subsequently feels. Hence, schizophrenia is regarded as a psychosis, where there is often a departure from reality, as opposed to a neurosis, where behavior may be abnormal but the patient has the same pairings of thought and emotion, shares the same constructs of reality, as most other people. Two types of schizophrenia have been proposed by the psychiatrist Tim Crow (1980) as Type I and Type II. Type I, or acute, schizophrenia need not last indefinitely and is characterized by abnormal thoughts and actions, hence positive signs. Postmortem examination of the brains of such patients reveals no obvious changes in the physical properties of structures of the brain. By contrast, Type II, or chronic, schizophrenia lasts indefinitely and is characterized by signs that are opposite to those of Type I. In this case the abnormality lies not in what the patient does but in what he does not do, hence negative signs. The postmortem brains of Type II schizophrenics are associated more frequently with clear structural abnormalities in that the cortex can be atrophied. There is also an important distinction in how well each type of schizophrenia responds to the conventional medication of blocking the action of dopamine.

It might be tempting to claim that these two syndromes are so different from each other that they should not share the name of schizophrenia at all. Indeed, the negative-symptom schizophrenia (Type II) is in itself indistinguishable from depression. Nevertheless, these two schizophrenias may reflect one and the same condition in that they could be different stages of the same disease:

Saint-Adolf-Grand-Grand-God-Father (1915): a painting by Adolf Wölfi (1864–1930), a schizophrenic. (Prinzhorn Collection, Heidelberg. Reprinted with permission.)

Type I with its florid symptoms of vigorous reaction to, and interaction with, the outside world could precede Type II, where patients turn inward, seemingly oblivious to all around them. Or perhaps the two syndromes alternate in short-term phases. Indeed, this temporary withdrawal into negative from positive symptoms is frequently attributed to the effect of medication. For our purpose, however, it is appropriate to consider the two forms of schizphrenia separately. It is Type I schizophrenia that turns out to be tractable to description in terms of abnormally sparse gestalts. We return, however, to Type II near the end of this chapter.

In what respects do the symptoms of Type I schizophrenia match the profile of consciousness composed of abnormally small neuronal gestalts? In Type I schizophrenia there is motor restlessness, which can include a phenomenon known as stereotypy, where the same action (which could be part of a normal behavioral repertoire) is repeated over and over outside of its normal context. This sign of purposeless movement is so cardinal as to be frequently used as an index in animal models of schizophrenia (Wing et al. 1974). Such an excess of movement for its own sake is directly in line with the prediction we made that small gestalts necessitate enhanced motor activity (and vice versa) since potential sensory epicenters could occur more readily. Such restless behavior would also be consistent with a state of abnormally high arousal, which we predicted would correlate with small gestalts.

In schizophrenia, patients report an enhanced quality in the physical properties of the objects around them. For example, everyday items may appear in vividly glowing colors and, even if not particularly special, may dominate consciousness much more than in normal people. This phenomenon matches the small gestalt profile of an exaggerated importance of sensory stimuli. There is a story of a psychiatrist interviewing a schizophrenic patient and tape-recording the conversation. After the session the patient apologized to the doctor that he was not responding as well as he might have because the baby crying in the background had distracted him. The psychiatrist, who had heard nothing throughout his talk with the patient, at first attributed the claim to some type of auditory hallucination. But when he played the tape back, to the doctor's astonishment, there was a baby crying in the background, far off, presumably in a neighboring room. This story could be interpreted, according to the concentric theory, as follows: Schizophrenics use a higher turnover of sensory epicenters than normal people do, who in contrast form fewer and bigger gestalts, thus allowing them to have more abstracted and longer lasting lines of thought and a deeper consciousness of fewer objects than schizophrenics.

This idea brings us to the types of thought Type I schizophrenics have. Although it is subject to debate, one theory has it that schizophrenics are far more literal in their thinking. We have already seen that they are more distracted by sensory stimuli and that their consciousness is less abstracted, more tied to the physical properties of what is around them, or perhaps evoking highly illogical or idiosyncratic associations. For example, one schizophrenic, when asked to identify a color, replied, "Looks like clay. Sounds like gray. Take you for a roll in the hay. Hay day. May day. I need help!" (Blakemore 1988). In this case we can see a clear predominance of the simple sounds of the words, not their more sophisticated cognitive significance, which serve as associative links. The vague, tangential associations that often occur in this type of schizophrenia, and can be seen as testifying to only the flimsiest continuity among small gestalts, are exemplified by a 1913 letter used in one of the earliest reports of the disorder by the pioneer psychiatrist Eugen Bleuler:

> *Dear mother. . . . I am writing on paper. The pen I am using is from a factory called Perry and Co. This factory is in England. The city of London is in England. I know this from my school days. Then I always liked geography. My last teacher in that subject was Professor August A. He was a man with black eyes. There are also blue and gray eyes and other sorts too. I have heard it said that snakes have green eyes. All people have eyes. There are some, too, who are blind.*

Since nonliteral, abstract thoughts would not be possible due to the restricted size of the neuronal gestalts, we have, instead, the sensory associations of words, including rhymes and puns, as the favored links in a rapidly shifting consciousness.

The psychologist Christopher Frith (1992) suggests that, in fact, the core impairment in schizophrenia is the inability to form metarepresentations. These are the types of thought where one is aware that oneself and other people experience individual, but different, types of awareness. More simply, a schizophrenic has difficulty attributing to other people appropriate thoughts and beliefs. This impairment leads to signs of paranoia, a seeming lack of logic, and a prevailing egocentricity. When asked even the basic question, "What time is it?" one schizophrenic replied, "Seven o'clock. That's my problem. I never know what time it is. Maybe I should try to keep better track of time."

In schizophrenia this limited and thus egocentric consciousness could quite easily mesh with the concept of small gestalts where strong emphasis is placed on the immediate, physical world; glowing, brilliant objects might well be construed as proof of a superhuman, godlike perception, which is a fairly frequent schizophrenic delusion. Similarly, the persistent use of the self as a reference point is the most obvious and literal epicenter, which would go hand in hand with an inability to use more abstracted cognitive epicenters to generate larger gestalts.

But what of the best known schizophrenic symptom, hallucinations? We have already seen that dreaming is describable in terms of small gestalts, as were the experiences of Penfield's patients (Penfield and Perot 1963). In these cases consciousness is viewed as unreal and has strong hallucinatory, dreamlike overtones, qualities which we have already attributed here to small gestalts. Perhaps the world of the schizophrenic is not that much different from our world of dreams or, rather, nightmares. Certainly the illogical associations, the unquestioned leaps from one scenario to another, and the lack of logic and space-time references would all be consistent with a disordered perception describable in terms of small gestalts.

We can see, then, that many of the signs and symptoms of Type I schizophrenia can be described in terms of abnormally small gestalts. As yet there is no hard neurological evidence, in terms of visualizing neuronal configurations, that this is so. Indeed, it would be impossible to demonstrate such an idea directly. We are obviously unable to inject voltage-sensitive dyes to record from isolated groups of neurons in the living brains of patients as they go about their lives. But a less direct way to judge if this classification according to gestalt size has true worth would be for it to encompass a range of completely different disorders.

Back in Chapter 4 we met two groups of patients purportedly suffering from disorders of short-term and long-term memory. We saw that a basic difference in the behavior of these two groups was that those with only long-term memory lived in a world of abstractions and generalizations, whereas those with only short-term memory were highly egocentric. In 1933 a nonpsychotic patient was described (see Goldstein) as someone for whom "things only have value in terms of herself." This woman might easily be classified as lacking any long-term memory, since she appeared to live entirely in the present. Rather like the schizophrenic, this patient, trapped in the present, interpreted all events as unique phenomena in specific relation to herself. An alternative interpretation, as we saw with the schizophrenic, is that this patient was unable to make any abstracted associations which might have linked her past with her present. Rosenfield (1992) identifies the problem, in this case, not as one of memory loss but as the inability to form abstracted concepts. The patient was unaware of the significance of many of the objects around her. Although she could name the objects, they seemingly triggered no associations. According to the concentric theory, such a patient would be unable to generate normal size neuronal gestalts.

A particularly interesting aspect of this case was that the patient's use of language was poor. She could not use language to form abstract concepts such as color. As we normally develop and become capable of free recall, our ability to form abstract concepts and our gestalts expand in parallel. It might be the case that the converse holds and that an inability to express ideas coherently is also part of the profile of someone with small gestalts. Indeed, schizophrenics are known to be linguistically impaired in this way.

The problem with the language of the schizophrenic is not one of actual articulation, as there is nothing wrong with the ability to make sounds. Rather, the problem lies in generating ideas to go with the sounds. As we have seen, small gestalts imply a poverty of associations with an object or idea, plus an inability to have abstractions and free recall. The speech problems of schizophrenics are not even ones of grammar but of an abnormality of thought. For example, there is poverty of content such that when asked, "Tell me what kind of person you are," one patient replied:

Ah, one hell of an odd thing to say perhaps in these particular circumstances. I happen to be quite pleased with who I am or how I am and many of the problems that I have and have been working on are difficult for me to handle or to work on because I am not aware of them as problems which upset me personally.

Other common features are irrelevant replies and lack of proper connections between phrases and ideas. Moreover, many schizophrenics cannot follow a chain of thought, but just repeat words or ideas. All these difficulties could be interpreted as a sign of weak associative connections amounting to small gestalts. There are certain similarities between schizophrenics and patients with only short-term memory. Both are highly self-referential and egocentric. Furthermore, there are problems common to both kinds of patients regarding an appreciation of the full context (associations) in which certain ideas occur, as well as an inability for handling abstract concepts.

As an illustration of the inability to form abstract concepts, B. Cohen (1976) asked volunteers to describe a colored disk in a way that would allow a listener to distinguish the disk from a group of others of diverse colors. This task proved impossible only for schizophrenics, and is reminiscent of the patient we heard about in Chapter 4 who had difficulty sorting skeins of wool according to color.

The problems in appreciating the context in which words occur is illustrated by an experiment where John Done and Christopher Frith (1984) asked patients to guess a missing word in a sentence—for example, "Coming in he took off his _____." Whereas the correct answer would be a word such as "coat," a schizophrenic might simply repeat the previous words or reply with an inappropriate word such as "dance." The language problems of schizophrenics could reflect a situation where the epicenter does not trigger the full complement of associations, where the individual is trapped in an egocentric world of literal and unique objects and events that have no wider significance and defy abstraction—in short, an inner world of small gestalts.

If this idea of poor language being connected to small gestalts is correct, then the reverse should hold and patients with language problems should display some of the other characteristics of the small gestalt profile. As it happens, aphasics (those who for a variety of reasons are unable to speak) display this precise *lack of continuity* in consciousness. We have already come across the claim of Henry Head (1926) that language provides a continuity to consciousness. To support this idea, he reported an aphasic patient who described a walk where each building he passed appeared as an "isolated event." It was all "in bits and pieces" such that he had to "jump from one thing to another."

Rosenfield attributes this problem to language per se, but we can go further and say that *both* language problems *and* a break in the continuity of consciousness would arise if a person had restricted size of neuronal gestalt where ability to form abstract concepts or to have a continuous and logical progression of consciousness were curtailed. "One image frequently ousts its predecessor, instead of adding to it," wrote Head of his aphasic patient. This type of phenomenon, then, is in direct line with our initial predictions, and we could include aphasics in the small gestalt category. Smaller gestalts mean a world of more objects but each with smaller significance. Indeed, one aphasic seems to bear out the consequent prediction of a reduction in significance of events and objects around him when he reported that he was "immune to happiness or sorrow" (Rosenfield 1992).

Another class of patient could be added to the constellation of abnormalities united by abnormally small gestalts. In this case there really is a change in personality. In manic depression the patient exhibits (for no apparent reason) wild swings of mood over periods of time ranging from days to months. In the depressive phase the patient is like other clinically depressed patients. In the manic phase he or she has boundless energy and needs very little sleep. Such patients are constantly distracted and appear to be living vehemently in the present. Such incessant movement and egocentric consciousness would be typical of the small gestalt profile, as indeed would be the behavior of participants at "raves." Frequently aided by the drug Ecstasy, "ravers" can dance all night making the same repetitive movements to the same repetitive beats of music stripped of all cognitive content—thus triggering no associations, generating no large gestalts. The ravers are at the mercy of external physical stimuli in their most minimal and literal forms.

If consciousness only deepens gradually as larger gestalts are able to form in our brains due to the development of more neuronal connections, we would expect children to have small gestalts and to display, albeit less excessively, elements of the small gestalt profile. Children are the best group to use to make predictions because they are the only group where we can assume gestalts are definitely smaller (since their brains are not fully developed). Whereas before we had to start with behavior and extrapolate gestalt size, here we can assume small gestalt size and make testable predictions regarding behavior. So, do the features of small gestalt consciousness also apply to the consciousness of children?

Children have poor linguistic ability and memory for past events; they form abstract concepts less readily; and their lack of experience means that most objects in their worlds have only limited significance. It is perhaps an enviable feature of childhood that they tend to live in the present. "Are we in Paris now?" asked a friend's four-year-old after we had been driving from Oxford for only five minutes. Moreover, children tend not to dwell on pain. Of course there is, in an adult view, usually an overreaction to a relatively trivial mishap, but the tears are frequently banished by some distraction such as a nearby bird, a kiss, or a bar of chocolate. The transient overreaction occurs precisely because the tumble or frightening noise or whatever happened in the immediate present is not rivaled by abstracted, internalized gestalts such as occur in adults. As soon as a new epicenter arises in the form of a chocolate bar, the new event in the external world, consciousness of the original pain vanishes. Other features of the small gestalt group also apply: heightened activity (at least compared to the average middle-aged adult), idiosyncratic logic, and interpreting the external world in terms of oneself.

But what of the other side of the coin? If the theory is truly robust, the profile of abnormally large gestalts should yield equally consistent predictions.

Living in the Past

Now let us imagine what an individual might be like if her gestalts, *for whatever reason,* were abnormally large. Perhaps the most obvious feature would be that any epicenter, by recruiting a large number of associations, might cause that person to dwell on an issue for an abnormally long time and be deeply conscious of it. Since these large gestalts would entail abstracted cognitive concepts, it is likely that the person would not be particularly sensitive to the immediate sensory environment. As either a result or cause of this subordination of the immediate sensory world, there would be very little physical movement. In contrast to the small gestalt profile, those with overly large gestalts would have an infrastructure of extensive neuronal connections to experience pain quite markedly. One epicenter would eventually take over from another as a result of well-established cognitive associations, but not at the haphazard mercy of the environment. Such individuals would thus dwell on the significance of the objects of their thoughts and possibly conflate them into more generalized or newer, abstracted trains of thought and states of consciousness. Let us now see if a range of familiar brain disorders could be classified into either of these two categories.

We have discussed how manic depressives in the manic phase resemble other pathological conditions in that their abnormal symptoms can be explained in terms of small gestalts. Can the opposite condition, depression, be described in terms of abnormally large gestalts? A clinical depressive is not at all interested in his immediate surroundings. The caricature picture is of a person sitting slumped in a chair obsessed with his inner world of despair and hardly moving at all.

This pattern of behavior could be explained by the depressive having so strong an epicenter that it recruits an enormous gestalt to the exclusion of any possible competition from the usual sensory candidates. A series of small separate anxieties can become conflated into one vast consciousness of despair, one large gestalt. The immediate sensation-laden events that dominate the consciousness of most of us, food and sex, do not become focal points in the consciousness of depressives because they are buried in their own inner worlds. For the depressed patient, the outside world is remote and gray; this demotion of the sensory world could be seen as both the cause or the effect of large gestalts. Similarly, depressives are often ill and in physical pain or, rather, illness and lack of mobility are frequently associated with an ensuing depression. Again, we must remember that causality is not the issue here. Instead, it is the *interaction*, the chicken-and-egg relation among depression, immobility, pain, and large gestalts.

In Chapter 9 it was suggested that large gestalts would be favored by increases in serotonin. Ecstasy, the drug favored by ravers, is believed to have a long-term action of destroying sero-tonin-containing neurons. Hence, it might indeed be reasonable to conclude that the incessant movement and purely sensory world of the raver is indeed a world of small gestalts. Following the line of reasoning developed here, we could also conclude that excess sero-tonin, in facilitating large gestalt formation, is also formative in depression. But now the conundrum: A widespread treatment of depression is to administer drugs that actually *increase* the avail-ability of serotonin. How can we explain this anomaly in terms of the theory? A clue comes from what actually happens when a patient takes an antidepressant drug. Nothing. The drug has no therapeutic effect for at least ten days, even though it might have succeeded at the biochemical level in increasing the availability of serotonin many days earlier. For some time now it has been thought that this therapeutic time lag could be attributable to the fact that the depressive state is not related to the availability of amines such as serotonin but to the status of its target receptors.

One of the advantages of the broad chemical diversity of the brain is that only neurons bearing a highly selective protein target receptor for a particular chemical to latch on to can be influenced by it. Hence a gestalt need not be defined by the passive diffusion of a substance, but would be actively demarcated by the distribu-tion of these receptors. In turn, the sensitivity of the target recep-tors for their chemical is highly labile. If there were lots of trans-mitters released, eventually the receptor would become less responsive, less sensitive; whereas in the absence of the chemical, it would become more sensitive.

A well-established answer to the problem of the therapeutic time lag at the physical level is that depression is associated *not* with a paucity of serotonin but with the target receptors being too sensitive. By bombarding these receptors with massive amounts of drug-induced serotonin, after about ten days they become far less sensitive. When the receptors to serotonin are less sensitive, serotonin is less efficient, and so large gestalts are not formed so readily. The all-embracing despair requiring a large gestalt is therefore no longer possible.

The idea that serotonin is needed for the formation of gestalts is borne out by the opposite situation, where the substance is less effective. Conversely, small gestalts would be favored if the action of serotonin was blocked. Any agent reducing the effectiveness of serotonin might be predicted to restrict gestalt formation, so that a small gestalt profile would predominate, resembling schizophrenia and dreams. This is exactly what happens. The hallucinogenic drug LSD, as we saw earlier, works in the brain by reducing the effectiveness of serotonin, and, as is well known, gives rise to hallucinations and a massive distortion of the senses. It can actually be used as an animal model of schizophrenia. Such a model would be validated by the concentric theory: LSD could be said to cause the formation of small gestalts, equivalent to those already postulated as characterizing schizophrenia.

But let us return to the large gestalt profile. A similar pattern can be seen in patients with short-term memory loss. In these patients there is an inability to hold in the mind immediate events; hence they seem to be withdrawn and, if anything, living in the past. We saw in Chapter 4 that Rosenfield eschews the distinction between short-term and long-term memory, and claims instead that the problem is one of perception of time. This type of patient has lost track of sequencing particular events; rather, he lives a generic lifestyle. In the case Rosenfield cites from 1913, Henry Baud lived his daily life as an automaton; he was indifferent to his surroundings, what he ate, whom he met, and so forth. By contrast, his efficient memory for the past, eighteen years prior to his hospital admission, was of a more generalized nature than for actual, present happenings. He remembered that he had "liked women" and visited his mistress on "last Saturday." He lived in the past where there were no isolated specific occasions, but simply a way of life. Note that where the immediate world does not intrude, there are no real candidates for new epicenters. Instead, there are the same, repeated associations devolving around, for example, women, that will not be subject to changes in the light of ongoing experiences or different external triggers. There will be an almost generic "liking of women" that forms part of an invariant inner world, part of a large and undisturbed gestalt.

Can we now test the concentric theory, as we did for the small gestalt profile, by seeing whether or not the large gestalt profile has any analogies in everyday life? If we turn to the elderly, we can see how in certain respects they resemble those with short-term memory deficit and depressives. The elderly do not move around much; they are very sensitive to pain and illness; and they tend to live in the past. Of course it could be argued that the elderly are more prone to illness and immobility; but the primary issue here is not one of cause or effect, in that gestalt formation is probably just as much influenced by factors such as ability to move as it can affect the degree of movement that might be generated. Similarly, heightened awareness of pain would take over as a major epicenter that generated a large gestalt just as readily as a large gestalt would furnish the infrastructure for intense sensation of pain. Rather, the task that confronts us is one of describing a variety of behaviors in terms of a single parameter, large gestalts, not of attributing a causality. Brain and environment are in constant dialogue.

A Subjective Index of Neuronal Gestalts?

Is there an unambiguous situation in which we might compare the two groups of small and large gestalts directly? Since we have seen the individuals in each case living, respectively, in the present and in the past, one possibility concerns the perception of time. Small children certainly have little sense of time passing; they are, after all, living in the present, where every day seems like an eternity. For many of the elderly, on the other hand, life can hurtle by and distant events seem like only yesterday. Perhaps, then, time perception can be viewed in terms of gestalt formation. The more gestalts are formed and changed, as with the schizophrenic or the child, the more time is perceived as passing slowly. Conversely, periods of prolonged concentration leave us with the feeling, for example, that the morning has rushed by. If there are no gestalts formed and no consciousness at all, as in anesthesia or sleep, time will pass most quickly of all, almost instantaneously.

We might venture, then, that the more rapid the turnover of gestalts, the more slowly time seems to pass. This idea would be corroborated by the way our consciousness changes during accidents. Everything appears to happen in slow motion; the passage of time slows right down. We are in a situation where the immediate sensory surroundings are of paramount importance and our sensations are changing very fast. As we move or are moved abnormally quickly, we are making small gestalts and are back in a dreamlike world as timeless, vivid, and unreal as that of the schizophrenic or the child. The consciousness of an accident could be the consciousness of abnormally small gestalts.

In general, time perception might indicate to us the speed or the turnover of gestalt formation. This consideration of time perception, and its accurate correspondence with groups of small and large gestalts, suggest a means for us to tell in ourselves how quickly our own gestalts might be changing in our brains. The comparisons we have been making so far might well be analogous to incessant, consecutive raindrops falling on a puddle, where each generates a modest and transient pattern of ripples (the small gestalt group), compared to a single heavy stone thrown in (the large gestalt group) and where the ripples are more extensive and last longer. Let us now imagine a third condition where neither is the case: that even though stones are thrown into the puddle, the water is too stagnant to generate ripples—hence no gestalt.

No Gestalts, No Consciousness?

We have seen so far that the size of a gestalt might determine the type of consciousness experienced. After all, if you have a small gestalt, the consciousness will be of short duration and not very profound, but there will be another contrasting one abruptly coming in to take over. But what if the gestalts were, for pathological reasons, dramatically diminished? This could be the situation in Type II schizophrenia. We have seen that Type II schizophrenia frequently follows Type I, and can actually be detected in a loss of brain tissue. The symptoms we saw were negative and insensitive to medication. Perhaps the potential gestalts and their neuronal connectivities are so vestigial that they can no longer be primed by the amines (either internally manufactured or given as medication) to generate an adequate consciousness to any epicenters, cognitive or sensory. In the end, the patient does not know who he is nor where he is; his consciousness sinks down toward the bottom of the continuum. This scenario of diminishing gestalts would provide the infrastructure for a continuum between the otherwise paradoxical yet frequent pattern of shift in dominance, during a patient's life, from Type I to Type II schizophrenia.

A similar situation occurs in Alzheimer's disease. This condition also involves degeneration of the brain and is very similar in signs and symptoms to Type II schizophrenia. Alzheimer's disease is not a consequence, as many once thought, of natural aging but a devastating insult to neurons that can occur at any time in later life or even in middle age (Jobst et al. 1994). The contribution of acetylcholine to consciousness in maintaining moderate levels of arousal (focused arousal) is particularly relevant in view of the fact that in Alzheimer's disease there is a marked deficiency in acetylcholine (Bowen and Davidson 1986) and an impairment in establishing normal neuronal connections (Woolf and Butcher 1990). In Alzheimer's disease, then, we could say that there is a reduction in both focused arousal and in the ease with which basic associative connections within gestalts might be formed. Hence, in initial stages of degeneration prior to complete loss of all gestalts, we might expect that gestalts start to *diminish* in size. The patient would thus go through a period resembling that of the schizophrenia or childhood profile outlined for small gestalts. This might well happen. In senile dementia, the patient is frequently restless and active, in accordance with the small gestalt profile (Finestone et al. 1982). In such cases, the patient is often agitated (as in amphetamine psychosis and schizophrenia) and may wander off or walk around inappropriately (Hope and Fairburn 1990). Such behavior and movements outside of a normal context would also correspond to the profile of small gestalts, where associations are sparse.

As the disease progresses, there would not be enough acetylcholine or the neuronal connectivity for even the formation of small gestalts. As with the transition from Type I to Type II schizophrenia, there would be a transition from the characteristic restlessness of small gestalts to no gestalts at all and, hence, no consciousness, just a persistent vegetative state. It is with the end of consciousness, then, that we come to the end of this particular journey.

Finally, however, we might also apply the concept of small and large gestalts to the phenomenology of our normal everyday lives. Having seen how gestalt size might be a relevant parameter for assessing consciousness, let us put to one side the extreme cases of size discussed in this chapter. If we think once again of gestalt size and thus consciousness *as a continuum,* we can easily imagine that our momentary states of awareness lie between large and small gestalt type profiles as we live out each day, progressing along a line of epicenters. There will be times of deep reflection, where an hour disappears while we nurse a grievance or fantasy or nudge away at some intellectual problem. These times will, however, be interspersed with moments when we open up to the full force of the vivid sensuality of the outside world and all it contains.

> *When I heard the learn'd asronomer,*
> *When the proofs, the figures, were ranged in columns before*
> *   me,*
> *When I was shown the charts and diagrams, to add, divide,*
> *   and measure them,*
> *When I sitting heard the astronomer where he lectured with*
> *   much applause in the lecture room,*
> *How soon unaccountable I became tired and sick,*
> *Till rising and gliding out I wander'd off by myself,*
> *In the mystical moist night air, and from time to time,*
> *Look'd up in perfect silence at the stars.*

Walt Whitman

EPILOGUE: A FUTURE

The discussions in this book have been based on an assumption. But it is an assumption that many have made before, simply because there is no plausible alternative. It is that consciousness is generated when vast groups of neurons work together collectively under specific conditions. However, in this book we have seen what those prevailing conditions might be and have envisioned how they might interact. Consciousness has been expressed in terms of a single final parameter (the rate of turnover of neuronal gestalts) that can be applied to both real brain events and the phenomenology of awareness in health, disease, and response to drugs. The more we can refine our knowledge of the conditions for the formation of gestalts, in both phenomenological and physical terms, the more we shall be able to predict the type of consciousness that will ensue and the nearer we shall edge toward having an objective way of looking at the phenomenology of awareness.

The philosopher Karl Popper (1959) has claimed that any proper scientific theory should be falsifiable. So how might the concentric theory be tested experimentally? The idea of neuronal gestalts is simultaneously applicable at both the physical and phenomenological levels; hence the common parameter of gestalt formation could provide a point of comparison for both clinical observations and laboratory experiments. Clinical scenarios offer a window onto the subjective feel of consciousness, but simultaneous, direct measurements of neuronal events are currently not very accurate without tampering in some unethical and/or irreversible way with the brain. The reverse, however, is true in the laboratory. Neuroscientists can study far more readily the physical characteristics of animal brains, but they get no idea at all of ongoing consciousness. Clinical situations invite a direct study of *changes in consciousness* as a result of net changes in gestalt formation. Conversely, laboratory models allow us to study directly *changes in gestalts* and thus manipulate consciousness. The next step is to relate these changes in gestalts in the laboratory to changes in consciousness in the clinic. Yet we cannot control and standardize the formation of gestalts in people, nor probably even in animals.

A pivotal conclusion of this book is that consciousness is a result of gestalt formation, which is in turn influenced by arousal and sensory inputs. In both clinical and experimental scenarios, we *can* standardize much more readily the level of arousal by using drugs that modify the availability of the fountains of amines—serotonin, acetylcholine, dopamine, and norepinephrine. It might be possible therefore to see how the concentric theory holds up to direct scrutiny by observing the effects of the same drugs on gestalt formation in animals and on reports of changes in consciousness in people. Obviously this type of proposal is extremely crude, since we would need a very precise way of relating the drug action to certain types of arousal rather than to any other actions the substance may cause. Furthermore, we would have to standardize the reports of human subjects with a questionnaire or some uniform laboratory protocol. This protocol would have to be very simple in order to determine any correspondence between the consciousness of animals and that of humans. For example, it might involve letting the subjects become mildly hungry, then monitoring the presumed response of pleasure at their being given food. These experiments are probably too basic and crude to be helpful as they stand, but at least this general type of strategy points the way toward a direct, neuroscientific means of experimenting with consciousness in the future, one that would actually attempt to address a specific hypothesis.

Of course, only real strides could be made by working with humans who are able to describe in some measure their conscious state. Imaging the human brain would overcome any ethical criticisms of the use of animals, and also would enable us to compare directly the subjective reports of consciousness as it changed under different experimentally induced conditions, simultaneously and directly with changes in gestalts. The biggest problem at the moment is a technical one. In order to test the validity of the concentric theory, much depends on the fidelity of the imaging of neuronal gestalts. We have already seen that by manipulating the environment and studying resultant activity of the brain, the changes can be identified in constellations of neurons, revealed by multiple recording of a population or by optical dyes. These two techniques in combination currently offer the best way of visualizing neuronal gestalts. The multiple recording of single neurons ensures a high spatial resolution on a scale of micrometers, whereas the use of dyes gives a good temporal resolution in milliseconds. This consideration is of the utmost importance in view of the fact that, for example, a gestalt in the rat cortex that is activated by the touch of a whisker is reduced to *half* its size at twenty milliseconds after stimulation, compared to what it was only *five milliseconds* before.

Unfortunately, in order to visualize the surface of the brain using the most sensitive methods of optical dyes and multineuron recording, a "window" has to be made by removing a portion of the overlying skull bone. Such invasive methods would not be feasible for routinely studying consciousness in freely moving humans. Presently there are noninvasive but less sensitive methods for imaging the conscious human brain at work. This approach can be broadly divided into two categories, those that require tracers and those that do not (Roland 1993).

Tracers are radioactive isotopes that are injected into the body and pass into the brain with the blood. The most active areas of the brain have a greater regional blood flow, so that the concentration of isotope is greatest where brain activity is greatest. The most sensitive method is one using isotopes of oxygen, nitrogen, carbon, and fluorine that emit positrons (the antimatter equivalent of electrons). This method, which is called positron emission tomography (PET), is widely used to map activities in the brain during sustained visual and linguistic tasks. But compared to the invasive methods that we were able to use as evidence to reveal neuronal gestalts, time and space resolution is very poor, at least a thousand times lower than needed. The spatial sensitivity is in the region of millimeters and the temporal resolution is, at best, in the range of tens of seconds. The problem is that tracers take time to cross into the brain and diffuse throughout the extracellular spaces.

On the other hand, there are also noninvasive, nontracer techniques such as nuclear magnetic resonance (NMR). When subjected to a magnetic field, the nuclei of certain atoms in the brain align with the field and respond to pulses of radio waves. The signals recorded indicate the number of active nuclei present and, hence, record the concentration of, say, sodium ions in a specific region. Although this system has a better time resolution than PET, it is not quite yet on a time scale commensurate with the ongoing activity of neurons. Moreover, the spatial sensitivity of the measurements still needs improvement, for at best it is about a cubic millimeter. Nonetheless, it may one day be possible to measure the difference between sodium ions inside and outside a particular cell and hence have an accurate measure of neuronal activity. The sensitivity required, however, is beyond that of present-day NMR detectors.

Another noninvasive technique, magnetoencephalography (MEG), has a better temporal resolution than does NMR or PET. This method involves measuring the magnetic field generated by the electrical activity of the brain. However, the spatial resolution of MEG needs improvements, and it actually deteriorates as one images deeper into the brain.

But then it could be argued that we need not have bothered with a theory of consciousness at all. All we need do is to take NMR, PET, or MEG scans of individuals and correlate what we see with what they say over a sustained period of time. But this would scarcely be in the spirit of scientific inquiry, where an experiment is run in order to answer a specific question suggested by a hypothesis. If we were "just looking," without any idea what we were looking for, or why, it would be very hard to interpret what we saw and to know how to proceed subsequently. We would simply be farming the brain, not studying it. Even though we do not currently have the technology for testing the concentric theory directly in human subjects, the theory *can* suggest empirically testable questions waiting for the methods of brain imaging to get just a little bit better. For example, are abnormally large

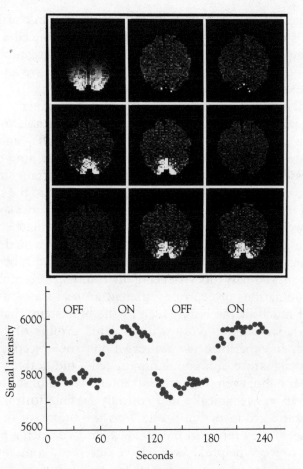

MRI: A noninvasive, nontracer technique, based on nuclear magnetic resonance. These functional magnetic resonance images (fMRIs) show a normal human brain during visual stimulation (from the work of Bruce Rosen and colleagues at the Massachusetts General Hospital, Boston). The baseline image depicts the anatomy of the slice of brain being studied; in the back of the brain the area monitored with fMRI is highlighted. The subject wore tightly fitting goggles that contained light-emitting diodes which were turned on and off as a rapid sequence of scans was obtained. The images show the prominent activation of the individual's visual cortices. Even more impressive, it was possible to actually appreciate the change in the signal over time, as depicted in the graph at the bottom. (Adapted from K. K. Kwong, J. W. Belliveau, D. A. Chesler, I. E. Goldberg, R. M. Weisskoff, B. P. Poncelet, D. N. Kenny, B. E. Hoppel, M. S. Cohen, R. Turner, H. M. Cheng, T. J. Brady, and B. R. Rosen, "Dynamic Magnetic Resonance Imaging of Human Brain Activity During Primary Sensory Stimulation," *Proceedings of the National Academy of Sciences,* 89 [1992], 5675–5679.)

and small gestalts really associated with the profiles described in the previous chapter? If the neuronal gestalts are indeed a sensitive measure of degree of consciousness, and if such gestalts can eventually be imaged in the brain, we might finally have an objective index of consciousness.

Beyond even these highly hypothetical experiments is the tantalizing possibility that in the future we might be able to reach beyond the correlation of neuronal groups (gestalts) and consciousness to understand a *causal* relationship. Just how does a transient assembly of synchronous neurons of a certain size and under certain conditions of arousal actually give rise to the subjective feeling of consciousness? Even the vaguest and most speculative of answers is currently beyond us. A more immediate concern is simply to appreciate the kind of knowledge that would reveal how neurons generate consciousness. Just how would it be done? If consciousness really does depend on transient assemblies of different populations of neurons, different arousal states, and the integrity of much of the brain (such as the brainstem, thalamus, and cortex), we cannot work with isolated groups of cells in dishes. Such an experiment would reveal only the objective physicochemical signature of a population of cells, and nothing more. On the other hand, even if we were to enter a world of science fiction where it was technically and ethically feasible to transplant the same static group of brain cells into the brains of different people to see if they reported the same experience, such a process would not be very helpful. As we have observed, consciousness depends on the dynamic formation of brain cells, not on a one-to-one relation between subjective experience and fixed bits of cortex. As I write these words in the last gasp of the twentieth century, it seems that it will always be impossible to demonstrate unequivocally and empirically how brain cells *cause* consciousness. But do we want to?

If we could explain exactly how consciousness is generated by groups of neurons under certain conditions, it would also mean that we had the ability to manipulate one another's consciousness to such a degree that it could lead to the effective annihilation of the individual. This specter is comparable to the ultimate, Frankenstein-like feat of the molecular biologist in creating organic life. Whether or not such a world would be a good place in which to live can only again be the stuff of science fiction.

Consciousness gives purpose to our existence. It is an inner world that meshes with the external one but is always distinct from it. Our lives are lived wallowing in the sensuality of the grass beneath bare feet and the sun on the face, or, alternatively, turned inward beyond objective time and space to the shadier realm of hopes and memories, successes and failures, and all the private associations that go with them. Each day we are on a roller coaster of grabbing at the outside world and retreating from it. The only way we can proceed at the moment to have any idea about what is happening in the brain is to say that under *certain* conditions in the brain, consciousness, that is, *certain* types of consciousness, is an inevitable consequence. We can now start to explore these conditions in increasing detail by framing questions generated by theories such as the one developed in this book. That, in conclusion, is at least a start.

REFERENCES

Aertsen, A., and G. L. Gerstein. 1991. "Dynamic Aspects of Neuronal Cooperativity: Fast Stimulus-Locked Modulation of Effective Cooperativity." In *Neuronal Cooperativity,* ed. J. Kruger. New York: Springer-Verlag, pp. 52–67.

Aghajanian, G. K., J. S. Sprouse, and K. Rasmussen. 1987. "Physiology of the Midbrain Serotonin System." In *Psychopharmacology,* ed. H. Y. Meltzer. New York: Raven Press, pp. 141–150.

Alonso, A., M. De Curtis, and R. R. Llinás. 1990. "Post-Synaptic Hebbian and Non-Hebbian Long-Term Potentiation of Synaptic Efficacy in the Entorhinal Cortex in Slices and in the Isolated Adult Guinea Pig Brain," *Proceedings of the National Academy of Sciences,* 87, 9280–9284.

Atkinson, R. L., R. C. Atkinson, E. E. Smith, D. J. Bem, and E. R. Hilgard. 1990. *Introduction to Psychology.* San Diego: Harcourt Brace Jovanovich.

Bailey, C. H., M. Chen, F. Keller, and E. R. Kandel. 1992. "Serotonin-Mediated Endocytosis of apCAM: An Early Step of Learning Related Synaptic Growth in Aplysia," *Science,* 256, 645–649.

Barlow, H. 1989. "The Biological Role of Consciousness." In *Mindwaves,* ed. C. Blakemore and S. A. Greenfield. Oxford: Basil Blackwell.

Bates, M. S., W. T. Edwards, and K. O. Anderson. 1993. "Ethnocultural Influences on Variation in Chronic Pain Perception," *Pain*, 52, 101–112.

Beaudet, A., and L. Descarries. 1978. "The Monoamine Innervation of Rat Cerebral Cortex: Synaptic and Nonsynaptic Axon Terminals," *Neuroscience*, 3, 851–860.

Beninger, R. J., S. B. Kendall, and C. H. Vanderwolf. 1974. "The Ability of Rats to Discriminate Their Own Behaviours," *Canadian Journal of Psychology*, 28, 79–91.

Blake, J. F., M. W. Brown, and G. L. Collingridge. 1988. "CNQX Blocks Acidic Amino Acid Induced Depolarizations and Synaptic Components Mediated by Non-NMDA Receptors in Hippocampal Slices," *Neuroscience Letters*, 89, 182–186.

Blakemore, C. B. 1988. *The Mind Machine*. London: BBC Books.

Blau, J. N. 1986. "Clinical Characteristics of Premonitory Symptoms in Migraine." In *The Prelude to the Migraine Attack*, ed. W. K. Amery and A. Wauquier. London: Balliere Tindall, pp. 39–45.

Blau, J. N. 1990. "The Nature of Migraine: Do We Need to Invoke Slow Neurochemical Processes?" In *Migraine: A Spectrum of Ideas*, ed. M. Sandler and G. Collins. Oxford: Oxford Medical Publications.

Bleuler, E. 1987. "Dementia Praecox or the Group of Schizophrenias," trans. J. Zinkin. In *The Clinical Routes of the Schizophrenia Concept*, ed. J. Cutting and M. Shepherd. Cambridge: Cambridge University Press.

Bliss, T. V. P., and T. Lomo. 1973. "Long-Lasting Potentiation of Synaptic Transmission in the Dentate Area of the Anesthetized Rabbit Following Stimulation of the Perforant Path," *Journal of Physiology*, 232, 331–356.

Bowen, D. M., and A. N. Davidson. 1986. "Biochemical Studies of Nerve Cells and Energy Metabolism in Alzheimer's Disease," *British Medical Bulletin*, 42, 75–80.

Bowman, W. C., and M. J. Rand. 1984. *Textbook of Pharmacology*, 2nd ed. Oxford: Blackwell Scientific Publications, p. 16.

Buzsaki, G. 1989. "Two-Stage Model of Memory Trace Formation: A Role for 'Noisy' Brain States," *Neuroscience*, 31, 551–570.

Carey, J., ed. 1991. *Brain Concepts: Sleep and Dreaming*. Washington, D.C.: Society for Neuroscience.

Churchland, P. S., and T. J. Sejnowski. 1992. *The Computational Brain*. Cambridge, Mass.: MIT Press.

Cohen, B. 1976. "Referent Communication in Schizophrenia: The Preservative Chaining Model," *Annals of the New York Academy of Sciences*, 270, 124–141.

Cohen, F., and D. Wander. 1993. *Handwriting Analysis at Work*. New York: HarperCollins.

Cole, A. E., and R. A. Nicoll. 1983. "Acetylcholine Mediates a Slow Synaptic Potential in Hippocampal Pyramidal Cells," *Nature*, 221, 1299–1301.

Cooper, J. R., F. E. Bloom, and R. H. Roth. 1991. *The Biochemical Basis of Neuropharmacology*, 6th ed. Oxford: Oxford University Press.

Cowan, M. 1990. "The Development of the Brain." In *The Workings of the Brain*, ed. R. R. Llinás. New York: W. H. Freeman and Co., pp. 39–57.

Cowey, A., and P. Stoerig. 1992. "Reflections on Blindsight." In *The Neuropsychology of Consciousness*, A. D. Milner and M. D. Rugg. San Diego: Academic Press.

Crick, F. 1994. *The Astonishing Hypothesis*. New York: Charles Scribner's Sons.

Crick, F. 1984. "The Function of the Thalamic Reticular Complex: The Searchlight Hypothesis," *Proceedings of the National Academy of Sciences*, 81, 4586–4590.

Crick, F., and C. Koch. 1993. "The Problem of Consciousness." In *Mind and Brain*. New York: W. H. Freeman and Co.

Crow, T. 1980. "Molecular Pathology of Schizophrenia: More Than One Disease Process?" *British Medical Journal*, 280, 66–68.

Dennett, D. 1991. *Consciousness Explained*. Boston: Little, Brown.

Desimone, R. 1992. "The Physiology of Memory: Recordings of Things Past," *Science, 258,* 245–246.

Done, D. J., and C. D. Frith. 1984. "The Effects of Context during Word Perception in Schizophrenic Patients," *Brain and Language, 23,* 318–336.

Dowling, J. D. 1992. *Neurons and Networks.* Cambridge, Mass.: Harvard University Press.

Eckhorn, R. 1991. "Stimulus-Specific Synchronizations in the Visual Cortex: Linking of Local Features into Global Features." In *Neuronal Cooperativity,* ed. J. Kruger. New York: Springer-Verlag, pp. 293–307.

Eckhorn, R., H. J. Reitboeck, M. Arndt, and P. Dicke. 1990. "Feature Linking via Synchronization among Distributed Assemblies: Simulations of Results from Cat Visual Cortex," *Neural Computation, 2,* 293–307.

Edelman, G. 1992. *Bright Air, Brilliant Fire.* New York: Basic Books.

Eliot, T. S. 1925. "The Hollow Men." In *Collected Poems 1909–1962.* San Diego: Harcourt Brace Jovanovich, 1963.

England, M. A., and J. Wakely. 1991. *A Colour Atlas of the Brain and Spinal Cord.* London: Wolfe.

Everett, H. 1957. "'Relative State' Formulation of Quantum Mechanics," *Review of Modern Physics, 29,* 454–462.

Finestone, D. H., D. B. Larson, A. D. Whanger, and J. O. Cavenar. 1982. "Hyperactivity in Senile Dementia," *Journal of the American Geriatric Society, 30,* 521–523.

Flaubert, G. 1857. *Madame Bovary,* trans. G. Wall. London: Penguin Books, 1992.

Flohr, H. 1991. "Brain Processes and Phenomenal Consciousness," *Theory and Psychology, 1,* 245–262.

Freeman, W. J. 1991. "The Physiology of Perception," *Scientific American,* February, pp. 78–85.

Frith, C. D. 1992. *The Cognitive Neuropsychology of Schizophrenia.* Hillsdale, N.J.: Lawrence Erlbaum Associates.

Frostig, R. D., E. E. Lieke, A. Arieli, D. Y. T'so, R. Hildesheim, and A. Grinvald. 1991. "Optical Imaging of Neuronal Activity in the Living Brain." In *Neuronal Cooperativity,* ed. J. Kruger. New York: Springer-Verlag, pp. 52–67.

Gazzaniga, M. S., J. E. Bogen, and R. W. Sperry. 1962. "Some Functional Effects of Sectioning the Cerebral Commissures in Man," *Proceedings of the National Academy of Sciences,* 48, 1765–1769.

Gerstein, G. L., P. Bedenbaugh, and A. Aertsen. 1989. "Neuronal Assemblies," *IEEE Transactions on Biomedical Engineering,* 36, 4–14.

Gleick, J. 1987. *Chaos.* London: Macdonald and Co.

Goldman-Rakic, P. 1987. "Circuitry of the Prefrontal Cortex: Short-Term Memory and the Regulation of Behavior by Representational Knowledge." In *Handbook of Physiology: Higher Functions of the Nervous System,* ed. F. Plum. Bethesda, Md.: American Physiological Society.

Goldstein, K. 1933. "L'analyse de l'aplasie et l'étude de l'essence du langage," *Journal de Psychologie Normale et Pathologique,* 30, 482.

Graham, G. 1993. *Philosophy of Mind.* Oxford: Basil Blackwell.

Gray, C. M., P. Konig, A. K. Engel, and W. Singer. 1989. "Oscillatory Responses in Cat Visual Cortex Exhibit Inter-Columnar Synchronization Which Reflects Global Stimulus Properties," *Nature,* 338, 334–337.

Greenough, W. T. 1988. "The Turned-on Brain: Developmental and Adult Responses to the Demands of Information Storage." In *From Message to Mind,* ed. S. S. Easter, Jr., K. F. Barald, and B. M. Carlson. Sunderland, Mass.: Sinauer Associates, pp. 288–302.

Harth, E. 1993. *The Creative Loop: How the Brain Makes a Mind.* Menlo Park, Calif.: Addison-Wesley.

Hazen, R. M. 1988. *The Breakthrough: The Race for the Superconductor.* New York: Summit Books.

Head, H. 1926. *Aphasia and Kindred Disorders of Speech,* vol. I. New York: Macmillan.

Hebb, D. O. 1949. *The Organization of Behavior.* New York: John Wiley & Sons.

Hobson, J. A. 1989. *Sleep.* New York: Scientific American Library.

Hodgkin, A. L., and A. F. Huxley. 1952. "Currents Carried by Sodium and Potassium Ions through the Membrane of the Giant Axon of *Loligo,*" *Journal of Physiology,* 116, 449–472.

Hollander, B. 1920. *In Search of the Soul.* London: K. Paul, Trench, Trubner & Co.

Hope, R. A., and C. G. Fairburn. 1990. "The Nature of Wandering in Dementia," *International Journal of Geriatric Psychiatry,* 5, 239–245.

Hubel, D. H., and T. N. Wiesel. 1962. "Receptive Field, Binocular Interaction and Functional Architecture in the Cat's Visual Cortex," *Journal of Physiology,* 160, 106–154.

Humphrey, D. R., and H. J. Freund, eds. 1991. *Motor Control.* New York: John Wiley & Sons.

Huxley, A. 1954. *Doors of Perception.* New York: Perennial Library, 1990.

Ito, M. 1987. "Memory System of the Cerebellum." In *Synaptic Function,* ed. G. Edelman, W. E. Gall, and W. M. Cowan. New York: John Wiley & Sons.

James, H. 1888. "The Art of Fiction." In *Partial Portraits.* New York: Macmillan.

Jasper, H. H., and J. Tessier. 1971. "Acetylcholine Liberation from Cerebral Cortex during Paradoxical (REM) Sleep," *Science,* 172, 601–602.

Jobst, K. A., A. D. Smith, M. Szatmari, M. M. Esiri, A. Jaskowski, N. Hindley, B. McDonald, and A. J. Molyneux. 1994. "Rapidly Progressing Atrophy of Medial Temporal Lobe in Alzheimer's Disease," *Lancet,* 343, 829–830.

Joyce, J. 1922. *Ulysses.* New York: Vintage Books, 1961.

Kaczmarek, L. K., and I. B. Levitan. 1987. "What Is Neuro-modulation?" In *Neuromodulation,* ed. L. K. Kaczmarek and I. B. Levitan. Oxford: Oxford University Press, pp. 3–18.

Kandel, E. R., M. Klein, B. Hochner, M. Shuster, S. A. Seigel-baum, R. D. Hawkins, D. L. Glanzman, and V. F. Castellucci. 1987. "Synaptic Modulation and Learning." In *Synaptic Function,* ed. G. Edelman, W. E. Gall, and W. M. Cowan. New York: John Wiley & Sons, pp. 471–518.

Kelly, D. D. 1991. "Sleep and Dreaming." In *Principles of Neural Science,* ed. E. Kandel, J. H. Schwartz, and T. M. Jessell. New York: Elsevier.

Kennard, C., and M. Swash, eds. 1989. *Hierarchies in Neurology: A Reappraisal of a Jacksonian Concept.* New York: Springer-Verlag.

Leonard, B. E. 1992. *Fundamentals of Psychopharmacology.* New York: John Wiley & Sons.

Levitan, I. B., and L. K. Kaczmarek. 1991. *The Neuron: Cell and Molecular Biology.* Oxford: Oxford University Press.

Libet, B., D. K. Pearl, D. E. Morledge, C. A. Gleason, Y. Hosobuchi, and N. M. Barbaro. 1991. "Control of the Transition from Sensory Detection to Sensory Awareness in Man by the Duration of a Thalamic Stimulus," *Brain,* 114, 1731–1757.

Libet, B., E. W. Wright, Jr., B. Feinstein, and D. K. Pearl. 1979. "Subjective Referral of the Timing for a Conscious Experience," *Brain,* 102, 193–224.

Livingstone, M., and D. Hubel. 1988. "Segregation of Form, Color, Movement and Depth: Anatomy, Physiology and Perception," *Science,* 240, 740–749.

Llinás, R. R., 1988a. "The Intrinsic Electrophysiological Properties of Mammalian Neurons," *Science,* 242, 1654–1664.

Llinás, R. R., ed. 1988b. *The Biology of the Brain: From Neurons to Networks.* New York: W. H. Freeman and Co.

Llinás, R. R., and D. Pare. 1991. "Of Dreaming and Wakefulness," *Neuroscience,* 44, 521–535.

Mackay, D. 1989. "Divided Brains—Divided Minds?" In *Mind-waves,* ed. C. Blakemore and S. A. Greenfield. Oxford: Basil Blackwell.

Marder, E. E., S. L. Hooper, and J. S. Eisen. 1987. "Multiple Neurotransmitters Provide a Mechanism for the Production of Multiple Outputs from a Single Neuronal Circuit." In *Synaptic Function,* ed. G. Edelman, W. E. Gall, and W. M. Cowan. New York: John Wiley & Sons, pp. 305–327.

Marr, D. 1969. "A Theory of Cerebellar Cortex," *Journal of Physiology,* 202, 437–470.

Martin, K. A. C. 1992. "Parallel Pathways Converge," *Current Biology,* 2, 555–557.

Mazzolini, R. G. 1991. "Schemes and Models of the Thinking Machine (1662–1762)." In *The Enchanted Loom,* ed. P. Corsi. Oxford: Oxford University Press.

McCormick, D. A., and D. A. Prince. 1986. "Acetylcholine Induces Burst Firing in Thalamic Reticular Neurons by Activating a Potassium Conductance," *Nature,* 319, 402–405.

McGhie, A., and J. S. Chapman. 1961. "Disorders of Attention and Perception in Early Schizophrenia," *British Journal of Medical Psychology,* 34, 103–116.

Murthy, V., and E. B. Fetz. 1992. "Coherent 25- to 35-Hz Oscillations in the Sensorimotor Cortex of Awake Behaving Monkeys," *Proceedings of the National Academy of Sciences,* 89, 5670–5674.

Myers, R. E., and R. W. Sperry. 1953. "Interocular Transfer of a Visual Form Discrimination Habit in Cats after Section of the Optic Chiasm and Corpus Callosum," *Anatomical Record,* 115, 351–352.

Nagel, E., and J. R. Newman. 1959. *Gödel's Proof.* London: Routledge and Kegan Paul.

Nagel, T. 1986. *The View from Nowhere.* Oxford: Oxford University Press.

Nedergaard, S., I. Engberg, and J. A. Flatman. 1987. "The Modulation of Excitatory Amino Acid Responses by Serotonin in the Cat Neocortex in Vitro," *Cell and Molecular Neurobiology,* 7, 367–379.

Nicholls, J., A. R. Martin, and B. G. Wallace. 1992. *From Neuron to Brain,* 3rd ed. Sunderland, Mass.: Sinauer Associates.

Noda, H., and W. R. Adey. 1970. "Firing of Neuron Pairs in Cat Association Cortex during Sleep and Wakefulness," *Journal of Neurophysiology,* 23, 672–684.

Olton, D. S., and R. J. Samuelson. 1976. "Remembrance of Places Passed: Spatial Memory in Rats," *Journal of Experimental Psychology,* 2, 97–116.

Orbach, H. S., L. B. Cohen, and A. Grinvald. 1985. "Optical Mapping of Electrical Activity in Rat Somatosensory and Visual Cortex," *Journal of Neuroscience,* 5, 1886–1895.

Ottoson, D. 1983. *Physiology of the Nervous System.* New York: Macmillan.

Parfit, D. 1989. "Divided Minds and the Nature of Persons." In *Mindwaves,* ed. C. Blakemore and S. A. Greenfield. Oxford: Basil Blackwell.

Penfield, W., and P. Perot. 1963. "The Brain's Record of Auditory and Visual Experience," *Brain,* 86, 595–596.

Penrose, R. 1989. *The Emperor's New Mind.* Oxford: Oxford University Press.

Perner, J. 1991. *Understanding the Representational Mind.* Cambridge, Mass.: MIT Press.

Pinault, D., and M. Deschenes. 1992. "Voltage Dependent 40 Hz Oscillations in Rat Reticular Thalamic Neurons in Vivo," *Neuroscience,* 51, 245–248.

Pinel, J. 1993. *Biopsychology.* Boston: Allyn and Bacon.

Plum, F. 1991. "Coma and Related Global Disturbances of the Human Conscious State." In *Cerebral Cortex,* vol. 9: *Normal and Altered States and Functions,* ed. A. Peters and E. G. Jones. New York: Plenum Press, pp. 359–426.

Poggio, T. 1988. *Time*, August 8.

Posner, M. I., and M. E. Raichle. 1994. *Images of Mind*. New York: W. H. Freeman and Co.

Premack, D. 1976. *Intelligence in Ape and Man*. Hillsdale, N.J.: Lawrence Erlbaum Associates.

Przuntek, H., and P. Riederer, eds. 1989. *Early Diagnosis and Preventative Therapy in Parkinson's Disease*. New York: Springer-Verlag.

Rang, H. P., and M. M. Dale. 1991. *Pharmacology*, 2nd ed. New York: Churchill Livingstone.

Rechtshaffen, A., P. Hauri, and M. Zeitlin. 1966. "Auditory Awakening Thresholds in REM and NREM Sleep Stages," *Perceptual Motor Skills*, 22, 927–942.

Rock, I., and S. Palmer. 1990. "The Legacy of Gestalt Psychology," *Scientific American*, December, pp. 84–90.

Roland, P. E. 1993. *Brain Activation*. New York: Wiley-Liss.

Rose, S. 1992. *The Making of Memory: From Molecules to Mind*. New York: Bantam Books.

Rosenfield, I. 1992. *The Strange, Familiar and Forgotten: An Anatomy of Consciousness*. New York: Alfred A. Knopf.

Saper, C. B. 1985. "Diffuse Cortical Projection Systems." In *Handbook of Physiology*, ed. V. Mountcastle, F. Plum, and S. R. Geiger. Bethesda, Md.: American Physiological Society.

Searle, J. 1992. *The Rediscovery of the Mind*. Cambridge, Mass.: MIT Press.

Seyfarth, R. M., and D. L. Cheney. 1992. "Meaning and Mind in Monkeys," *Scientific American*, December, pp. 78–85.

Sheer, D. E. 1989. "Sensory and Cognitive 40 Hz Event-Related Potentials." In *Brain Dynamics*, ed. E. Basar and T. H. Bullock. New York: Springer-Verlag, pp. 339–374.

Singer, W. 1990. "Role of Acetylcholine in Use-Dependent Plasticity of the Visual Cortex." In *Brain Cholinergic Systems*, ed. M. Steriade and D. Biesold. Oxford: Oxford University Press, pp. 314–336.

Skinner, B. F. 1938. *The Behavior of Organisms*. New York: Appleton-Century-Crofts.

Snyder, S. H. 1986. *Mood Modifiers in Drugs and the Brain*. New York: W. H. Freeman and Co.

Squire, L. R. 1987. *Memory and Brain*. Oxford: Oxford University Press.

Steriade, M. 1991. "Alertness, Quiet Sleep and Dreaming." In *Cerebral Cortex*, vol. 9: *Normal and Altered States of Function*, ed. A. Peters and E. G. Jones. New York: Plenum Press, pp. 279–358.

Steriade, M. 1984. "The Excitatory and Inhibitory Response Sequence of Thalamic and Neocortical Cells." In *Dynamic Aspects of Neocortical Function*, ed. G. M. Edelman, W. E. Gall, and W. M. Cowan. New York: John Wiley & Sons, pp. 107–157.

Steriade, M., and G. Buzsaki. 1990. "Parallel Activation of Thalamic and Cortical Neurons by Brainstem and Basal Forebrain Cholinergic Systems." In *Brain Cholinergic Systems*, ed. M. Steriade and D. Biesold. Oxford: Oxford University Press.

Steriade, M., R. Curro Dossi, D. Pare, and G. Oakson. 1991. "Fast Oscillations (20–40 Hz) in Thalamocortical Systems and Their Potentiation by Mesopontine Cholinergic Nuclei in the Cat," *Proceedings of the National Academy of Sciences*, 88, 4396–4400.

Thach, W. T., H. G. Goodkin, and J. G. Keating. 1992. "Cerebellum and the Adaptive Coordination of Movement," *Annual Review of Neuroscience*, 15, 403–442.

Tiitinen, H., J. Sinkkonen, K. Reinikainen, K. Alho, J. Lavikainen, and R. Naatanen. 1993. "Selective Attention Enhances the 40 Hz Transient Response in Humans," *Nature*, 364, 59–60.

Vaadia, E., E. Ahissar, H. Bergman, and Y. Lavner. 1991. "Correlated Activity of Neurons: A Neural Code for Higher Brain Functions?" In *Neural Cooperativity*, ed. J. Kruger. New York: Springer-Verlag, pp. 249–279.

Van Essen, D. C., C. H. Anderson, and D. J. Fellerman. 1992. "Distribution Hierarchical Processing in the Primate Cerebral Cortex," *Science*, 255, 419–423.

Von Neumann, J. 1955. *Mathematical Foundations of Quantum Mechanics.* Princeton, N.J.: Princeton University Press.

Watkins, J. C. 1989. "The NMDA Receptor Concept: Origins and Development." In *The NMDA Receptor,* ed. J. C. Watkins and G. L. Collingridge. Oxford: IRL Press.

Weiskrantz, L. 1989. "Some Contributions of Neuropsychology of Vision and Memory to the Problems of Consciousness." In *Consciousness in Contemporary Science,* ed. A. Marcel and E. Biasch. Oxford: Oxford University Press.

Weiskrantz, L. 1980. "Varieties of Residual Experience," *Quarterly Journal of Experimental Psychology,* 32, 365–386.

Weiskrantz, L., E. K. Warrington, M. D. Sanders, and J. Marshall. 1974. "Visual Capacity in the Hemianopic Field Following a Restricted Occipital Abalation," *Brain,* 97, 709–728.

Whitman, W. 1865. "When I Heard the Learn'd Astronomer." In *Leaves of Grass,* ed. G. W. Allen. New York: New American Library, 1955.

Wing, J. K., J. E. Cooper, and N. Sartorius. 1974. *Description and Classification of Psychiatric Symptoms.* Cambridge: Cambridge University Press.

Woolf, N. J., and L. L. Butcher. 1990. "Dysdifferentiation of Structurally Plastic Neurons Initiates the Pathological Cascade of Alzheimer's Disease." In *Brain Cholinergic Systems,* ed. M. Steriade and D. Biesold. Oxford: Oxford University Press.

Yeo, C. H., M. J. Hardiman, J. W. Moore, and I. Steele-Russell. 1983. "Retention of Conditional Inhibition of the Nictitating Response in Decorticate Rabbits," *Behavioral Brain Research,* 10, 383–392.

Yerkes, R. M., and J. D. Dodson. 1980. "The Relation of Strength of Stimulus to Rapidity of Habit Formation," *Journal of Comparative Neurological Psychology,* 18, 459–482.

Young, A. W., and E. H. F. De Haan. 1992. "Face Recognition and Awareness after Brain Injury." In *The Neuropsychology of Consciousness,* ed. A. D. Milner and M. D. Rugg. San Diego: Academic Press.

Zalutsky, R. A., and R. A. Nicoll. 1990. "Comparison of Two Forms of Long-Term Potentiation in Single Hippocampal Neurons," *Science*, 248, 1619–1624.

Zeki, S. 1993. *A Vision of the Brain*. Oxford: Blackwell Scientific Publications.

INDEX

Page numbers in *italics* indicate illustrations.